Journeys
and
Awakenings

Journeys
and
Awakenings

Wisdom for Spiritual Travelers

Edited by
Robert Peretz Corman
Devon Shahana Beckett
Darakshan Farber
Thea Halima Levkovitz

Foreword by
Robert Peretz Corman
Pir Zia Inayat-Khan

Sacred Spirit Books
Rhinebeck, New York

Journeys and Awakenings: Wisdom for Spiritual Travelers © 2019 by Seven Pillars House of Wisdom

Photo credits:
Hathaway Barry article: Wynn Bullock, Child on a Forest Road, 1958.
© 1958/2016 Bullock Family Photography LLC. All Rights Reserved.
Naomi Rose article: All illustrations by and with permission of Naomi Rose.

Hathaway Barry's excerpted from *BOY: A Woman Listening to Men and Boys*
Denise Boston's essay first appeared in RSF Quarterly, Winter 2014
Adam Bucko's essay first appeared in Huffington Post December 21, 2012
William C. Chittick's essay first appeared in Huffington Post, January 1, 2011
Charles Eisenstein's essay excerpted from *Sacred Economics*
Robert Karp's essay first appeared in the RSF Quarterly, Fall 2013
Winona LaDuke's essay first published in *Spiritual Ecology: The Cry of the Earth*
Yuval Ron's essay excerpted from *Divine Attunement: Music as a Path to Wisdom*
Wendy Jehanara Tremayne's essay adapted from *The Good Life Lab: Radical Experiments in Hands-On Living*

Cover design by Colin Rolfe
Book design by Darakshan Farber

ISBN: 978-1-948796-32-3
Library of Congress Control Number: 2018954248

Seven Pillars House of Wisdom
www.sevenpillarshouse.org
45 Brigham Street
Watertown, MA 02472

Sacred Spirit Books (an imprint of Monkfish Book Publishing Company)
22 East Market Street
Suite 304
Rhinebeck, New York 12572
USA (845) 876-4861
monkfishpublishing.com

Contents

FOREWORD

THE EDITORS AND PIR ZIA INAYAT-KHAN

In 2006, a remarkable story began that culminates in this book. At that time, Pir Zia Inayat-Khan, spiritual leader of the universal Sufi path named The Inayati Order, built on the inspired collaboration initiated in the magazine *Elixir* with the founding of Seven Pillars House of Wisdom. Soon a diverse community gathered, devoted to cultivating a living wisdom for our troubled time that would touch people's hearts, minds, and actions. It was to become a place of hospitality, exploration, and service to help create a more harmonious and thriving world.

Over nearly ten years, many advisors and collaborators, collectively known as "guiding voices," came together in various formations to develop key principles and methods, conferences, colloquies, and local events, as well as an innovative multi-media e-book titled *The Seven Pillars: Journey Toward Awakening*. Throughout that time, an extraordinary collection of writings and images from scores of authors and artists were circulated via an online newsletter and collected on the *sevenpillarshouse.org* website.

Recently, we Trustees of the organization decided to create a book to celebrate these contributions by carefully selecting a collection for a wider readership. *Journeys and Awakenings: Wisdom for Spiritual Travelers* is the result. It was only fitting to return to Pir Zia to help set the tone in this Foreword. Here then is his rendering of the story of Seven Pillars House of Wisdom.

> *Wisdom has built her house;*
> *she has set up its seven pillars.*
> *She has prepared her meat and mixed her wine;*
> *she has also set her table.*
>
> *Proverbs 9:1–2*

Of all the sayings of Solomon, these lines are among the most intriguing. Who is "Wisdom"? Where does she live? What is her aim? The Book of Proverbs provides no definite answers to these questions, but the picture it traces is alluring.

Imagine . . . Sophia Aeterna is hewing monoliths. She sets seven of them up in a circle, evoking the Ptolemaic planets, the days of the week, and the colors of the rainbow. This done, she prepares an aromatic feast and lays it out. Guests come from far and near to sit at her board. Under the benevolent eye of their hostess, the banqueters warm to each other. As the sun goes down, they find themselves articulating convictions and posing questions they had not known lay within them. The moon appears in the sky above. The conversation continues in hushed tones. An owl hoots. Silence follows. Sophia's eyes gleam. A transfigured world is unveiled. One by one the banqueters kneel and swear an oath, each one unique. Finally, as Sophia nods farewell, the company departs into the predawn twilight.

The implications of these verses inspired a number of scholars, poets, musicians, mystics, and activists to come together in a conversation that has spanned nearly a decade. Cognizant of a line of historical "houses of wisdom" including the Library of Alexandria, the House of Wisdom of Baghdad, the House of Worship of Fatehpur Sikri, and the Platonic Academy of Florence, we were moved to build a 21st-century house of wisdom. Drawing on the mysticism of Hazrat Inayat Khan, the ecumenism of Br. Wayne Teasdale, and the cultural creativity of William Irwin Thompson, as well as a number of other visionary sources, we commenced our collaboration in 2006.

Our banquet took the form of retreats at the Abode in upstate New York, colloquies and salons in several cities and towns in the U.S. and Europe, an immersive multimedia art performance in Los Angeles, conference calls, articles, and a marvelous e-book. We didn't always see eye to eye, but we trusted that a conversation undertaken in the right spirit would usher us into subtler and vaster territory, especially if silence was as much a part of the conversation as speech. Sometimes we got stuck. Other times, our Socratic dialogue showed us things we would not have otherwise seen. There were flashes in which we saw that we were united in something wider than our individual lineages and specializations. We were joined in the universal human quest for wisdom, and in our common intuition that wisdom is providentially renewed from age to age.

In 2015, the sun dawned on our soirée. The banqueters disbanded, and a new chapter began. It has been observed that while the Solomonic saying "there is nothing new under the sun" is certainly true, there may be something new under the moon. Our readiness to listen—to each other, to Nature, and to silence— was graced by the presence of Guidance, the lamp of the moon that always illumines the darkness for those who answer Sophia's invitation to dine.

Of the 140 contributions from the *sevenpillarshouse.org* website that we perused, we sought those that we felt would stir our readers as they indeed moved us. For the four of us, it has been a journey filled with awakenings; as we were individually touched by the writings, we were privileged to learn about each other through them. Every few weeks for the past two years we have answered "Sophia's invitation to dine," listening to each other and converging on what made most sense to us collectively. And, much like a mirror of the world, we did everything virtually, living at great distance from each other.

May this collection engender the spirit of listening to one another, the courage to express what seems fair and just, and the openness to collaborate and to trust in the power of the highest good we meet in the world around us.

Robert Peretz Corman
Devon Shahana Beckett
Darakshan Farber
Thea Halima Levkovitz

ACKNOWLEDGMENTS

This book is the result of the exquisite imaginations and talents of its contributing authors and the insights and selfless service of our advisors, collaborators and volunteers.

We especially want to thank: Shams Kairys for his skillful original editing of these articles, Lee Irwin for his wisdom and encouragement, Jennifer Alia Wittman for her early guidance and continuing enthusiasm, Wendy Jehanara Tremayne for her bubbling font of marketing ideas and friendship, Deepa Gulruhk Patel for her extraordinary navigation and creativity, Deborah Rabia Povich for her keen mind and warm heart, and Corin Lee Girard for her website prowess and lovely hospitality.

We are indebted to the founder and founding officers of Seven Pillars House of Wisdom: Pir Zia Inayat-Khan, Taj Inayat and Gayan Macher. We are equally beholden to its major funders: the Kalliopeia Foundation, the O'Halloran Family Foundation, New Earth Foundation, and many others whose investments, both large and small, buoyed and sustained this House of Wisdom. They all have helped to shape the body of this book. Thank you.

Finally, thank you dear Readers! You are holding in your hands a Dream Come True! May you be emboldened by these pages to share your gifts and helpful deeds in the world. Blessings on your Journey of Awakenings!

INTRODUCTION

ROBERT PERETZ CORMAN

Journeys and Awakenings: Wisdom for Spiritual Travelers calls for the recovery of our forgotten "perennial wisdom"— not as an end in and of itself, but rather as a fresh foundation for leaning into the possibilities of a bright future for the generations to come. Its contributors, enriched with splendidly diverse experiences, hail from cultures and ecosystems that robe the planet. With great heart and dedication to life-long learning, they have generously offered their inspirations and insights to us all.

This remarkable home we call Earth, blessed with a diversity of life-forms in partnership with all the elements, is a realm for wonderment and mystery. Insights into the way of the world and our life in it are at the heart of our personal and collective journey. Throughout the ages, women and men everywhere have longed to understand how we are tied to the whole of things and how we are, perhaps, a distinct presence in the vast flow of time. In moments when we experience an exquisite alignment with the fullness of all that is, we gradually open to the almighty realm of the unknowable, and, somehow, we do not feel at all lost. In fact, it feels like we have come home. The sweetness of this connection is truly divine.

For a scientist, this great "aha!" moment is the kissing cousin of the great "aha!" moment of the mystic. And they have good company on this path of uplifting discovery, for today we have at hand an ever-brightening treasure of stories and letters, drawings and sculptures, songs, symphonies and dances in celebration of these very moments and the insights drawn from them. They all honor the mystery and Source of Life itself. They raise new questions, perhaps, more than answer old ones; yet in the asking is a kind of trusting that the great mystery will lift its veil and reveal still more.

Through all this interplay there grows an ongoing self-discovery, a veritable liaison with the transcendent, and an aliveness that allows us to rest in the awareness that the riches of our human potential are truly within reach. Today we are blessed with the treasury of many mystical traditions evolved from the rare beauty of these experiences. Personal and communal practices have been received, taught and preserved in settings ranging from the elegantly simple to soaring architectural structures, all to honor the ineffable wonder of it all. While different languages, contrasting rituals, and diverse cosmological framings mark the distinct brilliance of each one, they surely are of a piece.

The writings within this book offer direct evidence of the common ground trod by spiritual travelers writing of their journey. The salience in the modern world of each of the articles is not at all limited to appreciating the author's individual experience, but more to bolster the collective stake humanity has in such shared experiences. If the words of this book could manifest as an ode, a dance, or a soaring song, it would deliver a clarion call for readers to know that when they attune to their own distinctive yet inextricable link to all of life, it is not only their birthright and a blessing upon them, it actually feeds and sustains the conditions for right action longed for and needed across the world.

To be able to engage the world with inner peace and clarity is a profound accomplishment. In the eloquent words of Pir Zia Inayat-Khan, one wise way is presented:

> *We are all fellow travelers.*
> *All pilgrims together*
> *emerging from mystery*
> *and returning to it.*

What if, when we gather,
we gather in the light of
this awareness —
that we are wayfarers
sharing stories of our journey,
knowing that our destination
lies in mystery.

The aggregate message drawn from the contributions in the book before you has lustre and fullness because they so broadly represent the human experience. Each contributor has passionately and deliberately plumbed the depths of their chosen work in the world and illumined distinctive lessons for us. While the writers seem quite disparate, there is a pattern that connects the inner city art therapist to the astrophysicist, the primatologist to the former president of an Asian nation, the musician to the social entrepreneur, the zealous atheist to the spiritual guide. Each engages their work in contemporary society much like those wayfarers Pir Zia speaks of above.

Together, the various contributions suggest ways to re-imagine a more peaceful planetary culture. We could start with the very personal, the value of self-discovery through music, song and dance as found in the rich offerings of Yuval Ron's *Sacred Ecstasy* and Robin Becker's *Belonging to Life*. Other titles begin with the cosmos, like W.H.S. Gebel's *Does the Universe Have an Inner Life?* or Omid Safi's *Heaven is Not a Zipcode*, but even these circle right back to the individual as the doorway to these seemingly distant realms, just as Ron and Becker discover the cosmos by going within.

Wherever we look, there is a reaching for the wholeness of life, for an experience beyond duality. Consider the lessons shared in the very personal stories from Wendy Jehanara Tremayne's *When the Whole World Is For Sale*, or Deepa Gulrukh Patel's *Journaling the Journey*. From the street-level viewpoint, Adam Bucko's *My God Is in the Street* and Denise Boston's *Expressive Arts Therapy* reveal the immediate, one-on-one call to serve those in need as they try to clear life hurdles to reach for their fullest place in the world.

Other essayists speak about their awakening to a vision of personal spiritual purpose that includes insights into how to actually embody that vision. Consider the soaring language of Christina Solaris's *From Vision to Action*:

> *When we awaken to the divine within us, we begin to have visions*
> *of what may be possible. We begin to have flashes of a healed*
> *Earth and a loving world. We have insights into how we can*
> *re-imagine old decaying systems and traditions in new life-giving*
> *ways. We begin to see how to become instruments of the highest*
> *good of all.*

The awakenings shared in these pages may well move the reader to deepen their sense of a personal calling. Indeed, the stunning ecological message heard in the voice of Diana Beresford-Kroeger in her interview with Gary Null entitled *The Mystery of Trees* beautifully joins the sacred practical with the universal unity of things while invoking a call to action. Llewellyn Vaughn-Lee speaks directly to the next generation as he shares his journey in *Spiritual Principles in Action*.

Richly woven through the fabric of the book are writings about the grand template that hosts the flow of all human exploration, and our history across cultures and traditions. How can the living wisdom at the heart of human knowing and sharing be harvested for the broadest common good? William Irwin Thompson's *The End of the Age of Religion and the Birth of Symbiotic Consciousness* offers a dynamic retrospective on the brilliant insights of many wise thinkers and leaders as they pondered the evolution of human spirituality and planetary culture, and hints at the danger of not taking action.

Finally, interspersed across these chapters, we are granted entré to a set of letters exchanged between mystics David Spangler, William Irwin Thompson and Pir Zia Inayat-Khan. This conversation was initiated by an inquiry from William Irwin Thompson to Pir Zia about the importance of the role the Sufis played in bringing forward the Renaissance and the role they might play on the troubled world stage today. Responding to the historical references in Thompson's letter, Pir Zia advances the conversation with numerous fascinating citations. He then refers to two distinctive contributions made by both Thompson and David Spangler, each of which could be seen as "harbingers of an integrated world view." In this most worthy trialogue, *On Prophecy and Time*, ten separate episodes reveal how these splendid teachers explore and appreciate the language and framings of each other's understandings. Follow the thread of this remarkable exchange to see where they go.

The personal journeys and awakenings of the contributors resonate with the teachers, role models, and mentors who inspired each of them along their varied paths, fueling them, in turn, to inspire you, the reader. This is a well-trod path across every tradition, rooted in the understanding, as Chief Arvol Looking Horse reminds us in *A Great Urgency*, "that what we create can have lasting effects on all life."

THE ODOR OF THE GODS

CHRISTOPHER BAMFORD

Smell is the oldest, most magical sense.

In *In Search of Past Time*, Proust tells how, returning home for a visit one cold winter's day, his mother offered him a cup of lime blossom tea with some plump little cakes, called "madeleines," molded in the fluted valve of a scallop shell. At first, he declined, but then, for no particular reason, he accepted. As the lime-tea-soaked crumbs touched his palate, a strange emotion overcame him. The world stopped, and an exquisite, transcendent pleasure, like the effect of love, filling him with joy, suffused his senses.

He concentrated on the sensation, but at first nothing happened. Finally, like a gift, a memory filled his consciousness. He remembered how, as a child on Sunday mornings, he would go in to greet to his aunt, who would give him a piece of cake dipped in tea. Immediately, he recognized the taste and smell. The moment returned, and with it a world of smells and experiences previously forgotten. Thus, "in the tiny and almost impalpable drop of their essence," taste and smell, like faithful servants, became the Rosetta Stone for the entire structure of recollection.

This so inward and personal epiphany at the beginning of the twentieth century has ancient and universal roots. Proust invokes "the smells changing with the seasons" as framing the life of the soul, but for the Andaman Islanders the year itself is a cycle of odors: a calendar of scents that follows the sequence of flowering trees and plants as they come into bloom and emanate their fragrance through the year.

More than that, for the Andaman Islanders, smell is not only creative of memory; it also magically evokes the scene of its origin. Smell is the spiritual sign of vital, generative powers. Each aromatic moment bears witness to the presence of a different spiritual power, and space becomes a shifting field of generative odors: a garden for the blind. Imagine walking through a landscape, as if blind and deaf, led only the scents permeating the air you pass through. If the odors and fragrances you walk though are the seminal powers of the creative beings whose expression nature is, then you had better be awake, for the ground you stand on is holy, and perhaps even dangerous if the spirits are not friendly. You had better know how to talk to them in their language, the language of smell, of perfumes, incenses, essential oils and fragrant herbs, whether fresh, rubbed, dried, or burnt.

Smell was thus once something quite different than it is today in our deodorized world. The scent of a rose, the scent of a lily, was that presence through and from which the plant grew. "The Odor of the Herbe Basil, being enclosed in the Seed, produces that Herb," the alchemist Van Helmont says. "Essential" or aromatic oil was just that: the essence or seminal being of a plant or flower. Extracting it was a secret, alchemical process.

A scent or perfume was thought to express the "inner essence" or spiritual nature of a thing. Think of the well-attested phenomenon of the "odor of sanctity"—the powerful fragrance emitted by and surrounding beautiful souls or saintly, purified human beings. Whether this was the scent of their own essence or the divine fragrance of the Holy Spirit—"like unto cinnamon and balsam and chosen myrrh"— or, in some ineffable way both, is moot. The fact remains. It is described many times in the lives of saints. The description of the death of Saint Polycarp of Smyrna, for instance, the earliest (AD155) testimony to the odor of sanctity, is strangely alchemical. Polycarp's martyrdom was by fire. Those who witnessed it wrote:

When he had offered up the Amen and finished his prayer, they
lit the fire. A mighty flame flashed forth. Then we witnessed a
marvel... The fire, which looked like a vault, like the sail of a
vessel filled with the wind, made a wall around about the body
of the martyr; and he was there in the midst of it, not like flesh
burning, but like gold and silver refined in a furnace. And, as
we watched, we perceived such a fragrant smell, as if it were the
wafted odor of frankincense or some other precious spice.

After Polycarp, the phenomenon of the odor of sanctity became
well known. The bodies of purified holy people "exhaled a perfume of
spices." "When Saint Hubert breathed his last, there spread throughout
Brittany an odor so sweet that it seemed as if God had brought together
all the flowers of spring." Many saints, like St. Francis Xavier, when
disentombed, were found to be whole and sweet smelling though no
spices or balm had been used to prepare the body. But this odor was
not simply a sign of heavenly blessing after death. Many saints while
alive were said to have emanated a heavenly scent and lived in a cloud
profusely fragrant with wild flowers, spices, and aromatic herbs.

Such smells were everywhere. Often the Virgin Mary or Jesus made
their healing presence known and felt by the presence of fragrances,
most often of roses or lilies. But not all such odors were celestial and
were exuded by benign beings or saintly souls. Demons, too, including
the devil, announced their presence by smell—in their case a foul odor.

All this was once traditional knowledge. At least into the Middle
Ages, it was a living part of culture, a vehicle for the expression of a
complex cosmology based upon a profound theology. It was science,
ethics, and aesthetics. With the modern age, however, Western culture
came under what Coleridge called "the despotism of the eye," the
tyrannical rule that believes that whatever can be seen can be known,
and what cannot be seen cannot be known and does not truly exist.
Sight became the pre-eminent sign of reason and civilization, while
smell, the most ancient and primordial sense, was denigrated to become
a symptom of savagery, madness, and poverty. George Orwell put it

well: "The real secret of class distinctions… can be summed up in 'four frightful words,' 'The lower classes smell.'"

Today, "a cloak of invisibility" has been thrown over the sensory world, particularly the world of smell. But when this cloak is lifted, as Constance Classen points out, "the cosmos suddenly blazes forth in multi-sensory splendor: the heavens ring out with music, the planets radiate scents and savors, the Earth springs to life in colors, temperatures, and sounds."

"The Earth, after a shower," Pliny writes, "sends out that divine breath of hers, of quite incomparable sweetness, which she has conceived from the sun. This is the odor which ought to be emitted when the earth is turned up, and the scent of the soil will be the best criterion of its quality."

Here we are on the boundaries of a different science of nature and the Earth. But we must approach slowly. First, we must appreciate the sheer volume of fragrance with which previous civilizations lived.

In the beginning, we may say, the world was a world of odors. Paradise, the Garden of Adonis, was a scented world, a perfumed, fragrant place. And this was because the world was alive, filled with spirits whose presence, whose medium, whose speech, all took place through the perfumes that filled—"smoked through," "per-fumed"—the air.

> Crocus, hyacinth, and blooming violet
> and the sweet petals of the peerless rose,
> so fragrant and divine –
> Such were the garments of the Graces for the ancient Greeks.

Imagine walking through a meadow filled with wild flowers—lilies, iris, tender narcissus, quince, and wild grape. What Presences would greet you! And if you wrapped sweet-smelling garlands around your neck or placed a special floral crown upon your head, what respect you would pay and how you would be recognized! Not only flowers, of course, and herbs, but everywhere smells of spices—cinnamon and cassia—and aromatic resins, the tears of trees: frankincense and myrrh. Scents were involved in all of Earthly life—religious, cultural, and scientific. For this reason, the ancient Zoroastrians created a sacred botany that linked flowers with the liturgy. Each archangel and angel had a flower and a scent as an emblem. To contemplate the plant was to become a receptacle for heavenly energies. Each archangel had a day of the month, each day therefore a flower and a perfume. As Henry Corbin writes:

> Contemplation of the flowers, which are their emblems, evokes psychic reactions, which transmute the forms contemplated into the energies corresponding to them; these psychic energies then dissolve into states of consciousness, into states of mental vision, through which the heavenly figures appear.

We are so far from that world now.

The story of smell begins for us in the West in Egypt. From the most esoteric realms of the temple to the everyday life of ordinary people, Egypt was awash with perfumes. Floral fragrances, scented oils, unguents, scented medicines, incenses were everywhere. In the court and on the street, people always smelt sweet with ointment of sweet moringa oil redolent of frankincense and cyperus grass. Herbs, resins, oils, and fats were highly valued. In the markets, you could find, among others, camel grass, cardamon, cassia, cinnamon, cypress, dill, henna, iris, juniper, lily, lotus, marjoram, mint saffron, spikenard, frankincense, myrrh, and the resins of fir, pine, bidellium, and mastic. The first documents attest that in the temple there existed a profound science, metaphysics, and practice of fragrant incense and oils.

Behind all this lay the intuition of the dual, mediating, communicating role of scent as interfusing inner and outer, heavenly and Earthly, essence and seed. Scent or odor lay between spirit and matter, cause and effect, seed and fruit. In the temple, the central rites, always accompanied by the sound of chant and the silence of meditation, involved incense, oils, and unguents. Daily, the statues were ritually anointed with aromatic oils and adorned with scents and perfumes. Specific incenses were ritually burned to the accompaniment of chant, for it was believed that odors came from the gods and could return there.

Incensing and oiling was thus a kind of "communion" and commemoration.

There was, for instance, a scent called "the Eye of Horus." Horus lost his eye in the struggle over the death of his father Osiris. Thoth then returned it to him. One chant, to accompany the incense called "the Eye of Horus," goes as follows:

> *The incense comes, the incense comes.*
> *The scent is over thee,*
> *The scent of the eye of Horus is over thee.*
> *The perfume of the goddess Nekhbet*
> *Which comes from the town of Nekheb*
> *Cleanses thee, adorns thee*
> *Makes its place upon thy two hands.*
> *Hail to thee, o incense!*
> *Take to thyself the eye of Horus,*
> *Its perfume is over thee.*

Burning and offering incense meditate between Earthly and heavenly worlds. They allowed the gods to work in the world, and at the same time, allowed this world to communicate with theirs.

The incense goes up, the incense goes down. Ascent meets descent. There is a release toward the heavens. There is a fine rain of grace from above. Heaven and Earth touch and begin to communicate, work together. Smell is the medium, a kind of Jacob's Ladder, with angels, spirits, and beings of all kinds ascending and descending. But there is still a little more.

The idea of the creative function of smell as it emerged in Renaissance alchemy, is therefore very ancient—and continuous. In Egypt, the vital coagulating fire, the creator-power of the Word, was metaphorized as odor. "Odor" was the seed specifying the abstract "fire" or creator-power of God. The "Fire" of the seed, which would make it burst forth in its true quality, was therefore called by the ancient Egyptians, the "odor" of the Neter, or god.

Consider the account of the divine conception of Queen Hapshepsut.

In the sacred "room of the theogamy" in the temple, devoted to the divine conception of the Pharaoh, the God Amun approaches the queen's mother. The seed is called "the odor of the god." She recognizes his presence, not by hearing him or seeing him, but by "smelling the divine scent." Because of this scent, she feels love for him flowing through her body. And, as conception of fertilization occurs, the palace becomes flooded with divine scent. "The odor of the god pervaded the palace." "It smelled like incense land." "The god found her lying in the depths of the palace. She awakened at the odor of the Neter... The palace overflowed in waves of odor of the Neter." Much in the same way, when Mary Magdalene "took a pound of ointment of spikenard, very costly, and anointed the feet of Jesus, and wiped his feet with her hair, the house was filled with the odor of the ointment." Odor here seems to signify incarnation, coagulation, a descent (as well as an ascent) of the spirit, for Mary anoints Jesus just as he is about to go to Jerusalem for the crucifixion. Here we might note that, each in its own way, every sense is fecundating: we can be impregnated through the ear, the eye, and touch. Nevertheless, odor plays a special role. In the ancient alchemical text of the Dialog of Mary the Prophetess and Aros, Mary who plays the part of the soul, is asked, "Can one make the work from a single thing?" "Yes," she replies, "...the root of our Science is a power that coagulates mercury by its odor."

We often forget in our haste or greed to literalize that the alchemical work was a work of prayer and was always said to be a donum dei, a gift of God. Ora, ora, ora et labora, "pray, pray, pray and work." Prayer has always been likened to a perfume, to incense rising, and grace has likewise frequently been likened to a celestial scent descending, while the process of prayer itself has been likened to the intermingling of heavenly and Earthly aromas.

The Neoplatonist Proclus' example is the heliotrope and its prayer:

What other reason can we give for the fact that the heliotrope follows in its movement the movement of the sun and the selenotrope the movement of the moon, forming a procession within the limits of their power, behind the torches of the universe? For, in truth, each thing prays according to the rank it occupies in nature, and sings the praises of the leader of the divine series to which it belongs…

"So there is a harmony," Proclus concludes, "a union, a connection, a sympathy between above and below, visible and invisible." The expression of this "sympathy" is prayer, and so, to the one who has a nose to smell it (and eyes to see it and ears to hear it), everything prays. The scented world constitutes a liturgy and to smell is to participate in the union of heaven and Earth, prayers ascending and descending.

And what are such fragrant prayers? For St. Bernard they are soul qualities. In his many sermons on the Song of Songs, which is filled with references to oils, scents, and perfumes, he always assigns them qualities: contrition (pungent), faith, devotion (soothing), love (healing), peace, courage, and so forth. Oils that have been poured out, as in "Your name is oil that has been poured out," St. Bernard interprets as effusions of Grace, as the presence of the Holy Spirit.

What shall we then make of our odorless world? What is the difference between a rose whose delicate perfume transports us to another state, and a rose that looks just the same but has no scent and may as well be made of silk? It is perhaps a work of art, but not one that "imitates nature in her mode of operation"—that is, not one that prays.

How can we help the world become a fragrant, praying place? Certainly, reawakening the senses, both the organs and the worlds to which they correspond, has much to do with it.

Shooting Arrows Blindfolded

A Modern Knight Describes His Training

Felix Idris Baritsch, Interviewed by Satya Inayat Khan

P*lease describe your formal chivalric training.*

In the early 1980s I entered a five-year study of the chivalric arts in France. The first year was an intensive study and training in healing, natural science, dream symbology and heraldry, martial arts and contemplation. It culminated in an exam that was an initiation into the first level of mysteries.

After two weeks of fasting and praying, I dressed in handmade knight's clothing—regular jeans and t-shirt, but with an overlying cloth portraying my own coat of arms, which had been revealed to me in a dream. This consisted of three golden-white lilies, a sword of golden-green, as well as some other symbols. For combat we used a bamboo sword and shield that had been personalized using breathing exercises, prayer and dream work—we always kept this holy armor with us, even while sleeping.

In the spirit of the unity of different levels of reality, we shot real arrows on real targets—but of course, like in the Zen art of archery, this practice was metaphoric of revealing qualities of inner states of mind. During the first year exam I fought twenty-one other knights who knew my shadows, weak spots and mental patterns. For me it was a question of life and death.

The second year, I studied holy art and scriptures and undertook extensive training in hermetic energy work. At its end there was a similar combat, but blindfolded, followed by a public presentation of music and poetry. The third year of training ended with an alchemist laboratory work of matter transformation. This started with a simple distillation and various processes on plants and metals, then progressed to complex detoxifications of poisons, and ended with transforming body and matter into light similarly to the laboratory accounts of Patanjali, the Tibetan tiglé and rainbow body practices. Finally, there was a performance of distant diagnostic and healing, and a pilgrimage to Santiago during which we performed several tasks at different places.

After successfully passing the tests at the end of the fourth year, I received a mission into the world as my fifth year training. In fact, it was the beginning of another four-year cycle in which I had to improve the medical care situation of an Indian reservation in Brazil. During the next four years my wise and compassionate master came three times to visit and to support my progress and the long-term outcome of my project. In that period I co-founded the first peace university in South America and organized the first inter-religious congress in Brasilia with 200 different religious groups participating. At the same time as the opening session of the congress, the wall in Berlin was torn down! Was it more than mere synchronicity? Anyhow it was a happy conclusion of my training mission.

What drew you to undertake training in chivalry?

During my childhood I already loved to play knight with my friends in our four acres of meadows, woods and gardens and my parents' two-hundred-year-old chateau on the outskirts of Paris. My classmates brought their costumes and musical instruments and we created a better world in our games and fantasy.

Later I was drawn to the chivalric training by its beauty, nobility and grounded-ness. Its visible power of transformation is oriented in a balanced way to the inside as to the outside. Easily accessible, deeply transforming, simple, clear and beneficial in the outcome, as all polarities and dimensions are oriented to find their natural expression in actions in the world rather than in mere words or speculations.

Have you ever experienced a situation in which the limits of your moral code were challenged by your personal beliefs?

Of course! All my moralistic, protestant, family and personal beliefs and preconceptions were constantly challenged and shattered during the training by my teacher, the power of reality, and by life itself. I had had personal issues with money, sexuality and war. Before my training I had judged any seemingly violent action indiscriminately. I had created a duality in my mind between spiritual and worldly activities and did not have enough faith to experience directly the unifying reality that connects and penetrates all opposites. Thankfully I was deeply cured of those limitations during my chivalric education.

I found that the 'ethics of the absolute' differ considerably from any single relative vantage point. Whenever I had resistance to letting go of my personal beliefs, I had to die painful deaths in order to integrate higher non-dualistic energies into my system. The chivalric approach accelerated this process immensely.

What do you mean by higher non-dualistic energies?

Well, just as childhood patterns are inadequate or counterproductive for an adult, progress on the spiritual path often means to integrate and unite contradictory and conflicting point of views and energies in one's own being—just as in the Being of God all opposites come together. You might start embracing at the same time 'your foe and your friend' or 'illness and health' and reach further until you embrace unwaveringly 'high and low', 'light and dark', 'good and bad' or 'life and death'. Every thought and concept is linked to a certain kind of energy; as a result of which any conceptual split or division between body, mind and heart risks enhancing duality in our Being, whereas the whole approach of spiritual chivalry is based on enhancing unity and its energy.

Would there be anything you would not do if asked within a chivalric context?

In relation to my teacher and in total trust of his wisdom, compassion and skilled means of training and developing my heart and mind, even if I resist his proposition at first, or if it challenges my personal convictions, I would still act according to it and jump off a cliff. Often of course his propositions are subtle hints and not to be taken literally—but you never know until the situation presents itself!

One year I picked up my teacher from Rio de Janeiro airport, and we had an eight-hour drive in order to reach his next seminar location in Brazil. I was tired, as I just had driven ten hours on poor streets to collect him. I had booked a hotel an hour from Rio to rest overnight. My teacher, however, wanted to go on traveling all night in order to arrive before sunrise. I didn't agree and considering my fatigue and the terrible light and street conditions it was really too risky.

Suddenly he asked me a single question: "Didn't you say you wanted to know more on the seven-pointed star figures according to Plato?" Surprised and excited I replied "Yes, of course! You want to tell me now?" "Well, he said, it's easy...just like this..." and he started to explain in precise details the meaning and application of the different seven-pointed stars, catching my full attention. When he finished his last phrase, we were driving into the courtyard of our destination and the sun was about to rise. Seven hours had passed by in less than a glimpse of time and I have no idea how it could be possible we made it. I had no memory of the route, the time that had passed, nor any of his explanations. I wasn't tired at all and worked for the rest of the day as normal.

The next night I had a dream on how to leave the body, time and space, and understood what had happened the night before. I fit the puzzle together and still use the symbology and power of seven pointed stars in many counseling situations today.

What are some of the challenges of upholding chivalric ideals in a modern society?

One of the challenges is the complexity of society and the speed of its development. Another is the polarization of rich and poor, north and south, healing and destroying, self-interest versus enlightened activity. Although polarization is still getting stronger, the impact of new economic, medical, political and spiritual forms of living is gaining increasingly more terrain. Humanity still needs many more individuals and groups with deep insight and integrated polarities to participate in concrete actions all over the world.

The modern world is definitely at the threshold of a new evolutionary phase. Everywhere I see the spreading of higher levels of consciousness based on new paradigms. Mystic knights participate in that natural event by holding up—or reintroducing, if necessary—the ethics of timeless wisdom in every field of life in order to keep a high level of truth and energy. As in any dawn, the possibilities of co-creating a new world are better than ever.

After the epoch of individuation, the moral code of our time will be more and more rooted in widespread authentic experiences of the Divine beyond concepts or cultural forms and will find expression in the energy of highly motivated groups dedicated to others. They will pacify and integrate by building bridges between opposites, benefiting life, nature, justice and the awakening of human consciousness. The more each conscious group takes specific action in the world according to the new paradigms the stronger the overall effect will be and the easier it will become to install and uphold an adequate ethics for a future world with worthwhile living for all.

Do you think a certain type of person is drawn to chivalry, or does it have a universal appeal?

His Holiness the Dalai Lama says that no one can really work or fight for peace who is not able to raise his sword. In all mystic traditions I see an aspect of chivalric training and whoever is attracted by truth has to pass in one way or another through the chivalric lessons. This is true for everyone, but for many inner and outer reasons only some are attracted to undergo this training and art of living directly. Others prefer the echo of it in other traditions.

Chivalry definitely has an archetypal and universal dimension in resonance with our time and a great potential to benefit the global issues of justice, change and survival of humanity.

ON PROPHECY AND TIME – PART 1

WILLIAM IRWIN THOMPSON TO PIR ZIA INAYAT-KHAN AND DAVID SPANGLER

Over the course of several months in 2010, three articulate and prolific mystics with very different backgrounds engaged in a dialog over e-mail. Stretching their knowledge and imaginations across a wide gamut of ideas, they are grappling with the role of mystic thought over history. They reflect how the evolution of human consciousness has shaped and continues to shape the issues facing our planet. Here we present their rich conversation, in ten letters scattered through the chapters of this book.

Dear Pir Zia,

I have been thinking lately about planetary culture and an earlier age of esoteric syncretism in the Convivencia in medieval Spain. I would say that the Sufis—and not the Italians!—actually brought us the Renaissance. Their Middle Eastern music and Persian poetry influenced the returning Crusaders like Guillaume of Poitiers and the later trouba-

dours such as Arnaut Daniel in Provence, and from there the influence
spread to Italy to Cavalcanti and Dante. Ibn Arabi's cosmology influenced Dante, as did the Hadith of Mohammed's journey to heaven and
hell, but to protect himself from the Church, Dante stuck Mohammed
in hell to appear completely Christian and unheretical. The poets,
musicians, and artists of the early thirteenth-century Renaissance
before the Black Death knew that Andalusia, Majorca, and Sicily were
the gateways of Islam into the soul of Europe. Just look at this picture
from King René's Book of Love (1456) of the chivalric knight from
Sicily and you see the Sufi emblem of the winged-heart atop his helmet
and on the coverings for his horse.

You can also see in the troubadour Arnaut Daniel's famous poem
Sestina that the lady in the heart is the esoteric figure of the inner
feminine—Tara in the East and the Donna of the Cathars in the West.
The whole poem is about an esoteric practice of meditation, as I make
clear in my translation since most literary scholars are not conversant
with this.

Sestina by Arnaut Daniel

The firm vow that enters me through my heart
no beak can strip away nor fingernail
of slanderer tear, cursed in his lost soul.
I dare not strike these branches with my stick;
instead of more family relations,
I'll know the joy of orchard and chamber.

When I reflect in my inner chamber,
I find none but the Lady in my heart,
closer than one's family relations.
No member but trembles down to the nail,
and like the infant awed by the stick,
I fear to be overcome by soul.

Would that she with body and not with soul
received me secretly in her chamber,
but that would injure me more in the heart
than if she beat me with a wooden stick.
Who leaves there never enters her chamber!
I shall be near her as finger and nail
and not be chastised by my relations.

Not even the mother of all relations
would I love like the Lady of my soul.
She's as intimate as finger and nail.
If it pleases her I'm in her chamber
then she'll make love of me in the heart,
better than a strong man with a weak stick.

Since dry twig has turned spring flowering stick,
Adam's stem has branched in all relations.

Never so fine a love entered my heart,
nor was before in my body or soul.
Whether she is out or in her chamber,
I'm no farther than finger is to nail.

As close as two boards hammered with a nail,
or as far as bark is to the rough stick,
is My Lady to my excoriate heart.
She is all—tower, palace, and chamber.
I can renounce all other relations,
with her in paradise inside my soul.

Arnaut plucks this song with a single nail
for those in the still chamber of the heart
who have stopped breeding dying relations
to turn a soul from a flowering stick.

All of which, is to say, Pir Zia, that I think the Sufis will need to do it again and serve to create a planetary Renaissance by transforming the Islamist fundamentalist threat into a positive cultural transformation. Just don't get yourself killed like Hallaj or Suhrawardi!

Islam rejected the Gutenberg Galaxy and Modernism—that interlocking causal system of the Scientific Revolution, Dutch capitalism and bourgeois democratic revolution, and mass distributed printed books. But now Muslim terrorism has adopted the Internet to inspire young men to violent Jihad and women to suicide bombings, so electronic society is now part of the *Unmah*. In this new planetary culture of East and West, we urgently need a new transformation of the Abrahamic religions and not new versions of Holy Wars, Crusades, and Inquisitions.

William

The next letter in this series begins on page 45.

Boy: A Woman Listening to Men and Boys

Excerpts from the book

Hathaway Barry

From the Introduction

Everywhere I go now, I see men differently.

I have loved and appreciated and felt exasperated by men in many ways—father, brothers, relatives, playmates, friends, lovers, mentors, colleagues, husband, ex-husband, son, long-term partners. I know the goodness of men. And yet, after more than a half century of living with them, I realize I am still mystified by much of their behavior.

There have been moments when I might have been tempted to give up on men altogether. Having a son keeps me hostage to the world of men. It's a kind of hostage I want to be. We're here such a brief time, I don't want to miss anything.

Here's how it began.

In my later fifties I fell in love again. I felt an inexplicable depth of connection with this man. He was the most open and vulnerable man

I'd loved and the most elaborately defended. So tenderly close and then . . . unreachable. My heart was scrambled. He didn't seem to be aware of his behavior or how hard it was to be on the other end. I'd wake up in the middle of the night, pierced with anguish. What do I not understand here? In the midst of heartache and confusion, stillness found me, and the word "BOY" appeared in my mind's eye. I had no idea what that was about, but I trusted it.

Writing is one of my ways of letting things sort themselves out. So I went to the wilderness to listen for poems. Not much luck. It dawned on me I needed to listen to actual men. To see what I could learn about some of the puzzling ways of relating I'd experienced. What's at the heart of it? And what's my part in it?

What if no one's "wrong"? Or "right"?

I am a woman living in a culture primarily thought up by men. I have carried a boy child in my body. He was part of me. I get it that it's human being first. And yet, because of his gender, my son has had to navigate a whole other world than that of his sister. I wanted to know more about this world. I wanted to know, what happens to boys growing up? Maybe I would need to listen differently if I wanted to find out.

I didn't want to close my heart. To me, at this time on this earth, it seems essential to stay open and embrace what I don't know and don't understand.

So I came closer and listened more deeply.

I just wanted to listen without blame or judgment to how it is for men, a whole half of the human species I knew less about. I wanted to hear their honest human stories, without gloss or performance.

Occasionally, I would catch myself wondering—what am I doing listening to all these males when I was someone who had muttered, more than once, about being tired of always listening to men, and men not listening in return? I really didn't know. I just knew I had to do it.

The more than eighty men and boys I interviewed (and dozens of mini-interviews wherever I'd go—people I'd never met on airplanes, on trains, in restaurants, waiting rooms, in a tow truck, at the gym etc.) range in age from 9 to 94 years. They are men of color, white men, gay and transgendered men, straight men, married men, bachelors, brothers and fathers. They are all American—and come from a variety of educational, religious and work backgrounds.

I've mostly chosen to share the more vulnerable responses, those perhaps less easily spoken about publicly—the ones that touched me most or just felt true.

From the Violence Section

"Because it is learned, it can be unlearned."

Any woman who has given birth to or nursed a boy, or anyone who even just looked, really looked, into the eyes of a newborn knows—there is no violence there.

So much of "being a man" sounded like a violence to the spirits of the young boys I listened to. Emotional as well as physical. The so-called "ordinary violence"—the daily violations that interfere with their being who they truly are. When I shared some of what I had been hearing with a friend in his 60s, he listened quietly, nodding in recognition. Then he leaned closer and spoke softly: "Yeah. And then, you have to be a man."

I am well aware of the fear and violence that many women live with, but I hadn't really let in how it is for men. The stories I heard when I asked the question—What was your first experience of violence?—changed that.

So many of these boys were beaten, yelled at, tickled to the point of tears, teased, mocked, put down, humiliated, hazed, called names. They suffered from absent, neglectful or abandoning caregivers, insensitive schoolyard bullies, mean big brothers, abusive coaches, unaware fathers and mothers passing on what had been passed on to them. In many instances, the brutality of their welcome to the world was searing. A man in his early 60s told me, "I was found unacceptable. It's hard to find your way back from that." If your caregiver is a source of terror and pain, where is safety?

Moment to moment we are impacting these boys by who we are and how we are. What do they see when they look in the mirror of our face?

I was trying to understand what it might be like to always be on guard, afraid that something violent is going to happen. What does that do to a boy's natural curiosity and creativity? How can you feel free to play and discover? It's heartbreaking what men have to go through to "be a man"—the uncomfortableness of it. I'm amazed at how much more limited the range of expression is for the men and boys I know than it is for women and girls. How easy it would be to pass on that uncomfortable feeling, without knowing why. Not out of malice, but because maybe nobody showed you another way of dealing with it.

If you could have the imagination and a way to express whatever you need to express—would you need to be violent?

From Thomas (40s)

My idea of a violent man was someone who fought with other men all the time, and was physically abusive to women. I wasn't those things, but I was using different types of coercion in my relationships that I wasn't aware of. After what I witnessed from my stepfather and the other violent men in my mother's relationships, I vowed to never hit a woman. I have kept that vow, but I wasn't aware of all of the other kinds of violence that I had been doing.

Men have the ability and the upper body strength to control and dominate. We think that we're in charge, because we can be.

It's really the rules of engagement, how you treat people. Now I say, "Equal is equal is equal." And that's something that takes a long time to soak in, because I always reserve the right to, if all else fails — I'm going to put my foot down here. Because somewhere in the back of my mind is the idea that I'm the boss and this is the way it's going to be.

A lot of guys, when we're first getting help, we try to minimize or deny responsibility for our violence. Blaming, really. It's culturally acceptable.

I got good at being passive-aggressive. I was losing control of my partner. When we up the ante, when we're challenged and our emotional or verbal or economic authority doesn't work anymore, as happened in my case, I finally crossed the line. I shoved her against the wall, and I threatened her.

She didn't call the police. She waited, and gave me a chance to explain myself. I remember the look on her face. She shook her head and said, "No, you're not going to do this to me." There was a quiet understanding between us at that moment — a pivotal, life-changing event. That look on her face, in her eyes.

Over the last few years, I've seen that look many times. I've seen it in my own mom's eyes when I raise my voice to her. It's a look of being hurt so deeply, and frightened. Fear of my rage. In my mother's frightened eyes, I saw myself as a terrified young boy. I felt ashamed, a very uncomfortable feeling, which was quickly followed by anger to justify myself. Men, we do that. It's a habit. Emotional violence — what it does is spiritual violence. It leaves a person worn down and off-balance.

The most difficult thing to deal with is when I feel justified. It stems way back. Growing up in a turbulent and unpredictable alcoholic household was a time of emotional violence. I remember as a boy when I had suffered humiliation and violence, I said, "This is not going to f—ing happen to me anymore." This emotional bomb shelter where you go into, it's a protective mode. Years and years of, "You're not gonna f— with me. I will not let anybody control and dominate me or challenge me ever again." I carried that attitude all the way up to domestic violence, controlling and dominating my partner.

That little boy is still there, and he's still afraid and he still doesn't want to be hurt again and he still doesn't completely trust people. I have to keep reminding myself, "You can trust her. She loves you." My default position is not to trust, not move towards intimacy, not be vulnerable. I have to make a concerted effort to overcome that automatic response.

From the Afterword

I wanted to learn to love well. I wanted to look into the violence in my own heart and not add to the aggression on the planet. "Everything included," a beloved older friend once said to me. "If you have any idea of 'us and them,' you're going the wrong way."

I got to practice listening and staying open. Whenever my heart clicked closed with thought, ideas of blame, judgment, making wrong, my own impatience or projection—reacting with the whole array of human habits—so did the exchange. When I took a breath and relaxed, suspended my beliefs long enough to put myself in their shoes, and let myself just listen and not know, the world lit up. It was like falling in love again and again with life ~

BELONGING TO LIFE
A Reflection on Movement and Meditation

ROBIN BECKER

Throughout my life I have been drawn to contemplation, meditation and movement. As a child, my love of movement carried me into the world of dance, where I have developed and worked as a dancer and choreographer for many decades. If you had met me as a five year old child, and asked me what I wanted to be when I grew up, I would have responded with full confidence that I planned on being a dancer and a nurse. I never became a nurse. However, a fundamental interest in healing, and serving the larger world shaped and guided my journey over the years. I also learned to love the natural world, and the animal world from my parents who were both from farming families. I continue to believe that this connection to nature has served as a foundation for the somatic inquiries in which I have been engaged.

Despite the many gifts of my childhood, another powerful shaping force in my life was paradoxically the feeling that I really didn't belong anywhere. I was a highly sensitive child who felt and expressed emotions deeply. I grew up with loving and well-meaning parents that did not have the emotional resources to respond to the depth of my feeling. The result of not being met emotionally was that I struggled with feeling abandoned and unrecognized. I spent many hours in an interior world of imagination, realms of light, prayer, and long conversations with the understanding community of stuffed animals on my bed. For years, I felt great secret anguish behind my very accomplished, public, outgoing persona.

I now value the wisdom of that child and her early choices. I see how my interior struggle was a guiding force for future learning. I eventually found my way into different therapy situations, and I have continued a life-long interest in the field of psychology. I met the teachings of Hazrat Inayat Khan, and the Sufi Order of the West [now the Inayati Order – ed.], where I felt an attunement to the perspectives and philosophy of that mystical path. I also had the blessing twenty-five years ago of meeting Emilie Conrad, founder of the somatic practice Continuum Movement. Continuum forever changed my understanding of embodiment, movement, and how we all intimately belong to life.

I am sharing a small part of my personal story to begin this reflection, because the silent worlds of movement and meditation are subjectively experienced. What follows is an offering from my experience.

~~~

When I began meditation, I considered it to be a refuge of complete stillness and release of thought: a place of rest where we would allow our spirit to leave the prison of our bodies and flow freely into higher realms of light and consciousness. I had many moments in my youthful meditating life when I wished I could just let go of the struggle of this physical life, and solely live in the magnificent realms of light I experienced. My problem was that I also loved the joy and physicality of dancing where I felt myself in total communion with the music. This was a passion that propelled my life, and I believe it often saved my life. I felt totally empowered when I was dancing. I considered the movement of my body to be an external activity that I was in absolute control of directing: such as the combinations of steps I did as a dancer, walking across the floor, stretching, lifting an object, or standing up and sitting down. That mastery was an important resource of self-confidence and identity in my early years.

As the years went by, I began to wonder how I could bring these two worlds together. I wondered how my dancing could reflect the realms of light and beauty I experienced in meditation. In meditation, I began to wonder how my body could go with me into those expanded states of consciousness. It was through meeting the somatic practice of Continuum Movement, that I began to learn my way into these questions.

Continuum offers a completely different understanding of the body than what Western Culture believes a body to be. It was world changing for me to consider that the body is an expression of an ancient unfolding planetary process, comprised of approximately 70% water that is in constant motion, instead of a solid stable form. I learned that water is liquid crystalline. Every cell in the body is made of this sensitive pulsing substance capable of receiving and transmitting information. Core teachings from many wisdom traditions, and the scientific world all emphasize that life is a process of constant change. I resonated with that idea, but I never fully grasped its significance. I needed the experience of life as movement for that truth to metabolize and grow within me.

When I speak of movement now, I am speaking about a primary movement of life. Most of us understand that any living system needs water to survive. However, we often overlook the fact that the movement of water itself has shaped all life forms: from our development in the fluid environment of our mother's womb, to the arcing shapes of trees, meandering rivers, curved stones, unfurling plants, and the wavelike landscape of mountains. Western culture tends to emphasize static form and facts. The perspective of Continuum is that all form is the result of movement. The entire living universe is a process of fluid movement.

An important principle of fluid systems is that they function in resonance or immediate communication with all other fluid systems. A characteristic of fluid movement is that it is radiant, spreading out and connecting, as rivers move toward the sea. My blood, my tears, my breath and my pulsing organs are in a dynamic exchange with all other living processes. As I have developed greater awareness of the sensory communication of my body, I have learned a new story of how I deeply belong to life. As an integral part of the fabric of life, I now understand

my body as a portal to the larger universe from which I am not separate, and to which I deeply and intimately belong. The angst of my
early childhood story began to shift as I experienced the ever-present
touch and response of the living universe.

With the perspective of all life as moving vibration, we can explore
a continuum of consciousness from the physical world into the subtle
movements, textures and vibrations of the invisible world. Conceptu-
ally, it was much easier for me in my early years to accept the idea of
spirit and energy moving into form, rather than to accept that we might
also follow the path from the denser more visible configurations of our
bodies to the finer realms of energy and vibration. I have learned a new
reverence for my body and its miraculous intelligence and capacity to
serve multiple functions as I have explored a path of conscious embodiment. I have come to consider my entire being, including my thinking
capacity, to be a sensitive, intelligent, perceiving world of movement
intimately and dynamically engaged with the larger universe.

Movement and meditation are practices in which we make ourselves
available to life as it unfolds in the present moment. We enter a much
broader field of engagement than the limits of thought and personal
preferences. Both contemplative inquiries are creative endeavors
that require courage, discipline, and a radical choice to be with the
tempo of a process that moves much slower than the acceleration
of our culture. We step outside the familiar context of daily life in
order to gain a deeper and expanded view of our lives where we may
encounter what is unfamiliar and unexpected. We have the opportunity to re-familiarize ourselves with the subtle textures and sensory
language of the natural world, which is the first language we mastered
as infants. Impulses of new and unexpected forms may begin to move
into our awareness through sensations, feelings, intuition, or inspirations of new possibilities for our lives.

The perspective of the body's role as an essential aspect of our intelligence is not always held as a value in western culture. Many people
find it difficult to engage in somatic practices. It is much easier to
engage in physical activities that have external goals to achieve or skills

to master: activities in which we feel in control and capable of directing all actions. After years of exploring movement, I have come to think of the body as a living library of a person's entire lifetime. The highly sensitive, responsive capability of liquid crystalline substance within us carries the memories and imprint of all our experiences. It is inevitable if we embark upon the path of embodied inquiry, that we will need resources in order to meet what emerges from within. I have found that many people are frightened of movement practices, as so many memories of pain and struggle reside in the body. The body becomes a landscape of fear instead of possibility.

As infants, we felt things throughout our entire bodies. If we were hungry, our entire body would cry out in distress. There was not the differentiation or development of consciousness to know that we were hungry and that our caregiver would be there in the near future to feed us. Every cell in our infant body would express the total global distress of the moment. There is not a developed sense of self in an infant. All conscious relationship requires a level of differentiation in order for the space of relationship to be possible. The extraordinary gift of our human consciousness is that we have the opportunity to be self-aware and in relationship with ourselves. The hyper-sensitive and brilliant awareness of the infant still exists within our adult bodies. As we grow in awareness of our embodiment, we gain the differentiated ground and spaciousness needed to be in relationship with that core sensitivity. We can learn how to encompass and value our vulnerability as an attribute rather than a weakness. I have found this journey of exploring movement and meditation to be a path in which I have grown in compassion for both myself and the larger world.

As a dancer, I have learned that if I want to leap into the air, I must first lower myself to the earth in order to gather my strength to push off the earth and rise up into the air. To rise up, I need ground. The two directions are in relationship with each other. I see the partnership of contemplative movement inquiry and meditation in a similar way: as we cultivate more sensory awareness, it is as if we grow a bigger container and broader field through which to receive and engage expanded dimensions of life. A larger sensation-body supports us in meeting the more subtle realms of consciousness.

The practice of movement and meditation is an unfolding path of discovery. We are never abandoned by the movement of life. To perceive all existence as movement is a very hopeful endeavor, as new possibilities endlessly emerge. The richness of what we are privileged to experience in life is boundless......

THE MYSTERY OF TREES

DIANA BERESFORD-KROEGER, INTERVIEWED BY GARY NULL

This interview with Diana Beresford-Kroeger was conducted by Dr. Gary Null, noted talk radio host, in May 2010 as one of his Conversations with Remarkable Minds (M-F, noon EST at www.ProgressiveRadioNetwork.com).

I'm going to give you a very broad canvas to paint with today, to give examples of the biological wonders and medicinal properties of trees; the destruction of our forest, and the threats to human and other life due to their demise; and the ways to introduce trees back into our lives. I have an enormous reverence for trees, and have planted more than 4,000 on my own farm in Florida.

Well, thank you, and good for you. I feel that the planet is for everybody, and to reduce and take down the global forest is an absolutely catastrophe for the world. Learning more about our forests is very necessary for the health and the safety of the world that is to come, and here on this continent there are extraordinary species that are matched nowhere else in the world, like the wonderful array of oaks and hickories. These species and the black walnuts will do something for the future that you all need to know and that you all need to be ambassadors for and pass this knowledge around. 400,000,000 years ago the atmosphere was filled with carbon dioxide and man and his babies could not live there, and the trees stepped into the stage of life.

They made an extraordinary marriage happen between carbon and oxygen. That marriage took place in the shade of sunlight that stimulated the manufacture of sugars and the oxygen that all the four-legged and two-legged species require.

I would ask you to right now just stop breathing and see how long you can support yourself. Now the oxygen that you are breathing comes from trees and the invisible global forest of the ocean, and they both hold hands with one another. Trees do something quite extraordinary and even as we are speaking they are doing it, which is to make both the wave form of light and the straight line form of light dance in an extraordinary molecular dance and that produces energy in a thermodynamic reaction that produces food. This is the source of all the food we eat! That's the food the animals eat and the oxygen we breathe. So this is what trees do and have been doing for 400 million years, but the trees on the American continent do it better than anywhere else, because they plug in carbon dioxide into their bodies and they get huge and massive, and they open their faces to the sun. These are the trees that will give us life, will give every baby in uteri life, and will breathe life back into the planet. So I say we have to protect our forest, and we all have to plant trees.

Thank you. I would like us to learn more about the energy of trees, and why people considered trees as sacred throughout history, as living entities, yet we tend to see them as floors, or a desk or a newspaper.

I brought many people to the Arnold Arboretum yesterday to show, amongst many more, one tree that I am particularly interested in, that was considered to be a sacred tree by all of the people of eastern North America for 6000 years. Ptelea trifoliata lived from Florida up into Canada, and its common name is wafer ash. This tree gave the first nations an extraordinary medicine, a biochemical synergist that is capable of looking at cancers straight in the face and saying, "You will not survive." It is an absolute boon to all of the oncologists and the people who are suffering everywhere all over the world from the massive exposure to pesticides and consequently the incredible problems with cancer. This chemical from ptelea trifoliate will give us one answer. But there are now only, I hate to tell you this, four or five or six left.

Now let us look at something that has a global impact. In the ancient world of China, Japan, Russia, going down into Europe, and indeed in America, we have 1000 species of hawthorns, and these are called crataegus. Now, these have been considered to be a magical species all over the world for all cultures in all times, and indeed there is magic in these trees. The magic has now been transmuted into a chemical called crataegun. Now you have to take your noses and you've got to find a hawthorn, and right now they're flowering, and stick them into these flowers. And when you put your nose into the flower, it is kind of a bitter smell, but what happens is like smelling a gorgeous apple pie that has just come out of the oven, your salivary glands start to work, and as they start to work, the lactone comes out of the flower and goes into your salivary glands and you actually drink the lactone of crataegus, and, here is the magic, here is the big answer, it opens the left ascending coronary artery. I will guarantee you will not have a heart attack while you are smelling that plant, and if you have had ascending artery surgery you will have been given this compound, but this one is for free.

The hawthorn produces a little red apple, and in the fall the farmers all over eastern North America, when they would go and get their dairy herds, they would pick this as a trail food. This gives them crataegus and that is why lots and lots have been so healthy. But the aboriginal people took it even further. Each fruit has got five tiny little nutlets inside, and they would wash and grind these up, and they had their first cup of coffee because there's caffeine in these little nuts and it gave them a little stimulant. So this is another example of the magic out of the forest.

Many people, not everyone, consider trees to be an intelligent life form, with their own immune systems, and even sexuality. Would you also share your observations about social lives of trees in the forest, how the forest as a natural habitat is actually a living community.

Well, you kind of have to sit back and listen to this one because it is an extraordinary story. I am an aristocratic mongrel. My father was from a titled family and my mother was from an ancient Gaelic family who were the kings of Monster, one of the five counties of Ireland, in the 5th century. And my father was killed, and my mother and brother, and I was made an orphan at age 11. Now, in the south of Ireland, an orphan is everybody's child, an orphan is the child of the whole community and the people who picked me up, who thought I was a valuable child, from, I suppose, a historical point of view because I was the last child left, they taught me for three long years, in and under the Brehon Laws. They taught me all of the ancient knowledge of Ireland, the ancient knowledge of druids, they taught me the Gaelic language, they taught me about the importance of trees, they taught me about the ability of trees to speak and how to listen and how to meditate into the forest. And they taught me all kinds of medicines, and cures and methods of withstanding the future world, because I would be an orphan child going into, they called it "the new world," for I would be their last child and I would have to speak for them there. Then I went to university and I studied and did all kinds of things, and as I got older this gift they gave to me became bigger and bigger, and these things that were told to me I saw they were extraordinary. And indeed I see now that I am the last child of that ancient world.

Now the forests are communities that have an extraordinary genome, they have extraordinary epigenetics, just like we do. They have an immune system and a biochemical pathway system filled with serotonin, similar to us, that links neuron paths. We have our brain at the top of our head, they have a cambia layer, and we can think of a cambia layer as a form of brain. But the tree is a chemical manufacturing system that is the wonder of the world. It is that chemistry that gives us 40% of our medicines that come from trees, like aspirin for example. So the chemical transmutations that the trees have produced over the centuries and millennia have become very important. And the tree can do something now, in the modern world, that we know very little about. We really don't know how the tree transports water from the soil, pulling up the aquifers into the great volumes of the tree and into the sky, and the aerosols that the tree produces has got legs, with hydroxyl groups on them. These attach to the moisture vapor above the trees and they're responsible for clouds and weather patterns, and they're responsible in the end really for our civilization, because if we have no moisture, we cannot survive. But the tree is awfully clever, and I will talk about the wonderful redwoods on the west coast in California, as they do something quite extraordinary in the upper canopy—they produce aerosols up there to pull in water vapor so that the sperm can swim along the tiny sheath of water and fertilize the ovule. This is a wonder of our world. I could go on and on and on. The trees have a low nutrient requirement, they drain sustainably into the lakes and valleys and down into the streams and the deltas of the world, and they put out a measured amount of nitrogen that is perfectly balanced for the ocean. If too much nitrogen goes downstream from farming, you get all of this algae that grow and you get toxic tide that grows and grows until the nitrogen is burnt up and the bacteria come in and draw off the oxygen such that some of the water areas are the graveyards of the sea. But the trees and the great forests of the world will stop this.

And that is why everything in the world is functioning like a unit, to keep it all together. We are the song of the universe, we really are the miracle of the universe in our mathematics, and the tree has this form of intelligence too. If you damage one tree, another of the same family next to it produces a phenol to help it heal and mend and cure itself.

Can you expand further on tree aerosols, their purpose for the trees and life in the forest, and how the tree is vital for our lives? And then juxtapose that with what's going on in Borneo, where they are destroying all the trees. You see it in South America, all over Brazil, they're burning the trees; the Chinese have contracted for genetically engineered soybeans, American companies have done the same, they're burning the trees. No one seems to care about the trees anymore!

I think what is happening here is that there is a dull roar coming from the human herd. We are listening to something that is quite extraordinary and ordinary people are starting to listen, though many across the world are a little deaf to this, and I think they all might be in for somewhat of a surprise in the near future.

But let me go to the aerosols. The tree functions by means of many mouths on many, many leaves, called stomata, that open and close by means of guard cells and emit these aerosols. The aerosol compounds are very, very important. As you go further north, some of these aerosols actually scrub the atmosphere and make it aseptic. Have you ever thought we are breathing in this dirty air, more or less, and most of us don't get lung infections? So the trees actually are doing that.

If you go out into the forest in a mountainous region on a warmish day that is a tiny bit humid, and you see a slight haze in the air over the forest, often people will say, "Oh it is kind of a hazy day today"—it's actually that the trees are producing vast quantities of aerosols! And you are seeing the aerosols in their tonnage being put into the atmosphere and cleaning the atmosphere with chemicals like alpha pinene and beta pinene from the pine forests. America has extraordinary pine forests, many, many types of pines, and pines are smart. If you have a child, or a teenager that has a learning disorder, and you bring your child into a pine forest, on a warmish day, when it is a little muggy with nice fresh air, the pinene is being released as an aerosol from the stomata of the leaves and the child will breathe it in. The pinene has a slightly narcotic effect on the brain, and it is a stimulant that acts as a carburetor for the brain, so the child comes out of the forest breathing a whole lot better, clearing and opening out its lungs, but with a higher IQ and better able to pay attention.

For those of you who live in cities, there are many, many areas in north America that have extraordinary urban forests, and we have to protect and build and strengthen them. Our urban forests are as important as the great forests of the world, and they do something really quite extraordinary. We have a deadly killer amongst us right now called particulate pollution, which is pollution of less and 2.5 microns. It's tiny, about a tenth the size of a pollen grain and its produced by cars and buses and planes. When these particles go into the deep area of the lungs they are very hard to get out. But the extraordinary thing that trees do, by the trinomial hairs, the hairy surface on most trees' leaves, is that they actually comb the air of this particulate pollution.

Let me tell you a little more about this particulate pollution because it also carries things called hitchhikers, which are the pesticides and herbicides that are being sprayed on fields. Along with large molecules like cobalt or lead or magnesium, metals, they are very dangerous for asthmatic people, and account for the rise in asthma of about 30% worldwide. So under a tree, the leaves comb the air of this pollution and it gets onto the leaves and the rain washes it down into the soil where microbes eat it and they use it for their daily lives. So if you sit under an urban tree, you are exposed to 25% less pollution. This is very important for people who have heart conditions or asthmatic problems, really important for our babies, and also for our dogs and our cats.

Can you talk about the nature of communication between animal species, humans and trees and between trees and other trees?

Yes, I would love to. The human body is made up of the spirit, the mind and the soul, and for us to have productive lives we have to have all of them functioning very well—all communities, all people everywhere have thought that. But there is one other thing that we have. We have the ability to listen to the trees and hear the forest, and not everyone can do this. Now the only way I can describe this phenomenon is when some people go to concerts and hear symphonies, and hear music when it is in its mathematical perfection because it's between the musical notes, what you don't hear, that makes the pattern that's so important. And they experience a rush of feeling that comes into their chest that is almost a choking, a cry, and it pulls you all into yourself. So for some people, walking in the forest is like the feeling of going into a cathedral, and indeed the ancient forest is the cathedral of nature. Here you feel this same emotional pull in your chest. I think that most of the children of the world when they are very little will go into the forest and feel this. For them it feels like the trees are their friends and they can indeed talk to the trees.

The trees are the most extraordinarily large species that are living on this Earth, make no mistake about it. They are alive. They have DNA. They are functioning like you and I are functioning. When you have a very large object, maybe an elephant, or a volcano, or a tree, it produces a low-frequency sound called infrasound. It's just recently been proven that the elephant can send out infrasound calls from one elephant to another in warning, and the trees do the same thing. These low level rumblings can be measured in our sound experiments.

You and I and the human family are created like a viola—we have our ribs, we have our chest, which is empty where there is a pair of lungs, so if you think about it, we're a receptor machine. So we can receive these sounds. Some people can receive them better than others, but children can definitely receive these infrasounds. Dogs can hear this low-level sound, birds can hear it, and I understand that monkeys can hear it also. In some ways some people are deaf to these sounds, but you can actually attune yourself by aligning yourself into unity, a form of all is one, a form of meditation. Then you can hear that sound. You have to listen and it will come to you. You don't go to it; it comes to you. And it is there in the trees. This is how birds can locate their own trees for feeding, perching and pruning, or for tuning up their bodies to the sun. This infrasound is just at the edge of coming into the radar of science because it means that the physicists have to work with the biologists and the biologists have to work with the biochemists, and there are not too many teams like that in all of the world. But there are a few people holding professorships of physics who actually do know about this.

As an organic farmer, I am very aware of the significance of trees. Not just what I plant, but the trees around the garden, and even the rich soil when a tree dies. As many listeners are starting to grow their own gardens, what would you recommend for trees that can benefit the growth of their gardens? And second, if you drive through much of the farmland in the United States, especially in the Midwest, you see that every inch of land has been utilized by the larger farmers. In the earlier past, the use of hedgerows was known to benefit the life and health of a farm. Could you explain to us what a hedgerow is and how they can benefit us?

Can I answer the question about the hedgerow first? When you have a hedgerow, you have a biodiversity of insects. It is a chain link fence of the forest around the field that provides the biodiversity needed for your crop, for predation and also for pollination. It has been proven that when you have your hedgerow, you have a 35% increase in your crop because of pollination and when you're talking about industrial farms, I don't really care if they are organic or are not organic, what happens is you have oceanic fields. All of our beneficial insects require one very essential amino acid called lysine; the queen bee, the queen wasp bee or whatever requires lysine for egg laying. Without that they are not able to produce the huge brood that they need to do all the massive pollination, stamen by stamen by stamen, and if you have oceanic fields you cannot produce lysine in the early flowering of the hedgerows, the bees cannot survive, therefore you cannot have pollination. Some of the bees are dying because they do not have sufficient food. And the birds are our first line of predation, running up and down the crops and protecting them by getting all of the deleterious insects. But birds cannot do predation when you have oceanic fields. And these industrial farms are also pouring the nitrogen from fertilizers into the oceans and destroying them. What do you expect when you attend the Church of the Holy Dollar and put everything into your fields and forget nature? You will end up destroying the planet!

Now, let me backtrack on this one. The price of food is too cheap, and the farmers are on their knees. Please, ask them to have smaller fields, so they can have areas where all of the native pollinators can live and grow. They are as good as you; a bee is as good as I am. So we have to hold hands with all of these agents of nature, and also allow these farmers to survive. What can you do as a consumer? You have a voting power in your purse. You go out with your purse and if and when you can you buy organic, but you try to buy organic from small farmers, local farmers, and keep them off their knees. And try to buy good quality food for you and for your growing babies.

Now we will go back to the first question you asked. What would be beneficial for little city gardens or country gardens would be any member of the Rosaceae family, like a pear, an apple, or other fruiting trees, and Amelanchiers, like the Serviceberry. All of those groups of flowering, fruiting trees are very good because the flower is a little five-petal flower, like the rose, that a flying insect, a wasp, a bee, a butterfly can fly into and rotate. When the insect can rotate, it feeds, when it feeds, it gets enough nectar, and when it gets enough nectar it keeps these beneficial insects primed for pollination. And so you have a win-win situation.

After all of your many years of observing and studying trees and forests, as a scientist and as a spiritual seeker to discover their hidden meanings, what is the wisdom you would most like to impart to us?

I would say that the tree is the king of the forest. The forests evolved to be the pinnacle of the green world with its chloroplastic structure, and we have evolved to be the pinnacle, I think, of the animal world. We have evolved our red blood cells, which contain hemoglobin, and the hemoglobin that makes us run is almost identical to the chlorophyll that makes the tree run. We have to hold hand to hand. The oxygen that is produced by the trees gives us the kiss of life, and we have to look to the trees and thank them like the ancients did in the long way past, because if we don't do that, when the last tree goes, like it did on Easter Island, we too, will go. No question, scientifically, spiritually, or otherwise about that.

Expressive Arts Therapy

Denise Boston

As a society, we have come a long way in the field of mental health over the past few decades. Improving the treatment and quality of life for individuals who live with serious mental illnesses as well as people who struggle with traumatic life events such as hunger and food insecurity, violence, cultural stigmatization, and social trauma, has been at the forefront of the work of many healing practitioners and therapists all over the world. The expressive arts therapy field specifically, has given increased attention to creative and liberatory approaches to health, wellness, and trauma intervention.

Expressive Arts Therapy (EXA) integrates a range of arts modalities in the service of mental health and self-actualization. EXA therapy practitioners have a wealth of aesthetic options to draw upon—music, visual arts, dance/movement, photography, creative writing, singing, storytelling, drama, poetry, and indigenous rituals. Through the creative process, clients and/or participants have the opportunity to explore and potentially transform emotional, social, and relational issues; identify patterns of personal success; and experience new and innovative insights.

Expressive arts therapists grounded in culturally sensitive and liberation psychological approaches—ones that aim to actively understand the psychology and social structures of oppressed communities—use the arts as a means of understanding and collaborating with children, youth, families, couples, and individuals dealing with varying degrees of threats that hinder self-actualization and a path to wholeness. Expressive arts processes in counseling and group therapy have been used in a variety of settings including, but not limited to, hospice, youth residential facilities, and homeless shelters.

One particular health challenge that therapists and counselors worldwide are currently being exposed to is emotional and psychological trauma. Environmental-contextual conditions such as chronic violence, bullying, human trafficking, abject poverty, war, and post-traumatic stress disorder, have necessitated an authentic and empathic therapeutic presence and practice with victimized populations and trauma survivors. An expressive arts-based approach has been effective in the treatment and intervention of trauma recovery, because an imaginative and creative process is a doorway into self-reflective inner work and self-empowerment. The body, mind, and in some cases, spiritual experience allow participants to articulate their feelings aesthetically when words are inaccessible and inadequate. Arts approaches used in the therapeutic setting are a powerful, sacred, and evocative tool for healing. The work of the therapist in this context is to increase hope and motivation, and create enough safety that the participants can become aware of their own agency and strengths.

In my work as an EXA educator and registered drama therapist, I have facilitated workshops and training sessions in collaboration with community-based service providers on the concept of arts, healing, and social consciousness. For more than a decade, my programmatic and research interests have been in the area of African American community mental health. African Americans are often at a socioeconomic disadvantage in terms of accessing mental health care and culturally sensitive counseling. Much of my work has been conducted collaboratively with community organizations and schools, and is aimed at promoting positive youth development by increasing cultural values and presenting an expressive arts caring approach for traumatized children and adolescents of African descent. The cultural-based research in the African American community has incorporated the use of drama, storytelling, dance, spoken word, and drumming to redress the disparities defined by historical trauma and the systematic loss of culture and self-identity. The data gathered through these projects have provided an important glimpse into the vulnerable and alienated voices of young people and the outcomes has indicated the positive and healing effects of expressing one's truth.

A memorable moment, which demonstrates the power of arts-based intervention, is an experience I had with an 18-year-old African American man by the name of Kevin (not his real name), who had been trapped in the criminal justice system most of his life. He participated in an expressive arts workshop that I facilitated for males living in a residential group home in Arlington, VA. As they entered the arts room, the young men were welcomed to the setting with the music of Tupac Shakur, a famous rap artist at that time, as well large pieces of paper and an assortment of colorful art materials. I instructed the group to allow the lyrics and the rhythm of the music to inspire them to create a collage that represented their stories, thoughts, and dreams. At first, Kevin was reticent and skeptical of this unfamiliar situation and stood with his arms folded, disconnected from the group. I did not intercede, but kept an eye on him as I moved around the room checking on the progress of the other teens. He stood for a while listening to the music, and then something moved him. He picked up the large oil pastels and immersed himself in the creative process. Once he completed one collage he approached me and asked if he could do another. In the two and a half hour session, he had the opportunity to channel his anger, trauma, and loss into two powerful, provocative works that represented his story. At the conclusion of the session, Kevin rolled up his work and left the room a different person than who he was when he walked in. I stopped Kevin on his way out and shared with him how moved I was by his work. I wanted him to know "I see you". We both shared a special transitional moment—never to see each other again. It is moments such as this that demonstrates the transformative and healing potential of the arts.

As a little girl growing up in Baltimore, MD, I loved using dance, music, reading, and dramatic play to express myself. At the age of twelve, I was diagnosed with juvenile rheumatoid arthritis. Bedridden with my knees filled with fluid, swollen, and painful to touch, I spent months in the hospital unable to be the energetic and vibrant child I was known to be. What I owe my recovery to was a supportive family and community, and my creative resources. I used movement and dance as my physical therapy to strengthen my inflamed limbs; and music to heal the sad places deep inside. It was from this traumatic childhood experience that I found my calling and a path to the creative exploratory process. I uncovered something profound within my spirit and my quest for optimal health and wellness, strengthened my love and compassion for others dealing with various aspects of pain and suffering.

I am appreciative of my arts-based practice and journey and will continue to use the arts with people who live within intersectional situations; race, gender, class and sexuality. This year, I have been invited to go back to my birthplace and to Washington, DC to promote the healing arts and provide training to mental health professionals working with children and families in traumatized environments. It is inspiring to connect with local people and plant the seeds of the arts in their promising communities and to imagine a thriving untraumatized world together.

ON PROPHECY AND TIME – PART 2

PIR ZIA INAYAT-KHAN TO DAVID SPANGLER AND WILLIAM IRWIN THOMPSON

Dear William,

Yes! In Count Jan Potocki's *Manuscript Found in Saragossa* a colony of Moors secretly resides in a system of caves deep inside the Sierra Moreno Mountains. These Muslim troglodytes are a fitting symbol, I think, of the traditions that "went underground" when the Reconquista overtook the Convivencia in medieval Spain. Their persistence is a largely unrecognized but crucially important factor in the cultural formation of Europe.

The Western assimilation of Sufi knowledge is difficult to track because the debt is rarely acknowledged in the original sources. A remarkable exception is Ramon Lull's introduction to his *Book of the Lover and the Beloved*, in which he credits the Sufis with supplying the inspiration for his meditations on love. (I wonder to what extent Lull's chivalry was informed by Sufi chivalry, or futuwwa. His *Book of the*

Order of Chivalry was a seminal work in the theoretical elaboration of knighthood.)

Dante is an interesting case. The "sweet new style" that he shared with Guido Cavalcanti appears not so new after all when seen in the context of classical Arab love lyrics (such as the *Diwan of Majnun*), the Persian mystical "School of Love," and the romantic psychology of Andalusian poets and aesthetes like Ibn Hazm (in his Ring of the Dove). As you point out, Cavalcanti's initiatory sect of Fedeli d'Amore has its spiritual roots in Sicily, where a century earlier Frederick II corresponded with the Sufi hermeticist Ibn Sab'in and commissioned an Arabic translation of Merlin's prophecies.

Dante's angelology is steeped in the Islamic Neoplatonism of al-Farabi, Ibn Sina, al-Ghazali, and Ibn Rushd, and as you rightly say, his heavenly ascent in the *Comedy* is modeled on the mi'raj of the Prophet Muhammad. So it is a matter of grim irony that he portrays Muhammad (peace be upon him) mangled and split open in the eighth circle of hell. Maybe, as you say, this was to camouflage his Sufi leanings, though I wonder, since he had the audacity to put popes in hell as well.

My friend Omid Safi suggests in his new book that Dante's portrayal of Muhammad is a malicious parody of the ninety-fourth chapter of the Qur'an, "The Opening Up," which describes how God opened the Prophet's chest and purified his heart. In any case, Dante is a good example of how attraction and repulsion coincided in the encounter between Orient and Occident in the Mediterranean basin. Another example is Ariosto, whose hero Orlando vanquishes Saracen warriors while pining for the Muslim princess Angelica.

So yes, I fully agree that cultural and spiritual contacts between Christendom and Islam in Andalusia and the Levant set the stage for the Renaissance. And I agree that if esoteric undercurrents could flow amidst the ideological fervor on both sides of the Crusades, they can flow again amidst Global Jihad and the War on Terror. To tap that flow is Seven Pillars' reason for being.

In Eschenbach's romance (borrowed from the Moorish astrologer Flegetanis), Parzival attained the Grail when he reconciled with his

Muslim half-brother. Today I think the Grail's price is higher. The rifts that we have to heal are not only religious and cultural; they are also ecological and spiritual. Your Entelechy and David Spangler's Incarnational Spirituality are, to me, harbingers of the integrated worldview of the coming Renaissance.

The next letter in this series begins on page 64.

MY GOD LIVES ON THE STREET

ADAM BUCKO

It's nighttime. I am walking outside the Port Authority Bus Terminal, that depressing brick behemoth on 42nd Street and 8th Avenue that is the main hub for buses arriving to and departing from New York City. I am looking for homeless kids, trying to spot new arrivals who might still be hanging out, unsure of where to go. I keep my gaze active, scanning the outside and the various crevices of the building.

Tonight, like every night, there are about 4,000 kids in New York City who will spend the night on the street. While most of us will be comfortably resting in our beds, many of these 4,000 will sleep on the subway, in an abandoned building, or with a person with whom they will have to compromise their dignity in exchange for a place to sleep. I want to reach them to offer help before they disappear into the Manhattan sinkhole. But I am not the only one looking for them. As soon as they step off the bus, there is a chain of pimps waiting for them, ready to promise them the future that they dream of. Ready to mesmerize their minds, stab their souls, and imprison their consciences.

In 2004 Taz Tagore and I co-founded the Reciprocity Foundation, an organization that offers street youth support and helps them build healthy and successful lives. Our job is to catch the kids before they become victims of this never-ending cycle of horror, abuse, and prostitution. It is just a question of who gets to them first.

A long time ago, I learned that if I want to be effective in my work, I have to walk the streets with certainty. I have to act and feel as if these streets are an extension of my living room. This aura of ease confuses all the pimps and the other sketchy characters here that are used to seeing fear in everyone around them. They are not sure what to make of me. They don't know who I know or who I run with, and so they leave me alone.

I walk into the station to see if I can find any newcomers. Kids come here from all around the country for various reasons. Some come because they were asked to leave by their parents. Some because their families were too poor to take care of them. Some because they aged out of the foster care system. Upon turning 17 or 18, they were simply dropped off at the Greyhound bus station and told to follow their dreams. Some come here because they have suffered abuse by a family member, and the only way to escape that—other than suicide—is to run away. Some kids come to New York City because they are gay, and they have been kicked out by religious parents who believe that the harsh reality of the street will convince them to "change their ways."

Over the years, I have met thousands of homeless kids. Some I was able to help, and some I lost. So here I am today walking these streets, prayerfully knowing that each time I see a kid, it might be the last time. Knowing this changes everything. Knowing this lends urgency to my work.

As I continue to walk, faces of kids I have known appear in my mind's eye. There is Tanisha, who got shot by a pimp. There is Nicky, who was kidnapped by two fellow shelter residents and turned into a prostitute. There is Larry, calling me on the phone crying, telling me he was just diagnosed with HIV. There is Tony, telling me how he is haunted by the memory of his father killing his mother, as he looked on, a frightened child. These stories are so horrifying and yet so typical, the daily experiences of thousands of street kids. I take a few more steps into a dark alley only to notice a kid I know getting into a stranger's car. God only knows what will happen once she gets into that car.

Seeing this, it is so easy to just give up. But I cannot do that. The kids we have helped through the Reciprocity Foundation tell me that we are their only family. They say our center is the only place they have ever felt loved. I stop for a moment and recall all the happy faces I have seen over the years. Kids who went through our program and whose lives were changed. Kids who discovered their talents and now work with other struggling teens. Kids who graduated from college and are now beacons of hope in this hopeless world of the streets. Kids who recently made a film called "Invisible: Diaries of New York's Homeless Youth." It aired on a major network, was nominated for an Emmy Award and showed everyone that homeless youth, once given proper attention and care, are capable of doing great things. All of them came to us in a state of despair, and through the Foundation got what they needed to lead purposeful and meaningful lives. Thinking of them, I know that I cannot, I will not, give up on those in need of help.

It is 3 a.m. and time to go home. As I walk towards the subway I try to hold all of those faces in my heart and offer them to God. Along the way I hear a mad street preacher desperately screaming, "Where is God? Where is God? Where is God?!" I look at him, and the words of Mother Teresa come to mind: "Jesus is the Hungry—to be fed. Jesus is the Thirsty—to be satiated. Jesus is the Naked—to be clothed. Jesus is the Homeless—to be taken in. Jesus is the Lonely—to be loved. Jesus is the Unwanted—to be wanted." Where is God? He is here on this street, laying naked in the gutter. He is here on this street, homeless. He is here on this street, in all the lonely and unwanted, waiting for our love.

As I continue my walk towards the subway I wonder, what will it take for us to notice Him?

THE ISLAMIC NOTION OF BEAUTY

WILLIAM C. CHITTICK, PH. D.

Mosque Mohammed Ali, Cairo Egypt

Anyone with the vaguest knowledge of Islamic culture knows that it has produced extraordinary works of art and architecture—Persian miniatures, the Taj Mahal, the Alhambra. Few are aware, however, that this rich artistic heritage is firmly rooted in a worldview that highlights love and beauty.

The link between love and beauty is clear. We love what we find beautiful. Beauty attracts, ugliness repels. Nor are beauty and ugliness simply physical characteristics. We all know people who are outwardly attractive but personally repellent, and vice versa.

Beauty makes a massive appearance in love poetry like that of Ibn al-Farid, Rumi, Yunus Emre, and countless others. Their verses stir up wonder and delight by evoking the beautiful characteristics of the beloved.

In explaining the relationship between love and its object, philosophers like Avicenna analyzed the universe in terms of a Necessary Being that combined the attributes of Plato's Good with those of Aristotle's Unmoved Mover. All contingent things, animate or inanimate, are in love with the absolute beauty of the Good and strive to reach it, hence the ceaseless activity that fills the universe.

Those with a more theological bent preferred to cite the saying of the Prophet, "God is beautiful, and He loves beauty." They understood both beauty and love in terms of the axiom of tawhid, "There is no god but God." If God is beautiful, then there is nothing truly beautiful but God. And if God is loving, then no one truly loves but he.

A bit of reflection on God's love for beauty leads to the conclusion that he loves himself before all else. God as the one true lover perceives his own true beauty and loves it eternally. As for the universe, God loves it because, by loving himself, he loves everything demanded by his beauty and mercy, and that includes an infinity of creaturely possibilities. This view was encapsulated in the oft-quoted hadith qudsi (divine saying), "I was a Hidden Treasure, and I loved to be recognized, so I created the creatures to recognize Me."

In discussions of God's love for the universe, theologians and scholars agreed that God loves both the way things are and the way things ought to be. The discrepancy between these two loves has given rise to the never-ending debate over determinism and free will, nature and nurture, science and values.

God loves the way things are because "He made beautiful everything He created" (Quran 32:7). All things are lovable because they make his beauty manifest. Each thing plays its own harmonious role in the infinite web of relationships that the Quran calls God's "signs." The signs in turn display the characteristics of what it calls God's "most beautiful names."

God loves the way things ought to be because he created human beings with freedom to change themselves. Unique among all things in the universe—so far as we know human beings have the capacity to recognize themselves as works in progress and to intervene in the manner in which they develop. Ghazali and other theologians pointed out that people are "compelled to be free." The expression points precisely to the creative tension between what is and what ought to be.

God's love for all things is often discussed in terms of the universal, all-encompassing mercy designated by the name, "All-merciful." His love for the way people ought to be is then tightly bound up with the particular, responsive mercy designated by the name "Ever-merciful." The formula of consecration—"In the name of God, the All-merciful, the Ever-merciful"—acknowledges both sorts of love.

To say that God loves all things reiterates the principle of with-ness voiced in the verse, "He is with you wherever you are" (57:4). By means of his all-embracing love and mercy, God tends to the welfare of the universe, including the posthumous realms.

To say that God loves things as they ought to be points to the human capacity to recognize God's with-ness. In order to live their lives in a manner appropriate to the divine presence within themselves, people must be merciful and compassionate. The fact that God is with them does not mean that they are also with him—that is precisely what needs to be achieved, what "ought to be."

Not being with God opens the door to the ugliness and evil that are apparent to everyone. To ask then how a beautiful God could create a world full of ugliness is to ask why each thing and each person is uniquely itself. From the standpoint of the role that beings and things play in the cosmic harmony, all are beautiful, but some are more beautiful than others, and the scale of beauty stretches not from "one to 10" but from one to infinity.

Whatever the scale we use to judge the discrepancies among things and people, no two fit exactly into the same niche. There is gradation without limit in categories without limit. The lower a thing may be on the scale of beauty, the more it is apt to appear as ugly.

More simply, the world is ugly inasmuch as we perceive it empty of God, the absolute good. It is beautiful inasmuch as we recognize the divine with-ness, the signs of the most beautiful names that fill the universe. Failure to recognize the signs goes back to ignorance—the "root poison," as Buddhists call it.

Islam has no notion of original sin, but the Quran does say that Adam "forgot" (20:115). Our inherited forgetfulness provides all we need to bungle the job of being what we ought to be.

SACRED INVESTING

CHARLES EISENSTEIN

The Dharma of Wealth

In a sacred economy, investment has a meaning nearly opposite of
what it means today. Today, investing is what people do to preserve or
increase their wealth. In a sacred economy, it is what we do to share our
wealth. Excess wealth, whether inherited from family or from an earlier
time in one's own life, is a dharma, a call to service. To squander it on
baubles, to give it away senselessly, or to devote oneself to its increase
are all ways of refusing that call. We live in a world of fundamental
abundance that we have, through our beliefs and habits, rendered arti-
ficially poor. At the most basic level, sacred investing is simply the inten-
tional channeling of abundance toward a creative purpose. This is the
kind of investment that is aligned with a future economy in which status
comes from giving, not having, and security comes not from accumulation, but from being a nexus of flow. It begins with the meeting of needs
and unfolds into the creation of beauty.

"Investment" means to clothe, as in to take naked money and put
it into new vestments, something real in the physical or social realm.
Money is naked human potential—creative energy that has not yet
been "clothed" with material or social constructions. Right investment
is to array money in sacred vestments: to use it to create, protect, and
sustain the things that are becoming sacred to us today. These are the

same things that will form the backbone of tomorrow's economy. Right investment is therefore practice for the coming world, both psychological practice and practical preparation. It accustoms one to the new mentality of wealth—finding channels for productive giving—and it creates and strengthens those channels, which might persist even when the present money system collapses. Money as we know it might disappear, but the relationships of gratitude and obligation will remain.

Just as financial investments won't survive economic collapse, so also does the end of life mean the end of all our accumulations. At that moment, what will give you joy? The memory of all you have given. Upon death, we take with us only what we have given. As in a gift culture, that is what our wealth will be. By giving, we lay up treasures in heaven. When we merge with the All, we receive that which we gave to all.

Robbing Peter to Pay Paul

Even before an economy realizing the core principles of the gift crystallizes, we can begin living it right now. This is far more radical than "socially conscious investing" or "ethical investing." While these ideas are steps in the right direction, they harbor an internal contradiction. For by seeking a positive financial return, they perpetuate the conversion of the world into money.

The venture capitalist identifies high-growth opportunities and provides the money to bring them to fruition. In a steady-state or degrowth economy, this model is no longer appropriate—hence the turn toward a different investment goal: the restoration, and not the more efficient exploitation, of the natural and social commons. I am talking about investing, not earning. It is one thing to receive rewards for doing good work in the world; it is quite another to add money to money by virtue of having money. For example, it would be fine for a corporation to charge enough to keep the business viable, to pay employees well, and to finance expansion, research, and so forth. But beyond that, corporations must earn an additional amount that goes out to investors in the form of interest payments or dividends. Where does this additional amount come from? From the same place all money today comes from: interest-bearing debt and the conversion of the world into money.

So if you really want to contribute to the good of the world, don't ask for a return on your investment. Don't try to give and take at the same time. If you want to take (and you might have good reasons for doing so), then take, but don't pretend you are giving. If interest-generating investments contribute to the despoliation of the natural and social commons, then obviously we should not invest money at interest. The same goes for any investment that drives the expansion of the realm of goods and services. As socially conscious investors, you don't want to contribute to the monetization of life and nature. There is no escape from this principle.

I am not advocating an age of altruism in which we forgo personal benefit for the common good. I foresee, rather, a fusion of personal benefit and common good. For example, when I give money to people in my community, I create feelings of gratitude that might motivate a return gift to me or an onward gift to someone else. Either way, I have strengthened the community that sustains me. When we are embedded in a gift community, we naturally direct our gratitude not only toward the proximate giver but toward the community as a whole, and we take care of its neediest members (gifts seek needs).

If we use today's money to create a large enough reservoir of gratitude, then our society can withstand practically anything. So badly have we damaged planet and spirit that it will require a full outpouring of all our gifts to heal it. The outpouring of gifts comes from gratitude. Therefore, the best investment you can make with your money is to generate gratitude. It doesn't matter if the gratitude recognizes you as the giver. Ultimately, the proper object of gratitude is the Giver of all our own gifts, of our world, of our lives.

To get ready for the gift economy, and to live today in its spirit, instead of investing money with the purpose of making more of it, we shift the focus of investment toward using accumulated money as a gift from the old world to the new, a gift from the ancestors to the future. It is analogous to the gifts of life, of mother's milk, of food and sensory stimulation and all the things that build us into adults, which we receive in order that we may enter adulthood and give onward of these gifts. The question, then, is how to use money in the consciousness of a gift.

Old Accumulations to New Purposes

The world sits on top of a huge pile of wealth, the end product of ten thousand years of culture and technology. We have a mighty industrial infrastructure; we have roads and airplanes; we have a vast apparatus already in existence that, for centuries, has been devoted toward the expansion of the human realm and the conquest of the natural. The time has come to turn the tools of separation, dominance, and control toward the purpose of reunion, the healing of the world. Who knows to what purposes we will turn the technologies of profit? When humanity is no longer under compulsion to grow its realm, we will turn our collective ingenuity and the amassed knowledge, information, and technology of the ages toward ecology, connectedness, and healing.

Whether it is the application of accumulated technology or accumulated money, we want to be sure that we are not using it in the old mode: as a tool to achieve more separation from nature or more financial wealth. The dynamics of usury-money are addiction dynamics, requiring an ever-greater dose (of the commons) to maintain normality, converting more and more of the basis of well-being into money for a fix. So too it is with our politicians' efforts to prolong the age of growth. If you are an investor, it is time to shift your focus entirely to the creation of connections, the generation of gratitude, and the reclamation and protection of the commonwealth. The time for the mind-set of wealth preservation is over.

That is why I suggest the concept of using money to destroy money. By this I mean to use money to restore and protect the natural, social, cultural, and spiritual commons from which it was originally created. Thanks to the efforts of generations of do-gooders, we still have a portion of our divine bequest. There is still goodness in the soil; there are still healthy forests here and there; there are still fish in some parts of the ocean; there are still people and cultures that haven't completely sold off their health and creativity. This remaining natural, social, and spiritual capital is what will carry us through the transition and form the basis to heal the world.

Right Livelihood

The same principles that apply to right investing apply also to right livelihood; indeed, right livelihood and right investment are two sides of the same coin. If right investing uses money as gift to support the creation of a more beautiful world, then right livelihood accepts that gift as it does that work. Traditional employment receives money for helping expand the monetized realm. We find that in order to earn money, we must participate in the conversion of the good, the true, and the beautiful into money. That is because of the money system—credit ultimately goes to those who can most effectively create new goods and services (or take it from those who create them).

Humanity possesses vast stores of wealth in many forms, the accumulation of centuries of exploitation, that can now be turned to other purposes, for example to preserve and restore natural, social, cultural, and spiritual capital. Doing this won't create more money; therefore whoever is paying for it is ultimately giving a gift. In other words, the key to "right livelihood" is to live off of gifts. These can come in subtle forms. For example, say you sell fair-trade products. When someone buys one, at several multiples the cost of a functionally equivalent sweatshop product, the cost difference is essentially a gift. They didn't have to pay that much. The same is true if your work is to install solar water heaters or build shelters for the homeless. Many traditional social service jobs, like social work, teaching, and so on, partake in the energy of the gift as long as they don't contribute to the more efficient operation of the earth-devouring machine. The source of the money could be a buyer, a foundation, or even the government. What makes it a gift is the motive—that it does not aim to get the cheapest price or generate even more money in return.

We are born into gratitude, born into the need and the desire to give. Trust that it is not your true desire to comply with the conversion of the world into money. Trust that you want to do beautiful things with your life.

THE KARMA OF NATIONS

NAMBARYN ENKHBAYAR

Buddhism explains that everything has been created by a cause or is the result of causation. In other words, there was and/or still remains a cause behind everything and every phenomenon witnessed in the world. One can say, in a very general way then, that in its search to understand the nature of every phenomenon or a complex of phenomena, Buddhist philosophy seeks the cause or a complex of causes lying behind a phenomenon or phenomena. We can draw a parallel between Buddhist philosophy and economics here in that economics should generally be a science to discover the reason or a complex of causes behind every economic and social phenomenon.

An understanding of the theory of causation regulating the very existence and activity of everything in the world according to Buddhist philosophy brings us to the next category of Buddhist philosophy—that is, the concept of karma. Karma is a kind of accumulated potential power or weakness gained as a result of each deed done in the past. Thus, every human being is unique, and all human beings and all communities and nations are different from each other because of their deeds. The economic development of each nation is unique in the sense that it is an accumulation of actions, both good and bad, that the leadership of a given country has carried out after being given power to rule a nation.

The responsibility of every individual and every nation is to be aware of the results of their respective actions and inactions because in the course of time these actions and inactions accumulate and form one's current condition. Put simply, one is responsible for one's present status, however good or bad it is, and each nation is responsible for the condition in which it finds itself. Karma indirectly means accountability. Every person, every government and every nation should be accountable for its deeds. There is no individual without his or her karma; similarly, there is no nation or government without accountability.

Understanding the principles of karma also provides a deeper appreciation for one's rightful place or location in the world and the appropriate time for undertaking an activity. Additionally, karma means that one should be aware of the necessity to stay within the limits of historical time and space for one's activities to accumulate good deeds.

In Eastern societies, especially those in which a nomadic culture is still alive and very much enriched by Buddhist culture, as in Mongolia, one can find a very strong feeling of community and cohesion. It is revealing to investigate the question of a link between Buddhist philosophy and economics from this nomadic point of view, because economics can be defined as a science that deals with finding ways for human beings to have sustainable and more fulfilling lives within a community, and now in the global society.

The strong community feeling of nomadic or seminomadic people in countries where Buddhism is the dominant religion can be explained in several ways.

First, nomads can survive only by gathering together and helping each other. Living in a community used to mean simply surviving. Members of nomadic societies survive not at the expense of other "weak" fellows but by forming a community in which distinguishing the "strong" from the "weak" is irrelevant, and where one's helping others to survive actually results in helping oneself to survive. Anyone who is more or less familiar with Buddhism knows that one of the Three Jewels of Buddhism is sangha, the Buddhist fellowship or community of monks and nuns. The community, or living in a community, is considered one of the treasures of Buddhism. Living in community means learning to share—sharing not only good but also, for example, sharing suffering, happiness and others' pain. This can be compared with the modern understanding of economic and social development. In the Buddhist model, development can be achieved not at the expense or exclusion of any person or any nation but rather in the larger collective community by including everyone and every nation in the process of development.

From living in a community, whose principles are based on learning to share others' pain, it is easy to come to one of the very important ideals of Mahayana Buddhism—the ideal of the bodhisattva. According to tradition, a bodhisattva is one who has already perceived the meaning of life and reached the condition of readiness to attain a higher, if not the highest, level of existence and nonexistence. But the bodhisattva chooses to stay at his or her present level of existence out of great compassion and mercifulness towards other human beings—because of her or his great empathy to feel the pain of others. The deeper meaning of the ideal of the bodhisattva in terms of the karma of nations is as follows:

If someone or some nations have reached a relatively better level of existence—in our sense, development—than other people or nations, it is immoral; and because of this immorality, it will be impossible to develop further without "feeling the pain of the underdevelopment of others" (both human beings and nations).

The meaning of the Buddhist ideal of the bodhisattva can be stated in modern economic terms, "The more you help others, the better, faster and more qualitatively you develop yourself." In other words, according to Buddhist philosophy, development means assisting others. The main difference between quantitative and qualitative development is that the latter means and includes morality, responsibility, account-ability, the feeling of community and of the necessity to assist others, and uniqueness in each example of development, while the former does not.

Another important category of Buddhist philosophy that we need to consider in our search to find links between Buddhism and economics is the one of attachment and nonattachment. According to Buddhism, attachment or passion for someone or something brings suffering.

Once a person or a society, such as a consumer society, is attached in a broad sense to everything that is transitory and subject to change, it starts turning into a body absorbed only by its desire to satisfy insatiable demands. Such a person or society starts to lose its mobility, flexibility and the ability to adapt to new challenges. In contrast, one of the main characteristics of a nomadic society in which Buddhism is the dominant religion is a relatively pollution-free lifestyle lived in a harmonious relationship with the environment, and with a readiness to give up the demands and things that become burdensome. Being unattached means not being occupied by prejudices, being objective and maintaining a harmonious balance between the material and spiritual and between cause and effect and karma.

Taking into account the preceding points, we inevitably arrive at the conclusion that Buddhism considers the creation of a good balance—or in a broader sense—the creation of a healthy environment where every being has the freedom to realize or improve its potential. This is a key for generating the conditions for qualitative economic and social development. This can be simplified further by stating that the realization or improvement of one's potential or karma is positive development. At the same time, when the material and spiritual, as well as cause and effect, are balanced, the interdependence, instead of independence, of every being is implied. Buddhism proceeds from the understanding that real, qualitative development is based not on the theory of contraction of two or multiple polarities or interests, but rather on the notion of interdependence of everyone and everything. The Buddhist theory of emptiness (shunyata) seems to be a philosophical basis for such an understanding of economic and social development. If one is logically loyal to the general implication of the emptiness concept, one has to accept that there cannot be permanent indicators of development in Buddhism because everything is dependent upon causation and is in constant motion and change—everything is impermanent and relative. The ideas outlined here could be the lines along which one can try to find indicators of development through the eyes of Buddhism. However, in the search for such indicators one must always proceed from understanding the main, ultimate indicator of development—a human being.

Finally, let us recall the fable when Buddha kept silent when he was asked what the ultimate meaning of life was. He said that if a person was wounded, he would not try to find out who did the shooting, what the size of the arrow was or what it was made of. Instead he should try to remove the arrow as soon as possible. Perhaps it is worthwhile to remove immediately the arrows that have wounded us through irresponsibility, lack of accountability, narrowness of mind and ignorance of the fact that everyone and everything is dependent on causation and on each other. Here we find that the indicator and ultimate aim of qualitative development is the human being.

On Prophecy and Time – part 3

William Irwin Thompson to Pir Zia Inayat-Khan and David Spangler

Dear David,

In response to our phone call conversation yesterday, I have just re-read your chapter on "the Pit Crew" in your new book, *Subtle Worlds: an Explorer's Field Notes.*

Yes, I would say that my concept of the Entelechy is different. I see my daily yogic practice of an invocation of energy in the movements of

my morning pranayama as a meditation that constellates (literally!) the five or six pointed star as a fractal of the Cosmic Mind. You could also call it, in Jungian terms, an "active imagination" of the Vitruvian Man of Da Vinci.

As I begin these movements that are like the movements of

ch'i in Chi Gung, I envision "God the Father" above and outside the physical body, the Divine Mother or Holy Spirit over the brain in the sahasrara or crown chakra, and the indwelling Cosmic Christ within the third eye or ajna chakra. At the left extended hand I envision the stellar angel, and at the right extended hand the Jinn of the lunar sphere. At the left foot I envision the earthly Angel of protection, the protective atmosphere of energy, air, wind and weather; and at the right foot, the elemental, the primordial spirit of the geological and geomantic forces of Earth itself. And in the center, behind the heart, as Sri Aurobindo would say for the locus of his "Psychic Being," or in "the cave of the heart" as it is described in the Upanishads, is the Socratic Daimon, the being of all one's incarnations and not just the personal ego of only one. This is the icon of the winged heart of the Sufis. So the day begins with a focus of attention on the self as microcosm, but a microcosm of interpenetrating dimensions and worlds and not just a hunk of meat in space as a container. And, as you can see, a planetary syncretism is my daily fare, as I draw off more than one tradition of spiritual practice. I do not invent this stuff; I receive it in the form of a Daimonic teaching, as you describe it in your book.

But, David, I do agree with your presentation about the Soul in your Field Notes—from your experience as a child of seven in the Sufi lands of Morocco—that the Soul is vaster even than the Daimon. I see the Daimon as a meta-personality, a vehicle created and projected by the soul for a whole cycle of incarnations into a particular world or solar-system. In the terms of the Egyptian esoterism I discussed in "Civilization and Initiation in Ancient Egypt" in *The Time Falling Bodies Take to Light,* I would say that this vehicle is a temporal function that lasts for one Magnus Annus, the Great Year of the precession of the equinox, or 25, 920 years. Rudolf Steiner says somewhere in one of his numerous books of lectures that the being takes on the male sex for half of that rotation, and the female sex for the other. But I wonder nowadays if it is that neat. Given modern "gender-bending," I would think the circle is more like the spirals and leaps an Olympic figure skater would make around the oval ice rink.

In my imagination, I see angel, daimon, jinn of the moon, angel of the earthly atmosphere of wind and weather, and elemental or primor-dial spirit of Earth like the mitochondria, plastids, nucleus, and cytoplasm of the cell. So for me this Entelechy is an emergent evolutionary form and is a vehicle of incarnation for a new civilization that we have not yet created but are invoking. Your "pit crew" I see as a team now assisting in one person's incarnation, but the Entelechy is preparing for a new kind of incarnation, a new kind of cell or organism in the Cosmic Mind—sort of like Lynn Margulis's laboratory films of the protist inside the gut of the termite.

Does this make sense to you, or am I being too fanciful?

Yours in the Fellowship of Lindisfarne,

Bill

The next letter in this series begins on page 92.

Returning the Soul to Poetry

Jennifer Ferraro

In a techno-consumer culture enraptured with externals and super-ficiality, the tendency toward poetry can represent a struggle to value, protect and embody those qualities that are most hidden in oneself, the qualities of the soul. This hidden-ness that lives within us form-lessly recognizes and loves beauty and is nurtured in being, as well as in doing. To affirm that that which cannot be seen exists, that that which is wordless and elusive to language has presence and power and reality, is no small feat.

In a time when our world grows increasingly wed to surfaces, we need to actively protect and foster that which is hidden from the eye of superficial vision. We need poetry more than ever now. We need it in order to remember, to revalue what we have left behind as the "childish" dreams of youth and innocence, to remind us of unseen and invisible worlds. So the task of poetry is not to simply describe or convey what is seen but to be a reminder of how, when what is seen penetrates the depths of our silences, vision opens and can transfigure reality. The real act of poetry happens in the heart, not on the page.

People need poetry in order to remember that soul exists. Sometimes our lives take us away from who we deeply are into a façade that we live in for years. Yet amidst this numbness an aching hunger for meaning and beauty, for a home in one's own being, persists. We long for a time when we will feel fully at home in ourselves and our lives, and wildly alive in ways which we have only glimpsed. We want life to be rich with love, full of gifts given and shared, a continual praising. The note we were given to sing pursues us, waiting for us to remember, to return to its urging. More and more I have come to feel that the only thing we really have to do here is to try to stay true to that note each one of us was entrusted with that is the unique signature of our soul. We must sing it clearly, with every ounce of our attention and faithfulness and strength.

In the wasteland of exile from your soul's note, how you wander and throw yourself into various occupations, trying to forget. How you long for one who might hear you and see you and coax you into the becoming you know is possible. You are vast as the universe, and inwardly you sense that nothing you do here will ever equal what you are actually a capable of. Redemption seems to spring from the very barrenness that you have let claim your life's voice. From the interior loneliness of finding yourself isolated from other beings, and from love, something new is often born. Ultimately you must stand up for innocence and soul sweetness, for beauty that is constantly assaulted by hollow, shallow and cynical images that repeat the mantra "There is no meaning here."

Each of us has a harsh, critical and often assassinating inner voice that functions as henchman to what is mysterious and soulful in us. When you feel sadness it tells you that you are a sissy, or irrational or pathetic. When you feel something in your gut, it tells you to be logical and to filter everything through rational thinking. It says discipline is what you need, and it rules through control. It tells you that you must achieve and conquer, that you are nothing except what you produce, that otherwise your life has no meaning or value. Success is tangible and worldly, and power is what you should possess and desire. This voice within tells you to get over yourself and your heartbrokenness, to forget what happened to your love as a child, with those people you called family.

There is a time when that voice is needed to move you through the ruts of self-pity or self-defeated lethargy. But more often that voice becomes a willful dictator, robbing your life of its vitality, its quiet joys and potential for true contentment. The voice of what you should be, do, or fix in your life distances you from your soul's innocent curiosity. There is a part of you, however small and buried, that has utter faith in life, that is willing to go wherever you are taken, that looks out upon this precious existence with wonder and praising, for the simple blades of grass, for the smell of the earth, for the warm flesh of your loved one and the laughter of strangers. This part of you sometimes breaks through the mask of control and affirms the childlike innocence of your heart. There is a moment when the rational discursive thinking breaks through to the symbolic, feeling language of rhythm and image hidden in your blood. This happened just now as I was writing this:

> In the land of image only
> of sound without word only
> I'll search for you
> I gather the golden leaves
> each one inscribed with a destiny
> a calligraphy no one has yet understood
> the meaning of which must be whispered

As I was writing about language and the inner voice my own inner voice rose up to speak. Notice how my third person objective prose turned into intimate address, into "You" all of a sudden. Where the limitations of rational language appear, soul must find a way through to greater truth. Poetry is both a veil and the rending of the veil covering Reality. It is a cover for the poet, yet it is designed to reveal much more than other kinds of language can reveal about the complex multidimensionality of experience. Is it straightforward? Is it the language of therapeutic self-disclosure? No it is not. Which kind of language glimpses a fuller, richer more mysterious experience? Which feels more real to you? Which is more vulnerable and exposed?

Poetry resists the overt statement; instead, it suggests. Mind would create a bottom line platform or position out of our rich lived experience of each moment. Mind seeks to reduce, categorize and control, to discriminate and choose this over that. It desires or rejects in each moment, constantly affirming yes or no to every thing that crosses our path. This is how we make sense of reality and make the choices necessary to live complete lives. Rationality is a beautiful thing. Yet beyond the logic of our rational mind is our utter bafflement before the mystery of being and non-being, birth and death, pain, loss and love. We know nothing. We know everything there is to be known. These contradictions can coexist within poetry, since poetry resists a bottom line, a black and white conclusion. Poetry is true to the grayness of the soul's terrain. We are separate and live most of our lives feeling bounded within our own skin and minds. And yet, since every life we encounter is ourselves, how can we pretend we are separate? Since everything in the universe exists within the soul, how can we say this or that is wholly other?

Poetry can contain and suggest this paradox, playing with it like a lover, coaxing it out and speaking to it from inside and outside. Poetry loves distance, and originates from closeness. But all of this is lost unless one has the courage to affirm the soul, the sacred inwardness of one's own precious vision. This is especially challenging when inwardness has been given no value in the world, in culture, yet it is where everything is conceived, ripened and born. There is an empty fertile darkness where all the forms are born. Without silence, no word could form.

Who will honor and protect the soul's darkness? Will you protect and value your own inner life, even if there is never any applause or money or accomplishment you can hold up as its outer sign? Will you give your life to becoming tender-hearted, to learning how to truly see? Will you make a space for poetry, even if it has no value in the world but affirms the value of that which is mysterious, dark and silent in us, that which lives, paradoxically, beyond words?

LISTENING TO THE HIDDEN HEART OF SEEDS

ANGELA FISCHER

Every seed carries a secret.

We will never come to fully know this secret, because it belongs to the mystery of creation. Yet we can learn again what hundreds of generations did before us, namely to live with the secrets, to use them as gifts, and to honour them as a source of life on this planet.

The first step in learning to live with a secret is to listen.

When I was a young child, my mother gave me a seed of a bean. She showed me how to plant it into a pot filled with black soil and how to keep it warm and moist. And then I had to wait.

For a young child this took a very long time. Every morning I would visit my seed, invisible in the darkness of the soil, and because I could not see anything, I remember that instead I tried to hear something. It was around the same time that my mother was pregnant, and I used to put my ear to her belly to communicate with the baby I could not see or touch. So I did the same with the invisible seed: I put my ears close to the soil and listened. I do not remember if I ever heard something, but I remember the listening. It was like an intimate conversation, though silent and unheard by anyone else.

The seed is a symbol for the deepest mystery of creation, and at the same time it is the mystery. For thousands of years farmers have known how to listen to these mysteries, and so found ways how to grow and to harvest, how to preserve the seeds, how to provide for them the best circumstances, considering the conditions of the earth, the soil, and the weather, and considering how much they connect us with the past and the future, our ancestors and our grandchildren. This goes back to an ancient feminine wisdom about the connection with the Earth, the knowledge of light being born out of darkness and an intimacy with the circles of life.

Every seed contains a light. Through greed and disconnection from the sacredness of life, this light is threatened. Genetically modified seeds become sterile. If the fertility is removed from a seed, its light is taken away; it withdraws. The divine light that is present in every seed is manifested through its fertility, through the potential to grow and to be a source for new life. When this light withdraws from a seed, it withdraws from the whole of creation, and our souls begin to starve.

As every seed embraces an outer as well as an inner reality, we need to care in outer and in inner ways. We need to protect the purity, diversity, and freedom of seeds through outer engagement, but we also need to protect the sacredness of life inwardly. The inner way is to hold the awareness of the sacredness in our hearts, to remember and to respect the feminine mysteries of creation—and to deeply listen. The same light that is contained in the heart of the biological seed is also present within our heart; it is the seed of love.

DOES THE UNIVERSE HAVE AN INNER LIFE?

W.H.S. GEBEL

Determinism and Uncertainty

Sir Arthur Eddington was a prominent astronomer and popular writer about the latest developments in science in the 1920's and 30's whose careful observations of a total solar eclipse in 1919 confirmed Einstein's theory of General Relativity. According to him, 1927 was the year when it became possible to reconcile science and religion. It was the year of the Solvay Conference in Belgium where leading scientists met to discuss the newly emerging field of quantum mechanics. In marking that year as a milestone, Eddington was referring to the replacement of the strict determinism of classical physics by the indeterminacy implied by the uncertainty principle inherent in quantum physics.

Using the laws of classical physics, the state of the universe, its structure, and the details of its elaboration, can be predicted, at least in principle, for any future time once it is specified for a particular moment. Therefore the universe as described by Newtonian mechanics is determined and mechanical like a clock. It evolves by random processes that, in principle could be predicted from a known initial state, and as a machine it has no apparent meaning, purpose, or direction. In contrast, quantum physics holds that an unlimited number of future states are possible at each moment. No state is determined exactly but rather could be in any one of an innumerable number of states, each with a well-defined probability. Thus it is not deterministic and it can only predict probabilities for the development of the universe. This difference between classical and quantum physics does not in itself add meaning, but it does take away the grayness and helpless feeling of a pre-determined fate.

And so in 1927 a major barrier to the coexistence of science and religion was removed. Sir Arthur, in The Nature of the Physical Reality and New Pathways in Science, went on to propose the terms of a peace accord whereby each field of knowledge would agree to limit its area of expertise to a specified domain.

> *The conflict will not be averted unless both sides confine themselves to their proper domain; and a discussion which enables us to reach a better understanding as to the boundary should be a contribution towards a state of peace.*
>
> *[Sir Arthur Eddington, The Nature of the Physical World, Cambridge, UK: Cambridge University Press, 1948 (out of print, available online), p. 177]*

Essence

How are the relevant domains to be specified? For Eddington, this requires an examination of the notion of reality. The scientific revolution began in the 17th century as a reaction to a dogmatic conception of reality tied to a theological view of the world. Rebelling against authority and tradition, adherents of science championed a consensus reality which required the results of experiments to be reproducible at least in principle by anyone.

Eddington probes deeper into the question of what constitutes reality. His criterion for reality is what is meaningful or significant. Science, by virtue of its method, must limit its domain to what is measurable. It attempts to avoid the subjective, relying on the input of the senses and rational deduction. Furthermore, using as an example an attempt to describe Einstein's theory of General Relativity, Eddington demonstrates that scientific explanations have a cyclic nature. As terms are defined, it turns out that every term depends on another for its definition. It's like trying to get to the bottom of a definition in a dictionary. He calls it a cyclic explanation because he finds himself cycling back to certain basic terms which must remain undefined. Eddington concludes that consensus reality is a skeleton or framework which can capture in great detail the incidental but always misses the essence.

The 12th century Sufi mystic Shahabuddin Suhrawardi struggled with the same problem, how can one find the basis of knowledge when it seems to be intrinsically referential? He concluded that the essence of knowledge is self-revealing. There is a knowledge that is direct, immediate, and spontaneous. It is independent of analysis. The Sufis call it presential knowledge. This knowledge is commonly experienced, for example, in the form of aesthetic sensitivity, conscience, striving toward a purpose, caring and feeling responsible, and experiencing sacredness. What is implied in Suhrawardi's description of presential knowledge is that there is an inner reality which fills consensus reality with meaning.

Eddington gives a metaphor to illustrate how the seemingly different realities of science and religion can be understood as two aspects of one thing.

> *Is the ocean composed of water or of waves or of both? Some of my fellow passengers on the Atlantic were emphatically of the opinion that it is composed of waves; but I think the ordinary unprejudiced answer would be that it is composed of water. At least if we declare our belief that the nature of the ocean is aqueous, it is not likely that anyone will challenge us and assert that on the contrary its nature is undulatory, or that it is a dualism part aqueous and part undulatory. Similarly I assert that the nature of all reality is spiritual, not material nor a dualism of matter and spirit.*

[Sir Arthur Eddington, New Pathways in Science, Wilmington, OH: Frazer Press, 2013]

He concludes that the proper domain of science is the realm of objective measures of the outer life that are perceivable through the senses. Direct or presential knowledge which comes from within is a domain science cannot probe. Our inner experience, our feelings, our imagination, our sense of meaning belong to the spiritual domain.

> *A defense of the mystic might run something like this. We have acknowledged that the entities of physics can from their very nature form only a partial aspect of the reality. How are we to deal with the other part? It cannot be said that the other part concerns us less than the physical entities. Feelings, purpose, values, make up our consciousness as much as sense-impressions. We follow up the sense-impressions and find that they lead into an external world discussed by science; we follow up the other elements of our being and find that they lead—not into a world of space and time, but surely somewhere.*

> [Sir Arthur Eddington, *The Nature of the Physical World*, p. 163]

Stated more simply we could say that the domain that science is so well suited to explore is the outer life and the domain of the spirit is the inner life. Eddington examined his own experience as a scientist and as a man of faith and concluded that the inner life is a domain for mystical religion, by which I think he meant experiential religion apart from theology and dogma. So far do the arguments of Eddington go.

The Inner Domain

If the scientist is well-suited to study the phenomena of the outer life, who would the scientist's counterpart be for the study of the inner life? I believe it is the mystic who is most qualified to discover the knowledge of the spiritual reality Eddington marked out as the other domain. It is the mystic who enters the silence of the inner life with patience and trust, who cultivates the breath as a gateway to deeper concentration, who develops the discipline of stillness, and who empties the psyche of self to more clearly receive the self-revealing knowledge coming from within.

In the literature of the religious traditions of the world, mystics have recorded their discoveries about the nature of spiritual reality. Often these insights revolve around the place of the human being in the greater scheme of nature. However, humans are newcomers to the realm of the universe. Science has determined that human-like ancestors go back perhaps 3 million years. Recent mapping of the cosmic microwave background, the remaining remnant of the Big Bang radiation, fixes the age of the universe at 13.8 billion years. Thus human-like creatures have been around for about .02 percent of the age of the universe. In other words, for 99.98 percent of its life the universe has existed without human intelligence. What is the nature of the inner life of the universe without human intelligence, which has only flashed on the scene in the very last instant, so to speak?

Eddington's analysis relies upon the common human experience of an inner life. Was there anything comparable to that inner life before human intelligence appeared in the universe? Putting aside the question of human-like intelligence arising elsewhere in the far-flung stars and galaxies, why might we suspect that intelligence has existed in the vast stretches of space beyond the earth and the enormous expanse of time before humans appeared? Isn't this idea simply an anthropomorphic projection? But what if we turn the idea of an anthropomorphic projection on its head? What if human intelligence is a theomorphic projection. By theomorphic projection I mean that cosmic intelligence has always existed and has taken upon itself a particular manifestation as human intelligence. (Though use of the prefix "theo" suggests "God," with all of its associations, for simplicity I am limiting the use of theomorphic here to cosmic intelligence.)

The idea that intelligence is universal is a widely shared belief among mystics. And the notion of theomorphic projection can be found in Biblical tradition, the human being fashioned in the image of God. The alchemists captured it in a maxim, "as above so below." The Sufi mystic Hazrat Inayat Khan pictured primal intelligence as a phenomenon seeking to know itself by assuming innumerable material forms.

The rocks are working out the same destiny as man, the plants
are growing towards the same goal as man. What is that goal?
Unfoldment. The spirit is buried in the creation and wants to make
its way out. At each step of evolution there is a new unfoldment, a
greater opening.

[Hazrat Inayat Khan, The Sufi Message, Vol XIV, The Smiling
Forehead, Part II The Deeper Side of Life, Chapter XIX The
Soul, Its Origin and Unfoldment, Katwijk aan Zee: Servire BV,
1982]

The universal push for unfoldment and the idea that spirit is working its way out through the denseness of material existence to finer and finer expression is summarized simply in an ancient saying by a Sufi dervish paraphrased by Inayat Khan.

There is a saying of the Sufis that "God slept in the rock, God dreamed in the tree, God became self-conscious in the animal, but God sought Himself and recognized Himself in man." *[Hazrat Inayat Khan, The Sufi Message, Vol IV, Mental Purification and Healing, Part III Mental Puri-fication, Chapter XXI, The Expansion of Consciousness, Katwijk aan Zee: Servire BV, 1982]*

The domain for the mystic to explore is not just the personal inner life but the inner life of the universal intelligence, in other words, the inner life of the universe.

Universal Intelligence

In recent decades scientists have turned their attention to developing a scientific theory of consciousness. Is this an encroachment on the spiritual domain? Is it an inappropriate method for the study of inner life? In studying the functioning of the brain, scientists are still in their domain, applying their methods to the outer material life. No doubt there is much to be learned by scientific study about how conscious-ness works in the brain. According to Eddington's reasoning, the best that can come out of such studies is a mechanical model of mind. A mechanical model is a skeleton of reality whose content, the essence of consciousness, belongs to the domain of the mystic.

> *The word intelligence as it is known by us, and spoken in everyday language, does not give a full idea; especially the word intelligence as used by modern science will only convey to us something which is the outcome of matter or energy. But according to the mystic, intelligence is the primal element, or the cause as well as the effect. While science acknowledges it as the effect, the mystic sees in it the cause.*

> *[Hazrat Inayat Khan, The Sufi Message, Vol I, The Way of Illumination, Section III The Soul Whence and Whither, Part II Manifestation, vii, Katwijk aan Zee: Servire BV, 1982.]*

How does a mystic know something about the essence of conscious-ness? Intelligence is known directly, as presential knowing. If I examine what is truly me, first I think of the body. But the body is substance borrowed from the earth, to be given back when it has exhausted itself. Am I my mind or my feelings? But both mind and feelings are subject to frequent changes. They come and they go and they change. What is there about me that is persistent, that has the continuity of a self? There is a bare sense of "I" that has always been with me. It doesn't seem to change with age. If I strip away my sense of identity from every-thing but this bare sense of "I," and if I examine it more deeply, I can further recognize it intuitively as pure intelligence, a capacity to know and understand. It is absolute intelligence, not relative intelligence. As a capacity, intelligence is present in everyone and everything equally.

Now a picture emerges of the inner life of the universe. Mystics report that intelligence has always existed and is seeking to know itself by unfolding its nature in ever more sophisticated and complex material forms. The universe has an outer life as the functioning of a plethora of materialized forms, organic and inorganic. It has an inner life as the essence of those material forms which accounts for their vitality and their desire to thrive. Taking human experience as a clue, I believe that consciousness, conscience, creativity, inspiration, motivation, and sense of purpose are aspects of the inner life of the universe. Think of these phenomena as prehuman templates that were present in a rudimentary way from the earliest manifestations of matter. As theomorphic projections, they are archetypes from which human experience has taken its familiar shape.

Theomorphism answers the question some scientists have pondered: how is it that our minds are capable of understanding the phenomena of the universe? If we are an outgrowth of the striving of the universal intelligence to know itself, then it is perfectly natural that our minds should be able to understand the greater nature from which we have emerged.

Scientists have viewed attempts at reconciliation sometimes with skepticism, sometimes with efforts to debunk or deconstruct. Another response is documented in Ken Wilber's Quantum Questions. The pioneering quantum physicists of the 1920's were open to the world of spiritual ideas. Like Eddington they felt that there is more to reality than what physics has revealed. They also made a point of respecting the boundaries suggested by Eddington.

An Integrated Worldview

I believe that a natural harmony between science and religion can be achieved with the help of a wider recognition of Eddington's domains and mutual respect for the methods of scientists and mystics. Eddington drew attention to the boundary where outer and inner life meet. Perhaps there is room for a sharing of perspectives at the boundary that would benefit both fields of knowledge.

Teilhard de Chardin expressed a similar wish for an integrated understanding of the universe in his ground breaking work The Phenomenon of Man. He noted the longstanding tension between science and spirituality and characterized the shortcomings of each discipline.

> On the one hand the materialists insist on talking about objects as
> though they only consisted of external actions in transient relation-

*ships. On the other hand the upholders of a spiritual interpretation
are obstinately determined not to go outside a kind of solitary intro-
spection in which things are only looked upon as being shut in upon
themselves in their "immanent" workings. Both fight on different
planes and do not meet; each only sees half the problem.*

*[Pierre Teilhard de Chardin, The Phenomenon of Man, New
York: Harper Perennial Modern Thought, 2008, p. 56]*

Recognizing the within of things, he foresaw a time when science in
its study of the without of things could join with spirituality to establish
an integrated worldview.

*I am convinced that the two points of view require to be brought
into union, and that they soon will unite in a kind of phenome-
nology or generalized physic in which the internal aspect of things
as well as the external aspect of the world will be taken into
account. Otherwise, so it seems to me, it is impossible to cover the
totality of the cosmic phenomenon by one coherent explanation such
as science must try to construct.*

[ibid]

The discovery in the twentieth century of the vast expanse of the
universe—100 billion galaxies each on average studded with 100 billion
stars, the whole assembly fixed in a space-time matrix that has been
expanding for 13.8 billion years—has impressed upon us a stunning
physical vision of the universe. Further revelations about Dark Matter
and Dark Energy, as well as speculations about the earliest moments of
the Big Bang have kept public attention focused on a material framework in which we might wonder, what is our place?

It is natural to imagine that life on our planet, including human
life, is utterly insignificant in such a mind-boggling vastness in whose
description the word "billions" is cast about so casually. Is human life
simply a chance outcome of physical processes working mechanically?
Or is our existence just the consequence of the existence of innumer-

able possible universes in which, like monkeys typing randomly and eventually producing Shakespeare, one universe happens to have the right conditions for life, again without any meaning or purpose? As Eddington pointed out, since science only attempts to explain how things work, it can at best offer a functional description of nature, without essence.

If the universe has an inner life, what are the implications for revising our worldview? Imagine that pure intelligence has always existed, that it is the essence missing from the picture science has discovered. The unfolding of the universe according to mystical insight is a result of pure intelligence seeking to discover its secret by working its way first through the simplest forms of matter and then into ever more refined and able instruments. In this picture our existence as a complex material form capable of self-awareness is a most significant stage in the story of the universe.

Furthermore, in this view the very same intelligence is at work in every material form from the most elementary quantum particle to the stars and galaxies. Therefore the universe is our home. We can know it with a degree of intimacy because its essence is the same as our essence.

This vision of the inner life of the universe can coexist with the spectacular discoveries of the scientific worldview. It doesn't contradict scientific ideas. And although it stops short of religious doctrines, it needn't conflict with any religious point of view. It comes from the insights of mystics who have dived deep into their own inner life and have found their way to the universal inner life. To arrive at this understanding, they have dedicated themselves to a demanding discipline and a self-denying life. Yet every soul potentially has access to a direct knowing.

I believe that in the course of evolution, humanity has developed a sensitivity, refinement, and awareness that makes it possible for all of us to have a glimpse of spiritual essence. This opens up the possibility of a broader, meaningful worldview in which a new understanding of the purpose of human life in this vast universe may emerge.

Conversations with Remarkable Minds

Jane Goodall, interviewed by Gary Null in 2009

Would you please share your insights about why it is important for humanity and ecology to protect various species from extinction? How we can best go about challenging globalization and corporate privatization of resources that threaten natural habitats? In light of this problem, how have you been able to remain so hopeful?

Well I travel the world a lot. I meet people all over the world, and everywhere I go I meet extraordinary people, people who tackle seemingly impossible tasks and won't give in. If you think back across European and U.S. history, there was a lot of bloodshed and bitterness, and now the United States are under one star-spangled banner and we have the European Union. So things do change.

The corporate greed that you talk of, the dark side of globalization, is indeed a huge obstacle if we're talking about saving a piece of forest somewhere in Africa, where the government feels they could sell that piece of land and get lots and lots of money, which very often goes into a Swiss bank account because there's a lot of corruption all over the world.

But at the same time I think it is important to realize that many corporations today have understood the problems that are being caused by, for example, climate change with the emission of CO_2 into the environment, the methane gases from intensive farming of animals, and the overexploitation of ground water for irrigation. All of the big corporations are beginning to realize that these things are devastating, that they are causing a cataclysm, and they truly are beginning to change.

I was just in Greenland where the ice is melting, and it was horrifying—beautiful, but horrifying. I was there with about 25 very wealthy real estate developers from North America and Europe, and they were so moved when they realized what was going on that they made written pledges to reduce their emissions by up to 60 percent over the next few years. So there is change afoot. There are people who realize that this preoccupation with materialism is simply destroying the planet. If we care about our children and grandchildren, and theirs, then we simply must realize that each one of us has got to do our bit. It may seem tiny, but if the millions and billions of people on the planet are all doing their bit that's going to make a huge change.

I appreciate your insights. Thank you. Go back to Greenland for a moment. Greenland is an enormous body. It's three times the size of Texas. It has so much ice that if it were to melt it could raise the sea level over 20 feet, and that would threaten about 265 million people. Could you explain what you were seeing there?

Well, I went up to this great cliff of ice that goes up and up and up to the icecap that covers the whole country, and it's considerably shrunk over the last 20 years. It's much lower than it used to be, and a great river pours out of it where there never was a river at all. In fact it never melted even in the summer, and standing there with some of the Inuit elders who hadn't been back there since they were children, they had tears pouring down their face. As we stood there, there would be this huge crack and then a silence and then a thunderous roar that reverberated as a vast slab of ice broke off and crashed down. Then the river became turbulent with pieces of broken ice. It really was terrifying to know how fast these great glaciers are moving, and then to fly over the sea which used to be frozen and see it now covered with icebergs, and to actually land on a piece of ground which until a few years ago had been under the ice since the last Ice Age. It's happening much faster than anybody predicted, and it's melting from below as well as above.

I came away shocked, but I came away just like the real estate people, absolutely determined. The message that I now shall give is that each one of us must do everything we can to slow down climate change. Yesterday in the U.K. they launched 10/10, getting people to pledge reductions. They've already got 2,000 corporations, companies, individuals, schools, universities that will reduce their CO_2 emissions by ten percent in the year 2010. So it's called 10/10. And it's fantastic—it's really involving people, which will then push the government to act.

I recently spoke with Dr. James Lovelock and asked him, do you believe that with China, India, and Brazil becoming the major polluters along with the United States that we have the political will to reduce greenhouse emissions by 60 percent minimally, or 80 percent, realistically? And he said, no we will not be able to do that—it's too late for this current crisis. What we have put into the environment will stay there and there will be an accelerating series of tippings. He said we would have to have a radical change immediately, and he personally does not believe that people are willing to make the sacrifices.

I said, well look I'm a vegan. I eat organic. I don't support multinational stores. I buy from greenhouses. I grow my own food. Ninety percent of what I eat at the table I grow. I said lots of people could become vegans. If we just became vegan one day a week, if we had no animal products one day a week, we could do more than any other effects of CO_2 from cars, ships, planes, and trains. And he said you're right, but now you've got to get the people to be willing to give up their tastes and their comfort and their foods.

What are your thoughts on the vegan diet as a major contribution, which would actually contribute more than ten percent? It would actually contribute close to 55 percent.

Well I'm not a vegan because traveling to so many weird places in the world it's very hard to do. If we could all become total vegans it would do exactly as you say, but that would be a very hard thing to get people to do. One day a week, maybe. So I've taken a slightly different tack, which is less perfect but it seems to work quite well in getting people on board. That is, first become vegetarian, and if you must eat any animal products they must be free range and organic. If we went back to the days when cows wandered in the fields and we just took a little from them it wouldn't be such a bad thing, and it certainly would make a vast difference to the methane gases produced.

The average person doesn't have a clue that the meat they're eating is causing all this havoc. They don't understand about the effects on the environment or on human cells. The suffering of the animals they might try to turn away from. So how to make them listen and understand is difficult, but it's happening. You know that my last book, Harvest for Hope, was all about food and many people have become vegetarian from reading that book, and it's very successful in France, in China, in Korea. It's being used by university students. So I completely agree with you, but maybe we need to take smaller steps and then bigger steps.

Okay. I accept that. What about another small step buying locally?

Oh that's so important, but you see here again you and I are lucky. We can grow quite a bit of our food in our gardens. There are an awful lot of people in the cities for whom it's difficult to grow their own food, and sometimes it's difficult for them to afford that extra that it takes to buy organic, or from small shops. So you know first of all you want people to understand why they should do this, and second we must make it cheap enough for them to do it. So one of my passions is urban farming, like what started in Cuba after the American embargo there. They started growing their own food in Havana and it started feeding the starving people of the city. It's happening in other parts of the world too, like China and India.

Let me build slightly on what you just said. I would like to see inner city organic farming, and here's how it could be done. There are 60,000 abandoned buildings and lots in New York City alone, and through the city turning those over to a foundation you could have hundreds of community gardens with greenhouses paid for by corporate sponsors giving a two dollar tax deduction for each dollar they donate. Any corporation in America would love that, no matter what their ultimate interest is. Once corporations pay to have these greenhouses and gardens built, local community leadership can get the people involved. Then produce can be grown 12 months a year, from sprouts to micro-greens to garden vegetables that become a regular part of those people's food at minimal cost.

I completely agree. I think that we should be doing this urban farming. I tried to set that up in North Korea for the starving people there so they could grow some food of their own even in the city, and it also brings children back in touch with nature again. They get to understand that potatoes grow in the ground and tomatoes grow on a stem and that they are fruits, which lots of children today haven't a clue about. And also you can get all of your food composted with worms and create fantastic fertilizer and grow your food even better and not discard any waste.

India and China are two of the most problematic countries, both because of the amount of pollution that they create and the amount of starving people and poor they have, and also their middle class and upper middle classes' ravenous appetites for everything Western including animal foods. What would be your suggestion for these two countries to help in their future development?

Well, we have this program for young people called Roots and Shoots, which has been going since '91 and now is in 111 countries. It's involving young people of all ages who form groups and choose three kinds of projects to make the world better, first of all for their own community and then reaching out to other communities, second for animals including domestic animals, and third for the environment that we all share. In China we now have four offices all run by Chinese. We've got about 600 active groups across China. We could grow even more if we had more money, but we service these groups. The same program has begun and I think will spread quite fast in India, and we hope to launch it in Brazil once the Jane Goodall Institute has the funds.

As I'm traveling around the world I find somebody who gets the idea and says, yes I'm going to champion this. And then if the moment is right and the person is right it takes off, and it really is making a huge difference. So my answer to China or India is get more and more youth involved, particularly at the university level, though even the younger children are influencing their parents and their grandparents. Since I first went to China about 13 years ago there's been an enormous change. I know that the demand for raw materials is skyrocketing in a very unsustainable way, but too the awareness of the problems has grown and the young people are very, very aware of and concerned by what's happening. And they want to see change.

I appreciate these insights because most people are not aware of the grass roots movements in every one of these countries. Now I feel our postmodern infatuation with high tech gadgetry and the concrete jungle of consumerism divorces people from their connection to nature. What have been the consequences of us separating ourselves from our natural origins in the community of life forms on the planet?

Well I think this separation from the natural world is very, very drastic. Psychologists have shown that young children need nature to grow psychologically healthy, they need grass and bugs and sky and flowers There was an experiment done in Chicago where they took two areas of high crime and in one they made gardens in the empty lots. They put in window boxes, they planted trees along the streets, and the other they left as it was. And the level of crime dropped really substantially in the place that was green.

So we need nature for our psychological wellbeing. And if you don't understand something, how can you care about it? And when kids grow up glued to video monitors, and all these things, they become divorced from nature.

It is my view that the environmental threat to biodiversity is a spiritual crisis. What are your thoughts on the connection drawn between an environmentally oriented consciousness and a spiritually directed consciousness?

I think that material society has been crushing out the spiritual aspect of us humans. One of the things that could really lead us into a glorious future if we allow it to develop is that this materialistic culture is actually making people very dissatisfied. They can't find the meaning in their life, and they're left with nothing except getting more and more stuff that they don't either want or need whereas the other three-quarters of the planet has nothing. So nature and spirituality to me is all interconnected, and I certainly feel that personally from spending so much time on my own in the forest and feeling very close to a great spiritual power.

In your own work with children both in the developed and developing world have you noted any fundamental differences in children's development between those who live closer to nature and those who are completely alienated?

I think it's hard to pinpoint what's causing these differences because for children learning through a computer and websites seems to be quicker, but apparently less deep, so they tend to forget it. They tend to think differently, and they seem to have much shorter attention spans. They want instant gratification, and then of course at the same time they're in a society where if their attention seems to be off they're given medications. You don't find any of that if you go out into the rural part of Tanzania or into the Congo jungles with the pygmies. People don't live that way, and they seem much more whole. They may not have academic learning, but they're certainly learning how to live and how to be decent human beings.

I have one final question for you. You have a great affinity for Africa since you've spent so much of your life there, and I'd like to hear your views about the slaughter of the rhino, the hippo, the great apes, the chimpanzees there, and also how prepared Africa is for the crisis due to climate change forecast by various UN agencies involving a large group of people affected by unrelenting drought, lack of water and starvation. Could you take us on that little journey also to give us a perspective we don't have?

Well if we take Gombe National Park where the chimpanzees are that we've been studying coming up to 50 years, in the early '90s I flew over this whole area in a small aircraft, and although I knew there was deforestation outside the park, I had absolutely no idea that it was virtually total. There were more people living there than the land could support, and they had degraded their farmland with terrible erosion and were struggling to survive. So the question came up, and this applies to all wilderness areas right across Africa or anywhere else in a poor country, of how could we try to save these famous chimpanzees if the people living around were struggling and starving?

So we started a program called Take Care, which is now one of the most successful of its kind. It's improving the lives of the people in now 24 villages, and we're about to expand hugely. The program takes a holistic approach including everything from growing their food in a sustainable way to restoring fertility to overused farmland, free nurseries, fast growing tree species for building and firewood, and micro credit loans for women, which I think are tremendously important. We provide scholarships for girls and place emphasis on women because all around the world as women's education improves family size tends to drop and this is desperately important in many parts of the world. This program has been very successful and now the villagers appreciate it. They realize that their water supply is improving because they're managing it better, by protecting the forest along the watersheds for example. So now they're allowing the land around Gombe to regenerate, and it's very resilient and it regenerates fast. So now the Gombe chimpanzees have a buffer between them and the villagers, and an opportunity for interaction with other well-known chimp groups, which is their only chance for long-term survival.

I think it's important to say that poverty is one of the worst destroyers of the environment. Poverty on the one hand and over-consumption on the other. We in the developed world can deal with our over-consumption by just taking a firm grip on ourselves and saying as an old wise Indian once said, I ask myself every time I think of getting something new can I live without it. If we start thinking like that, if we start thinking about how our actions today will affect our children and their children, and if we then realize that extreme poverty must be alleviated if we hope to protect the environment in the developing countries.

Regarding your point about cultural insensitivity to animals, we have sanctuaries for orphaned chimps, and the local people make the most amazing keepers. They have a real affinity with chimpanzees, with monkeys and with the other creatures. And the local people who come to visit go away saying, "I'll never eat another chimpanzee again. I didn't realize they were like us. I've never seen a monkey close up. I have been fascinated to watch this hippo mother and her baby." So we have to realize that they need exposure to it. They need to understand before they can care.

ON PROPHECY AND TIME – PART 4

DAVID SPANGLER TO PIR ZIA INAYAT-KHAN AND WILLIAM IRWIN THOMPSON

Dear Bill,

I'm appreciating very much that you are enjoying Subtle Worlds, my first new book in some years and one close to my heart. I have for so many years kept the details of my interactions with the non-physical and spiritual worlds close to my heart, sharing their effects through my teachings and outer work and with a few close friends such as yourself, but reserving the deeper sense of partnership to myself. This was never through any sense of wishing to possess secrets, but only through shyness and self-protection. Having come out of a scientific culture in University, where I was training to be a molecular biologist like Tim Kennedy, I knew that in that environment my converse with spiritual beings would not be accepted and would lead to being ousted—in those days at least—from the fellowship of scientists. And I had professors in those days who were outspoken in their intent to strip away from their students all "illusions" and "delusions" pertaining to any kind of spiritual life. "If you believe in anything when you are done with my class," one professor told us, "then I will have failed in my duty." So I held my inner knowledge sacred and secret, and in the end took myself out of that fellowship myself in answer to a larger calling from the subtle worlds.

But even in the metaphysical and New Age movements where I found my first audiences, I discovered that being open about my inner experiences and contacts led to unwanted projections and glamour which only hindered my work. Ironically, I found that I needed to be as discrete and reticent around my putative allies as I was around my former classmates and professors in the science departments of the University. So I have a history of holding my cards close to my chest. The book Subtle Worlds represents for me my first attempts to begin laying my cards on the table.

I would like to also thank you, Bill, for your description of the role of the Sufis in the opening of the Western mind and heart that we call the Renaissance. As you said, I was raised in Morocco, which has always had a special place in my heart. I have felt for many years that my childhood there, which saw my awakening to my own soul and the true beginning of my spiritual work, was a recapitulation of at least one other life in that land, very likely as a Sufi or certainly as someone engaged with the esoteric and mystical pursuits of the winged heart. There were many times as a child when I encountered echoes and "ghosts" of past associations with that land and, I think, with my former self or selves.

This had an interesting result in this life. When I left college and went to Los Angeles in 1965 to test the waters of spiritual teaching to see if I could swim in them and not drown, I was assisted by a wonderful gentleman who was in many ways a Sufi himself, though not in any organizational sense. It was his organization that sponsored me in the City of Angels and gave me my first speaking gigs. I was visiting him in his apartment one day and found Idries Shah's book The Sufis lying on a table. It had just been published the year before. I was immediately drawn to it and looking through it, I felt a jolt of recognition that said to me "I am a Sufi." Then, years later, at a college in England where a group of spiritual teachers had been gathered for the making of a television show, I met Pir Vilayat Khan for the first time. We felt a spark together, a bond that later grew into a treasured friendship. My association with the Sufi Order International [*now the Inayati Order – ed.*] began then as a partnership that I have always appreciated.

But I am not a joiner, and it has not been my path in this life to become part of any organization. I've had my own work to pursue, a task given to me from the subtle worlds, but I've been honored to follow that pursuit with such good friends and colleagues as I have found the Sufis to be.

So, Bill, about your Entelechy. You are correct that this is a very different phenomenon than that of what I call the "Pit Crew." This latter is made up of those subtle beings, both human and otherwise, that for any number of reasons act to support and further the incarnational aims of this one particular life. Those who are part of a Pit Crew in one incarnation may not at all be involved in a subsequent one. My mentor and non-physical friend, John, was part of my Pit Crew but he said that at another time, I had been part of his when he was in embodiment and I was not. Tit for tat!

But the Entelechy is indeed something else. I see it as a geometry of forces that promotes and structures or shapes an incarnation rather than simply assisting or accompanying it. In this regard, if I look at it through the lens of my own cosmology and experience, it is akin to what I think of as the "incarnational system."

One of the main elements in my teaching on incarnation is that we incarnate into systems, that only the geometry of a relational field can hold the higher-order energy of the soul in contact with the world. Your Entelechy seems to me to be an expression of such a system.

What I call the "incarnational system" is a process within each of us that enables incarnation to occur. It posits a set of connections that make it possible for the higher-order nature and energies of the soul to engage in a stable manner with the differently-configured and lesser energetic state of the physical world. I might picture these as the guy wires that hold a radio tower erect or as the stakes in the ground to which the support struts or ropes of a tent are fastened.

This incarnational system can be fairly complex, its geometry depending on the nature of the particular soul, the nature of the incarnation which it is attempting to manifest, and the particular work it wishes to accomplish, among other things. It can also change during the incarnation itself, so it is not totally fixed. For simplicity's sake in my classes, I portray it as having a four-fold structure, and for me, this is the basic structure, to which more can be added.

In describing this structure, I use the term "connection" to refer to two of its components. In effect, these represent the connection of the Incarnational Soul (and the newly emerging incarnate life) and its participation in larger, collective fields. These fields are that of the planetary Soul, which may be called Gaia, and which includes both the forces of the land and of the biosphere, and that of the collective Soul of Humanity. These "connections" can legitimately be seen and experienced in different ways. They can appear as actual beings—angels, devas, or elementals, depending on how you conceive of such things—connected to us and to some extent residing in us or alongside us, or as beings who are representatives of much large entities and collective forces. They can also be seen as functions and activities, living principles, within us, rather like organelles in a cell. Or they could be seen as subtle energies that we take on and hold as a means of connection to the aspects of the world to which they are related. I have experienced them in all of these modes.

In my classes I also discuss these elements using the metaphor of the plastids, mitochondria and other organelles within a cell, and in fact they behave somewhat like that. I have found there are a number of parallels and similarities between incarnation as a process and manifestation and cellular life and biology. Of course, that may simply be because my early training in college was in cell biology and chemistry.

This four-fold structure includes:

• The Incarnational Soul. This, I think, is my term for what Bill calls the Daemon. It is the part of the Soul that undertakes and focuses upon the incarnational process itself, relating the Soul as a hyperdimensional intelligence to the earth itself.

• The World "connection." This is a portion of the World Soul (or Gaia) that we take on or that becomes part of us—it could be seen, as I said above, as a being, such as a deva, an energy state, or a function or activity within us. It connects us to the physical, chemical, biological processes of the earth and to the energies of the land and of the biosphere, making us one with and part of the world and of nature.

• The Human "connection." This is a portion of the Soul of Humanity as a single collective Being but as shaped its by current incarnational status. The same applies here as with the World connection: this may be experienced as a being, such as an angel, an energy state, or an activity within us. It connects us to the collective energy and purpose of incarnate humanity (not to Humanity as a cosmic Being), and thus to whatever challenges and opportunities humanity is facing at this moment of history. I might think of this as the Zeitgeist or the Spirit of the Age as manifested through humanity at any particular moment. So, generally speaking, if I were incarnating right now, I would take on the energies relevant to 21st century Humanity, not the energies that defined Humanity during the Age of the Pharaohs or during Imperial Rome or the Renaissance. But whatever the Soul of Humanity is facing within a particular historical moment, it also has universal qualities and tasks, and this connection enables me to participate in those as well.

• The Personal Soul. This is the specific Intelligence, a fractal of soul paired usually with a body elemental, which oversees and patterns the specific individual life. It holds the "I" that gives the flame of individuality within the incarnate personality, and holds as well the matrix of karma and potentiality that affects the development of this personality. In many ways, this is an emergent condition rather than a fixed or given one, so that the Personal Soul at the end of the life is not the same, or I should say, in the same condition, as when it began the life. In the Post Mortem Realms following death, the Personal Soul reintegrates with the Incarnational Soul and then eventually with the Soul itself, at least as I understand it.

One of my projects this year is to write a book on what I call "incarnational spirituality" which will go into all this kind of material. These topics are not really part of the Subtle Worlds book or of the new book, Facing the Future.

Anyway, I can certainly see parallels between my incarnational system and your Entelechy.

However, there are other "incarnational systems" —other geometries of subtle connection and invocation—that can be deliberately shaped and invoked by a person during his or her life. A person would do this to invoke new energies or open up new potentialities in his or her life, thereby transforming the incarnation. From what you describe, Bill, this sounds a bit like what you're doing with the Entelechy attunement and exercises you are doing.

And there are also "connections" or "elements"—guy wires or tent stakes—that stay in the background until invoked by the personality. For example, there are solar and stellar energies to which our souls are connected but which may not play a role in the individual incarnate life unless proper conditions are created for them to do so.

I also understand that there are new patterns of incarnation—new kinds of incarnations—taking shape in our time. This may be a process that is always going on as far as that goes. But at this time in human history, a Gaian Human is a necessity; I see such a being as having a new subtle body or inner configuration, and I've always seen my own work as involved with this process. It could well be that the configuration you feel and describe is part of that process as well. The kind of beings you describe are certainly among those who would be involved in such a new birth.

Love to you, my brother, and all blessings to your life,

David

The next letter in this series begins on page 113.

NOCTILUCAE

From the book Shadowings, published in 1900.

LAFCADIO HEARN

The moon had not yet risen; but the vast of the night was all seething with stars, and bridged by a Milky Way of extraordinary brightness. There was no wind; but the sea, far as sight could reach, was running in ripples of fire—a vision of infernal beauty. Only the ripplings were radiant (between them was blackness absolute)—and the luminosity was amazing. Most of the undulations were yellow like candle-flame; but there were crimson lampings also—and azure, and orange, and emerald. And the sinuous flickering of all seemed, not a pulsing of many waters, but a laboring of many wills—a fleeting conscious and monstrous—a writhing and a swarming incalculable, as of dragon-life in some depth of Erebus.

And life indeed was making the sinister splendor of that spectacle—but life infinitesimal, and of ghostliest delicacy—life illimitable, yet ephemeral, flaming and fading in ceaseless alternation over the whole round of waters even to the sky-line, above which, in the vaster abyss, other countless lights were throbbing with other spectral colors.

Watching, I wondered and I dreamed. I thought of the Ultimate Ghost revealed in that scintillation tremendous of Night and Sea—quickening above me, in systems aglow with awful fusion of the past dissolved, with vapor of the life again to be—quickening also beneath me, in meteor-gushings and constellations and nebulosities of colder fire—till I found myself doubting whether the million ages of the sunstar could really signify, in the flux of perpetual dissolution, anything more than the momentary sparkle of one expiring noctiluca.

Even with the doubt, the vision changed. I saw no longer the sea of the ancient East, with its shudderings of fire, but that Flood whose width and depth and altitude are one with the Night of Eternity—the shoreless and timeless Sea of Death and Birth. And the luminous haze of a hundred millions of suns—the Arch of the Milky Way—was a single smouldering surge in the flow of Infinite Tides.

Yet again there came a change. I saw no more that vapory surge of suns; but the living darkness streamed and thrilled about me with infinite sparkling; and every sparkle was beating like a heart—beating out colors like the tints of the sea-fires. And the lampings of all continually flowed away, as shivering threads of radiance, into illimitable Mystery....

Then I knew myself also a phosphor-point—one fugitive floating sparkle of the measureless current—and I saw that the light which was mine shifted tint with each changing of thought. Ruby it sometimes shone, and sometimes sapphire: now it was flame of topaz; again, it was fire of emerald. And the meaning of the changes I could not fully know. But thoughts of the earthly life seemed to make the light burn red; while thoughts of supernal being—of ghostly beauty and of ghostly bliss—seemed to kindle ineffable rhythms of azure and of violet.

But of white lights there were none in all the Visible. And I marveled.

Then a Voice said to me: "The White are the Altitudes. By the blending of the billions they are made. Thy part is to help to their kindling. Even as the color of thy burning, so is the worth of thee. For a moment only is thy quickening; yet the light of thy pulsing lives on: by thy thought, in that shining moment, thou becomest a Maker of Gods."

WISDOM AND THE WAY OF SELF-AWAKENING

LEE IRWIN

The topic of Wisdom is a deep and difficult subject because, as a limited human being, the scope and depth of Wisdom exceeds my grasp. I cannot start from a position of authority because Wisdom, whom I will personify as feminine, knowing she is so much more, cannot be contained by the authority of any personality or subjective state. For me, Wisdom is a Mystery inseparable from the sacred ground of Being from which we all come and in which we live and breathe and co-exist.

I am reminded of an image from the ancient Egyptian world, a larger-than-life-sized statue of the Goddess Isis, carved from black stone. She sits on a throne, veiled, with the Ankh (symbol of life) in one hand and flowers (symbols of luminous beauty) in the other. On the front of the base is carved the following saying: "I am everything that was, everything that is, that will be, and no mortal has yet dared to lift my veil." Isis as an image of the Goddess of Wisdom, of innumerable attributes inscribed in the Isis aretalogies, reflects the Mystery of the Veil that hangs between seeing and being seen, a translucent barrier that reminds us of our mortality and limitations. Wisdom, in the image of the veiled goddess, solicits our sense of awe and reverence before the unspeakable depth of divine origins. As it is written in The Wisdom of

Solomon (7:10–26): "Her radiance is unceasing." . . . "She penetrates and permeates all spirits, all things" for "She is the breath of the power of God, a spotless mirror of divine activity."

The human circumstance, embodied in the circumscriptions of sensory, emotional, and intellectual perception, holds a revelatory potential. The depths of the sacred human are, I believe, inseparable from the divine ground in which Wisdom sustains our capacity for new insights, creative manifestations, and a lucid maturity of care and concern for the well being of others. In this sense, I perceive Wisdom as a nurturing presence, a veiled potential able to illumine any circumstance, relative condition, or situation. She is discovered in the moment of inspiration, in the outward flowing energies of love that manifest as a concern for the health and vitality of another, in the joy of discovery, and in the affirmation of what is truly sacred in life.

We grow into Wisdom, into a maturity of insight that challenges us to constantly refine and deepen our understanding and values. And each step is part of a dance, a partnership with all those we encounter, to find the appropriate response that will manifest the potential of Wisdom in each and every circumstance. Wisdom is not a content, nor a set of precepts or rules for behavior, nor is it a particular philosophy or coded symbolism of a spiritual practice. Wisdom is a process, a dynamic interaction that penetrates every person and being, every creature and created thing which seeks to solicit insight; it is unconfinable in static images, irreducible to fixed ideas.

It is my conviction that Wisdom in its depthless Mystery is emergent, revelatory, and infinitely capable of newness [in the context of the preservation and enhancement of life]. Whatever content we attribute to Wisdom, however viable and central to human life, such content reflects only the interface between our shared mortalities and the conditionality of the human situation. Our relative needs for greater maturity or insight depend on the development and refinement of the known in the face of the unknown. Beyond the content, or through the content, the Mystery of the depthless wonder of human possibility, of creative discovery, manifests the heart of Creation [— to make a world, beings, the web of life —] as living, dynamic, and evolving toward deeper insights and the embodiment of sacred potential.

Wisdom as an emergent ground, as a dynamic process of discovery and affirmation, is deeply rooted in the pathways of mystical tradition, in the branching Tree of human spiritual realizations and embodiments. The roots of this Tree sink deep into the sacred ground, drawing sustenance from every tradition that hallows life, nurtures human relations, and promotes communication and understanding between and across traditions. Every tradition embodies wisdom in the life of its community, in our human capacities to actually manifest wisdom in our interactions with others. And out of those interactions comes yet more revelatory insights because? Wisdom is not bound by human law or custom or tradition.

Wisdom, as an ever deepening current within the World Soul, I believe offers all humanity the opportunity to be fully participant in the forthcoming of new insights and revelations. These insights, arising through all the branches of human activity—artistic, musical, mathematical, scientific, political or economic—reflect the self-surpassing nature of our human potential. We are not defined by what was but stand, as individuals and as communities, on the threshold of what might become, what calls us beyond our limits into an expansive horizon of shared insights, new spiritual realizations, and the reaffirmation of the sacredness of creation.

As a global community, we bear a responsibility to foster the health and well-being of all humanity, and through Wisdom to find the ways that lead to peace and cooperation. The very ground of Wisdom manifests in the energies and creative interactions of those who can love and be loved, where love is the medium of Wisdom, and creative trust and cooperation are the weft upon which is woven the imagery of our greatest accomplishments. And every act of selfish concern, every violent reaction and self-serving decision, unravels that imagery and leaves only the disjointed remnants, the disturbing incongruity of uncaring beings in pursuit of their own pleasures, needs and appetites.

Chivalry, in a spiritual sense, is caring for others, protecting the weak and less empowered, and serving a cause greater than one's own needs and aspirations. Wisdom requires chivalry, a surrender of pride in knowing, deep humility, a willingness to not know, not see, not comprehend. Then the loving heart can be informed, in service and devotion, by what next is needed, inspired by insight, for the healing of our many wounds and scars, for the recovery of our dignity in light of our renewed potential for transformation.

We do not need teachers of Wisdom; what we need is a shared context within which the processes of inspiration can be fostered for the good of all, not the few. We must all seek to be wise, however simple that wisdom might be. In the deep Mystery of Wisdom, we are asked, led, persuaded to be more, to prepare our hearts for a lifting of the Veil that we might receive inspiration, guidance, direction that demands our utmost creative abilities to actualize. Wisdom does not give us "answers"—She teaches us through the gifts of our own potential, reveals a resolution based on the integrity by which we live, by the honesty and truthfulness between our thoughts, words, deeds and promises.

The importance of integrity is crucial—every seeker of Wisdom takes on the burden of living in accordance with his or her most profound insights. It is not only the teachings, but the practices, and even more, the embodiment that manifests the values and commitments of the individual, that reveals the deep congruency between thought, feeling, will and creative actions. As Wisdom flows into our lives, every person becomes an embodiment of sacred potential, every individual a medium of possible insight. The clarity, depth and fullness of that insight arises through an inner coherency, a healthy-mindedness, a loving heart, and a flexible will that seeks to foster growth and development in both self and others.

We are all teachers of Wisdom through the acts and commitments of our lives. We must awaken our deep potential through the inner sacrifice of selfish intent and the surrender of unconcern for the well being of others. Wisdom asks us to recognize our limits, to acknowledge our lack of insight, and to affirm our desire to be uplifted through a gracious receptivity of the Infinite. Within nurturing Presence, our stance or attitudes toward our unknown potential is a crucial index of our capacity for growth. As I give myself to Wisdom, She gives Herself to me, the greater giving to the lesser for purposes of shared human development.

There is a mystical ground within Wisdom, an ocean of endless reach without a shore, a vast clarity whose light is a source of quickening life, a profound energy of creation. And we, as limited beings, stand in the midst of that Ocean, surrounded by the currents of transformation, breathing our life gift for the purposes of creation. And the self in that context goes beyond "identity" and becomes something else, it becomes a gate, a mirror, a window through which the light of transformation can reach the incarnate world, cast its rays on sorrow and suffering, and offer healing warmth.

Can we clean the glass? Can we remove the smoky darkness of inner preoccupations, the ashes of hurt and the dust of illusion cast by our poor choices and misdirection? Can we polish the mirror of the heart and make a place within our engaged and active lives for unexpected revelation? Can we hold open through love and care, an inner expectation, a purity of motive seeking new insights without preconception?

The awakening of self-awareness is the very basis of spiritual insight because the ground of our humanity is not different than the ground of Wisdom. What we desire for the well being of the world, without imposition or arrogance, without fear or qualification, is born through self like a lens polished to focus light, to spark the fire of inspiration. Wisdom's light teaches us not to abandon self but to perfect the self as a medium of engagement within the world; Her light is a subtle vitality that heals excess and extremes and encourages the grafting of individual insights onto the Tree of Life.

Wisdom teaches engagement, dedication, loving kindness, and the joy and humor of our limitations. Whatever we know, there is more— immeasurably More—and the excitement of that fact is that there is no end to creative discovery and world transformation.

May Wisdom guide our steps, may we find the courage
to surrender and in our willingness to learn,
discover Her Endless Depths.
May we rejoice in the fellowship of Wisdom, in related
harmonies of soul and loving embrace,
affirming Her Luminous Presence.
May we overcome the illusions of self through courage
and thus discover the self-in-relation,
manifesting Her Joyful Grace.
And may we work in concert, in solidarity to discover
our differences, each unique, rare and precious,
as a witness to Her Unity and Diversity.
Amen, Now and Always.

Agriculture and the Sacred

Robert Karp

To live, we must daily break the body and spill the blood of Creation. When we do this knowingly, lovingly, skillfully, reverently, it is a sacrament. When we do it ignorantly, greedily, clumsily, destructively, it is a desecration.

— Wendell Berry

In ancient times agriculture was intimately connected with the sacred. We find evidence of this in a host of texts and in many traditions which survive to this day. We know, for example, that for the indigenous people on the American continent, the corn plant is believed to have come into being through a long process of cooperation between human beings and the gods, and to grow corn is still a sacred activity for many Native American people today.

If we try to discern the ultimate source of these traditions, we discover that people in ancient cultures experienced the natural world much differently than we do. Where today we might see, for example, simply a corn plant (tall stem, tassels, ears, husks, silks, yellow kernels, etc.), they saw the body of a spiritual being whom they felt to be the ultimate source of the unique traits and gifts of that particular plant species. This vision of the spiritual in nature endowed all creatures and all creation with a special kind of dignity.

It was thus not enough for ancient cultures or indigenous people to simply plant a corn seed at the right time in the right soil, and then cultivate the plant during the growing season until harvest. Growing corn also required prayers and rituals that would invite the spiritual being of corn to participate in the growth of the plants and so bless the people with her radiant wisdom and health-giving powers. Maintaining this sacred connection with the gods through agriculture was at the heart of the life of ancient cultures and echoes of this religious feeling toward nature survived in indigenous and rural farming communities for centuries.

Through his research, Rudolf Steiner discovered that the gradual loss of this way of experiencing the world among the majority of the world's population was an inevitable and necessary part of the evolution of human consciousness. This loss paved the way for a much clearer way of seeing the physical world, and eventually led to the discovery of the physical laws of matter and to modern technology. Through this process, we have also come to experience ourselves more and more as unique individuals independent of nature, culture, race and one another. With this independence comes freedom: the freedom to choose our own vocations, community and ideals—as well as the feeling that we are responsible for our own actions. This sense of individual freedom and responsibility is the gift, the silver lining, you could say, of materialism.

The healthy age of materialism has long since passed, however, so that today we bear witness primarily to the shadow side of materialism rather than its gift. We have become so enamored of our seeming power over nature, that we are undermining the very fabric of life on earth. This is perhaps nowhere more evident than in agriculture. Practices like confined animal feeding operations (CAFO's) and genetically engineered plants and animals (GMO's) betray a consciousness completely devoid of any remaining sense of the spiritual dignity of landscapes, organisms, creatures and species.

There is also a silver lining to this era of post-materialistic devolution of values, however. In the depths of the crisis brought on by these destructive trends, a new, individualized, eco-spiritual consciousness of the world is emerging. From thousands of humble, everyday people—farmers, eaters, scientists, educators, artists and business people—a grassroots awakening to the ecological and spiritual realities that sustain the earth and her creatures is taking place. This new consciousness, I would suggest, is the ultimate source of inspiration for the growth of the ecology movement of the 1960's, the health food movement of the 1970's, the environmental movement of the 1980's, the organic farming movement of the 1990's, the local food movement of the 2000's, and a host of other allied movements too numerous to mention. It is also, of course, the inspiration for the biodynamic movement which seeks to demonstrate the many practical ways this new consciousness can bring renewal to the earth and to the practice of agriculture.

Yes, the sense of the sacred is reemerging in the food and agriculture movement of today, as the quote from Wendell Berry at the beginning of this article so beautifully expresses. But, this new consciousness of the sacred is not the same as that possessed by ancient cultures. This awakening is not embedded in collective religious practices or cultural norms, but rather has emerged as a natural extension of healthy scientific inquiry and in the context of a cosmopolitan confluence of diverse philosophical perspectives and cultural traditions. This new sense of the sacred is thus rooted in and sustained by a contemporary sense of individuality and freedom of thought. In this otherwise deeply troubling moment in human history, this awakening, this tender, growing movement toward a reunion of agriculture and the sacred, can give us hope.

Dispelling Ignorance and Developing Harmony

Sister Joan Kirby

In July 2011, Yogaville, an Ashram founded by Gurudev Satchidananda, cele-brated the 25th Anniversary of its LOTUS temple with a gathering called "One in Spirit." The following was a response offered by Sister Joan Kirby, RSCJ, of the Temple of Understanding, to the panel topic, "Dispelling Ignorance and Developing Harmony."

Introduction

What ignorance are we addressing here? I am considering ignorance here from the point of view of a westerner. We live in the global village, we share the same roof, we are interdependent and co-responsible for care of the Earth. And yet, we still think of ourselves, and our religion, as separate, distinct, and unique. We see the world as dualistic, as I/Thou—I am sepa-rate from you, the exterior world is separate from me. We continue to think of doing things, hearing sounds, seeing things outside of our subjective self, and we remain separate. The suffering of the world is out there, over there and does not necessarily touch me. Further, our practice is to reason things logically, rationally. We are a subject observing an object. Our direct expe-rience is less important than syllogistic reasoning drawing us into self-reflective thought. Is this ignorance? I believe so. To live harmoniously as one universal family we will have to dispel this ignorance.

Dispelling Ignorance

We westerners should reflect as well on the Euro-centrism of our culture. A perhaps distorted reading of our sacred writings instructs man to dominate the Earth. But the message to use the Earth for our purposes sets up a dualistic hierarchy. This, as well as greed, has brought us to the exhaustion of the Earth's resources that we face today. Notice also that it is man who is the highest creation. Today women struggle for equality with men.

Separate from the Earth, it follows that we are separate from other humans. European culture is indebted to a Greek heritage of the matter/ spirit separation. Brilliant as they were, the Greeks taught of a dualistic world where we are separate from the other and from the world in which we live and move. Our fascination with this static universe has fostered the effort to impose assimilation, sometimes using bullying tactics based on a so-called superior civilization. This led to a haughty mentality and a falsely arrogant position with neo-colonialist attitudes. A hierarchical position places one above others exacting an attitude of submission.

Finally, as Christianity spread it was seen as the One True Revelation, the one true Church. In fact, many religions proclaim this uniqueness. In past centuries we westerners traveled to other continents with explicit missionary proselytizing in mind. The concept of the "one true religion" has directed much of Christian activity. The grave danger here is that if there is only "one true religion" we will never see all the others as equal— Christians will always be superior. Many traditions, particularly the religions of the Book, consider themselves to be the "one true faith," and some make every effort to bring all of humanity into the fold. Is this based in ignorance? Perhaps. However the many people who cherish their own belief system while humbly seeking to recognize the truth in other systems seem to escape this ignorance.

Educated to this world-view, we find it difficult to go beyond our customary frame of reference. Yes, it is probably strong education that has shaped our western mind. But as we look to develop harmony, our educational philosophy has to reflect a different awareness of reality if we are to address the brokenness, violence, and disunity of our world. To develop harmony, we have much to do.

Developing Harmony

Faced today with exhausted resources on the Earth, we are questioning our use and manipulation of the planet. Are we master of or partners with the Earth? Bolivians at the United Nations have re-introduced the concept of Mother Earth. A recently formed partnership among NGOs at the United Nations, the Interfaith Coalition for Ecological Civilization, is working toward a transformation of consciousness that recognizes our interdependence with the universe. Because we are in grave danger of leaving an uninhabitable Earth to the next generation, a life in dynamic relationship with the Earth, our mother, is a universal calling today. I believe there is a new revelation here.

If we are one with the Earth, then we are not separate from other humans. Our whole epistemology has to be transformed. Instead of considering ourselves as separate, we can learn from the eastern understanding of interconnectedness and oneness. "Not One, Not Two." When there is difference, not separation, harmony becomes possible.

As we place ourselves on an equal, respectful, and friendly footing with others, we learn to respect differences and to love diversity. This is not limited to educational philosophy—its application is wider and demands a way of being that cherishes collaboration and reciprocity.

I want to quote here a passage from my Religious Society's documents on this subject:

Collaboration is recognition of the dignity of persons and of peoples; it implies welcoming and sharing what each one is and offers. It requires attitudes of trust and mutual support, vulnerability and openness. It recognizes the need to learn from others and it requires flexibility and imagination in discovering new possibilities together.

How will the richness of many cultures and spiritual traditions enlarge our experience of God and the ways of God's actions in ourselves and our world? As we travel the globe encountering many different cultures and religious traditions, our hearts are opened to understand the vastness of creation and the appropriateness of different traditions for varied and rich cultures quite other than our own. God, Holy Spirit present in every corner of creation, has opened many paths to Godself. God births us at every moment and there is no separation from the Creative Spirit given us by God. The cosmic Christ is present, not in a subject/object relationship, not as an I and Thou, but as one with all creation through His Spirit. This way of openness makes possible new growth for us Christians.

I believe this way of life is not an option. It is the opportunity and responsibility of our age. The future of humanity depends on our dedication to establishing harmony.

Conclusion

To our credit, many are recognizing the beauty, intelligence, and inspiration in the different cultures we encounter. If we claim to recognize and respect human rights we are compelled to go beyond social differences and acknowledge legitimate religious differences. Seeking the face of the One Holy God, manifested in many forms, we are compelled to go beyond our traditional, historical understanding to the depth of the mystery of diversity.

Contemporary insights into the ever-changing, dynamic universe raise the question: Is revelation finished? Or are we at a truly new moment? Is this a time when our presence in the universe is holistic, not dualistic—when consciousness is being transformed from self-consciousness to an ecological consciousness?

It is a wake-up call from the universe—a call for all, not just a few insightful ones. As an act of justice we are called to recognize universal unity, a radical unity in diversity.

This is the great opportunity, our duty to the future.

On Prophecy and Time – part 5

Pir Zia Inayat-Khan to David Spangler and William Irwin Thompson

Dear David,

I enjoyed Subtle Worlds immensely. I admire your knack for expressing the most delicate perceptions in ordinary workaday language. Subtle Worlds is a book that people of all spiritual traditions, and those of no tradition, should be able to appreciate with equal relish.

I understand William's Entelechy as the constellation of presences whose interactions establish the human being as a microcosm of the whole. The function of these interactions, I think, is the "circulation of Light and vital energies" that you describe in your book. Subtle Worlds is really a wonderful account of how the ecological principles of interdependence and circulation extend beyond the visible world into the unseen.

You and William have spoken of how mitochondria and other microscopic symbionts have their counterparts on other levels. At the psychic level, the Sufis call these animalcules *muwakkals*, which means literally, "commission holders." They are called this because they receive commissions from the heart that is awake to its own life, knowledge, power and desire. One finds an allusion to this in the legend of Solomon when he built the Temple of Jerusalem by commanding the djinn. In other words, the awakened heart establishes sacred space by appealing to the best instincts within the myriad entities that populate its mindscape.

I agree with you both that the Entelechy is not the same as the Pit Crew. The Pit Crew, as I understand it, is a being or group of beings that guides the human soul in the course of its journey. Sufism posits the existence of a "spiritual hierarchy" (your holarchy is a better word!) made up of incarnate and disincarnate masters, saints, prophets and angels whose task is to consciously mediate between the visible and invisible realms of being. Ibn 'Arabi uses the term wiratha ("heritage") to describe how different prophets shine their light on the mystic's path at different stages. Though Ibn 'Arabi remained a Muslim thoughout his life, he came under the esoteric tutelage of Jesus, Moses, Hud and other prophets at various periods. Ibn 'Arabi's prophetology breaks open the horizon of what we call interfaith. Recognizing the validity other faiths is just the beginning; the real work is accessing the living guidance of the prophets through inner initiation. I think your concept of the Pit Crew is an excellent articulation of that opportunity.

With heartfelt good wishes,

Zia

The next letter in this series begins on page 141.

LIVING RELATEDNESS
An Ecocentric Worldview

SATISH KUMAR, INTERVIEWED BY GARY NULL

I *used to have a friend named Krishnamurti. Were you familiar with him?*

Yes, he was also my friend. When he said, "the truth is a pathless land," that resonated with me. I also believe in this approach, that we need to be pilgrims, which is not to get dogmatic, not to get fixed, not to get stuck in any one kind of ideology, but always remain open and move on to a new, fresh experience. So that is very much an influence of Krishnamurti on my life.

Why is focusing on fear aspects of environmental catastrophe less constructive than reorienting our consciousness and thinking about our relationship with the Earth based on love? How would you describe your experience of relationship to nature and how does it compel you to act and live your life?

When people were warning about Katrina, they were giving a scenario of doom and gloom and fear. That makes people feel impotent, or they get into a kind of numbness. If you create a kind of spirit by which people are inspired to take positive action and that inspiration comes from love of nature, love of people, love of communities, love of good values, then I think people will act.

So the reason people don't act at this moment is that there is a lot of media coverage about global warming, a lot of government leaders are talking about climate change and how oil is running out and how resources are depleting and how our life will be difficult and water is running out, and food will run out, all with fear, fear, fear. That is causing a kind of numbness and that numbness is causing a kind of impotence and that is when you get the phenomena of "watching Katrina."

So my solution to that problem is that the inspiration from within each and every human being and within every community, each and every town, and each and every state and each and every country, has to come from inside—that we are not only talking about changing our lifestyle because of the fear, the doom and gloom and disaster, but we are changing our lifestyle because the kind of lifestyle we are going to be changing and transforming to is a good life in itself! When you change out of love and out of desire for elegant simplicity, the new lifestyle will be joyful and delightful, and build a relationship with the natural world and with the human community.

So if we want to move people to act, we have to inspire a positive vision, and that vision is love of nature. We tend to see nature as some thing out there, like rivers and mountains and forests and animals and birds. We don't think that we are nature; rather we think we human beings are superior to nature, we are the masters of nature, and nature is there only for our consumption, so we can kill the animals as we like for our food, we can destroy the rainforest as we like for timber or fields to produce more meat, or we can pollute the rivers and scour the oceans to get more fish, it is all for us, us, us. So fear, combined with greed, leads to the kind of society we have today.

So, my strategy is not to dwell in fear and a kind of telling people they are greedy, therefore, don't do this, don't do that, but I want to inspire people from inside and say "when you love the sea, when you love the forest, when you love the rivers, when you love the animals, you will not destroy them." This perennial wisdom has been forgotten.

So we need to return to that more positive, optimistic, and intrinsic value of nature, and see that we are part of nature, and what we do to nature, we do to ourselves. If we destroy nature, we are destroying ourselves, because we are an integral part of nature. That way, I think the "watching Katrina" phenomenon will come to a solution.

I appreciate your insights. Now, let me ask you to go a little further with that. There is a certain element of hypocrisy amongst many of our educators and leaders in that they tell us that our educational system and our other institutions are there to inspire us, motivate us, and help us, and yet they never encourage us to be disobedient or to look critically at those institutions.

Education at this moment is very problematic, and the problems of the world today are mainly caused by so-called educated people. Global warming, climate change, nuclear weapons, wars, all the kind of problems we face today, are managed or even created by people who have been educated, often at prestigious universities. So education is not a panacea; it has caused many problems, because nuclear weapons are not created by uneducated peasants of Africa, and global warming is not created by uneducated women of India. They are created by highly educated people, but they are half educated.

I was invited to speak at the London School of Economics, which is one of England's prestigious and well-known universities, where young people come from all over the world to be trained in economics, and I asked them, "You teach here economics, all right, but where is your department of ecology?" They said, "We don't have one." I said, "Do you mean to say that you are teaching people economy without teaching ecology?"

Because "ecology" is made of oikos and logos. Oikos means our Earth home, our planet home, how relationships work. Logos means knowledge. And with "economy," oikos links with nomos, which means management. So you are teaching your students, young people from all over the world, how to manage your home without knowing your home!

Half educated is worse than uneducated, like half-baked bread. And most of our world problems that we face today are created by half educated people. So we have to bring a total transformation to the educational system where ecology and economy are joined, which will also lead to ethics and morality and spirituality. Education is really a double-edged sword, and unless it is more holistic it can destroy as much as it can build so I think we need to reexamine how and what we teach.

I believe that, with, rare exception, we do not inspire our students to challenge our ideas. And therefore, they may end up knowing some limited skills, but do they know about life?

Wasn't it Soren Kierkegaard who said, " Life can only be understood backwards, but it can only be lived forwards." And Henri Amiel said, "The man who has no inner life is a slave of his surroundings." Yet in our society today, we are virtually cultish in the individuality that dominates just about every area and discipline, and has been a fundamental cause of the loss of humanity's sense of community and connectedness.

What are your thoughts about this, and what is the necessary awareness in order to restore the need for community?

We are individuals, but the word "individual" means "indivisible." We are not separate, we are not disconnected as individuals—this is a corrupted meaning of individual, that we are autonomous units separate and disconnected from the rest of the world, or the community, or the natural world. So the individual must be indivisible, and the individual does not exist separately.

The French philosopher Rene Descartes separated mind and matter, and individual and community, with "Cogito ergo sum." I think therefore I am. That is a kind of beginning of individualism and separation from the natural world, and from the community. We are all connected, we are related in this web of life, Indra's net we call it in India, the network of nature and humans and animals and the sky and the sun and the moon and the stars, all life is interconnected.

We are all connected and we are all related. You are, therefore I am. The Earth is, therefore I am. The forests are, therefore I am. My ancestors were, therefore I am. That message is forgotten. Descartes' philosophy and his science dominate our educational system, particularly in Europe, and America, and we become so rational and intellectual, at the expense of our spirituality and our emotions and our feelings.

So education for me is only true holistic education if you combine the head, the heart and the hands. So education needs quite a lot of new thinking and reforming so that we truly become holistic. Once we have that kind of relatedness in our consciousness, then we will not destroy the planet that sustains us, we will not cut the branch on which we sit.

If our environment is destroyed, our oceans are polluted, our rain-forests are gone, our biosphere is filled with greenhouse gasses, what will happen to humanity? We are not going to feed ourselves with computers, cars and televisions, we have to depend on the natural life and natural resources. So humanity, which genetically engineers seeds, and creates industrialized agriculture, and manipulates animals in factory farms, this kind of technological future that we are building is not going to be resilient and sustainable.

So I am working to create a new consciousness, a new kind of education. This is why I established Schumacher College in England, where we have people coming from all over the world to study and understand the world in an interconnected, interrelated, interdependent way, so that we move on from Cartesian dualism of individual against community and mind against matter and humans against nature.

Well, I commend you for that. Cardinal Newman said, "Growth is the only evidence of life," and when I read that years ago, I thought no, it is just the opposite. Our mistake has been that we must always show that we are grow-ing, to establish a sense of the quality of our life, while in fact consciousness is what determines, in the end, the evidence of life. Those who have a deeper consciousness have a profound respect for life.

Absolutely. If you look at the definition of "consciousness" in the dictionary, it is mutual thinking, thinking together, awareness together, and that togetherness is the lost course at the moment. We are always thinking me, me, me, and what I am saying, and also the magazine that

I edit called Resurgence, is that we have to move from this egocentric thought to ecocentric thought.

When you go from egocentric to ecocentric, you are going away from an individualistic, separational worldview to a more communitarian and relational worldview. Then we are in the delight of life, and celebration of life, and joy of life, rather than the domination and control and fear that lead to ownership and possession and acquisition and consumerism.

Our whole philosophy has to be reexamined and re-explored, so that we create a worldview where we can be at ease and relax, and the universe is working in our favor and not against us.

I really appreciate these insights, and I want to thank you for all the good work you do. Please give people your contact information.

Thank you. It has been a pleasure to be with you on your program. The link for Resurgence Magazine is www.resurgence.org, and this is my website. If you would like to know more about Schumacher College, visit our website at www.schumachercollege.org.uk, or maybe come and do a course here. That way we can build a more relational world where harmony and prosperity and peace prevail, rather than this competitive, conflicted, dominating, control-oriented worldview that is prevailing at this moment.

In the Time of the Sacred Places

Winona LaDuke

And while I stood there
I saw more than I can tell
and I understood more than I saw,
for I was seeing in a sacred manner
the shapes of all things in the spirit
and the shape of all shapes as
they must all live together
as one being.

> *– Black Elk*

It's not like a church where you have everything in one place. We could describe how sacred sites are the teachers…. We don't want the American dream…. We want our prayer rocks.

> *– Calleen Sisk, Winnemum Wintu*

IN THE TIME of Thunderbeings and Underwater Serpents, the humans, animals, and plants conversed and carried on lives of mischief, wonder, and mundane tasks. The prophets told of times ahead, explained the causes of the deluge of past, and predicted the two paths of the future: one scorched and one green, one of which the Anishinaabeg would have to choose.

In the time of the Thunderbeings and Underwater Serpents, it was understood that there was a constant balance and a universe beyond this material world that needed to be maintained and to whom we would belong always.

The Anishinaabe people, among other land-based peoples, undulate between these worlds. The light of day, the deepness of night remain; the parallel planes of spirit and material world coexist in perpetuity. All remains despite the jackhammer of industrial civilization, the sound of combustion engines, and the sanitized white of a dioxin-bleached day. That was then, but that is also now. Teachings, ancient as the people who have lived on a land for five millennia, speak of a set of relationships to all that is around, predicated on respect, recognition of the interdependency of all beings, an understanding of humans' absolute need to be reverent and to manage our behavior, and an understanding that this relationship must be reaffirmed through lifeways and through acknowledgment of the sacred.

Millennia have passed since that time, yet those beings still emerge: lightning strikes at unexpected times, the seemingly endless fires of climate change, tornadoes that flatten, King Tides, deluges of rivers, copper beings in the midst of industrial society. So it is that we come to face our smallness in a world of mystery, and our responsibilities to the life that surrounds us.

> *We are a part of everything that is beneath us, above us and*
> *around us. Our past is our present, our present is our future, and*
> *our future is seven generations past and present.*
> *—Haudenosaunee Teaching*

In the midst of this time, land-based peoples work to continue such a lifeway, or to follow simply the original instructions passed on by Gichi Manidoo, the Creator, or those who instruct us. This path often is littered with the threats of a fossil-fuel and nuclear economy: a uranium mine, a big dam project, or the Tar Sands. People work to restore or retain their relationship to a sacred place and to a world. In many places, peoples hold Earth renewal ceremonies, for example, or water healing ceremonies. In an Indigenous philosophical view, these ceremonies are how we are able to continue. This essay tells some of those stories.

This essay also tells a story of a society based on the notion of frontier. Born of a doctrine of discovery, terra nullius, and a papal-driven entitlement to vanquish and destroy that which was Indigenous, America was framed in the mantra of Manifest Destiny. This settler-focused relationship to this North American continent has been historically one of conquest, of utilitarian relationship, of an anthropocentric taking of wealth to make more things for empire. That society has named and claimed things: one mountain after another (Mt. Rainier, Harney Peak, Mt. McKinley, Mt. Lassen, Pikes Peak) all named, and claimed, for empire. Naming and claiming with a flag does not mean relationship; it means only naming and claiming. Americans have developed a sense of place related to empire, with no understanding that the Holy Land is also here. To name sacred mountain spirits after mortal men, who blow through for just a few decades, is to denude relationship.

Americans are also transient, taught an American dream of greener pastures elsewhere. This too belittles relationship to place. It holds no responsibility, only a sense of entitlement—to mineral rights, water rights, and private property—enshrined in the constitution.

In the times we find ourselves, with the crashing of ecosystems, dying out of fish and trees, change and destabilization of climate, our relationship to place and to relatives—whether they have fins or roots—merits reconsideration.

On Sacred Places

Since the beginning of times, the Creator and Mother Earth have given our peoples places to learn the teachings that will allow us to continue and reaffirm our responsibilities and ways on the lands from which we have come. Indigenous peoples are place-based societies, and at the center of those places are the most sacred of our sites, where we reaffirm our relationships.

Everywhere there are Indigenous people, there are sacred sites, there are ways of knowing, there are relationships. The people, the rivers, the mountains, the lakes, the animals, and the fish are all related. In recent years, US courts have challenged our ability to be in these places, and indeed to protect them. In many cases, we are asked to quantify "how sacred it is … or how often it is sacred." Baffling concepts in the spiritual realm. Yet we do not relent, we are not capable of becoming subsumed.

The Nur & the People

In Northern California, the Winnemem Wintu have known since time immemorial of their relationships to the Nur, the salmon people. They have known that they have a sacred responsibility to protect and care for the salmon that have sustained them on the slope of Boyum Patuk, the sacred mountain, now known as Mt. Shasta. It was the Nur who gave the Winnemem their voice, who taught them to sing. The Winnemem were told long ago that if the salmon disappeared, so would they.

The salmon only sing as they course the rivers of the Northwest, and are only to be heard by the Wintu. Legends talk of a time when the Nur took pity on the Wintu people and gave to them their voice. The Wintu, in turn, were to care for the Nur always and were to sing. Millennia later they still try to fulfill this responsibility.

"The people believe that when the last salmon is gone, humans will be gone too," Caleen Sisk, traditional spiritual leader of the Winnemem Wintu, explains.

Millennia on the river did well for both the people and the salmon, in an area whose remoteness from white civilization was its protection. But in time that civilization encroached, and although they were signatories in good faith to what would be an unratified 1851 treaty, and later identified as the tribe who would be drowned in the 1941 federal act that created the Shasta Dam, the Winnemem Wintu ceased to exist as "Indians" under federal law. This strange irony, that the government created by the settlers and intruders who took your land and killed your people gets to determine if you are still an Indian, remains particularly bitter to many tribes. The Winnemem Wintu are particularly caught in this quagmire.

In 1941, the Shasta Dam drowned more than 26 miles of the lower McCloud River system, engulfing sacred sites, villages, and history under a deep lake destined to benefit cities far away, agriculture for the world, and tourists who could afford the way of life. The dam drowned much of the history of the Winnemem Wintu, and the dam blocked the passage of the salmon people—the McCloud River salmon. The Nur either interbred with the Sacramento River salmon, or died out in California.

Fish Rock was blown up to make room for a railroad track in 1914, which was, like so much else, drowned by the waters that would become known as Lake Shasta. What is left of Dekkas Rock, a prayer site, now protrudes from the reservoir, as one reporter notes, "… a malformed atoll." It was here, next to the river, that the Winnemem held what other tribes in the region call "Big Times," where disputes were adjudicated, songs and ceremonies were held, and marriages were arranged.

The Wintu grieved the loss of their salmon, and their sacred doctoring rocks, and the loss of the river, though their prophecies had foretold the loss of the salmon: "Our old people said that the salmon would be hidden behind a river of ice. Indian doctors and prophets had been with the Wintu long ago, and prophesied the time when the salmon would disappear," Caleen Sisk tells me.

That was almost unimaginable to the Wintu—or to those who "discovered the salmon" of the McCloud River. Livingston Stone, a fish culturist arriving in Wintu territory, noted that the spawning Chinook were so plentiful he could have walked across their backs from one side of the river to the other. In the 1870s, he established the Baird Hatchery on the McCloud, originally as an effort to breed a Pacific salmon to replenish the now dwindling and overfished Atlantic salmon stocks. The Winnemem Wintu, initially opposed to the fishery, made peace with the white men of the fisheries on the condition that the salmon would always be able to come home.

Then in a strange turning of events, in 1890, Livingston Stone decided to transplant the Wintu Nur to another world, Aotearoa, or

New Zealand. Moved in sphagnum moss over a vast ocean, the Nur salmon people came to live in the Rakaia River on the South Island in Aotearoa (New Zealand).

So it was that the Nur, the salmon of the McCloud, disappeared from the Wintu world, but just as had been prophesied, they returned elsewhere, in a "river of ice"—the Rakaia River emerges from a glacial mountain. In 2008, the Wintu went to Aotearoa to visit their salmon. And, for the first time since the dams had destroyed their relatives, the Wintu sang once again for the Nur. It is fifty years since the dam destroyed the homeland of the salmon and much of the sacred world of the Wintu, but the Wintu believe that through prayer, prophecy, and hard work, there will be a return.

Copper & Iron, Wild Rice & Water, & Wolves

> Sometimes it seems like people aren't interested in
> sticking around for another thousand years.
> – Mike Wiggins, Bad River Anishinaabe Tribal Chairman

Two thousand miles to the East, on the shore of Gichi Gummi (Lake Superior), the Anishinaabeg Akiing ("the land to which the Anishinaabe people belong") stretches throughout the Great Lakes region in a territory of lakes and rivers, wild rice, and wolves.

On this land the Underwater Manidoowag, the Miskwaabik and Biwaabik spirits of copper and iron ore, have lived, omaa akiing, since the time of the Thunderbeings. As one early European explorer recorded, "Copper was said to belong to the Underwater Manitouk.... One often finds at the bottom of the water, pieces of pure copper.... I have several times seen such pieces in the Savages' hand, and since they are superstitious, they keep to them as so many divinities, or as presents which the gods dwelling beneath the water have given them and on which their welfare is to depend."

The Underwater Manidoowag, Miskwaabik and Biwaabik, were viewed not as spirits by the American government, but as objects of empire. Some of the first incursions by the US government onto

Anishinaabeg land, in the early 1800s, were to secure access to iron and copper deposits. Within a very short period, four treaties were signed by the United States, each providing for mining in Anishinaabeg territory. By mid-century, more than 100 copper companies had been incorporated in the Anishinaabeg Akiing. Many of today's US-based transnational mining companies, including Kennecott, Anaconda Copper, and 3M, were founded in this era on the wealth of the Anishinaabeg.

The wild rice has also been here since the time of Thunderbeings. Indeed, it was a part of the Anishinaabeg migration story and of a set of prophecies instructing the people to "go to the place where the food grows upon the water." Called manoomin ("a seed of the Creator") by the Anishinaabe, wild rice is the only grain endemic to North America and is one of the greatest gifts imaginable to the land and waters. There are few other places in the world where such a bountiful gift is delivered to those who live there, whether they have wings or hands. Owing to the unique nature and adaptability of the manoomin, the lakes and rivers each year offer a wild rice crop at some place in the region. That is an amazing food security for a people and for the waterfowl who nest and eat in these same waters. It is because of this bounty that where there is wild rice there are Ojibwe or Anishinaabeg people, and where there are Anishinaabeg, there is wild rice. This is a sacred food and a keystone of the ecosystem of the Great Lakes region, or Anishinaabe Akiing. As copper and iron mining despoiled the waters of the lakes and rivers, so it devastated both the manoomin and those whose life and ways depended upon it.

The decimation of the Anishinaabeg by plagues, starvation, and federal policies closely mirrored the destruction of the ma'iingan, the wolf. The Anishinaabeg relationship to the ma'iingan is deeply sacred in the traditions and history of the people. It is said that the first friend of the half spirit/half human being Naanaaboozhoo, a central figure in Anishinaabeg culture and teachings, was the ma'iingan. In Anishinaabeg prophecies, that which befalls the wolf will befall the Anishinaabeg. The limiting of territories—to reservations for the Anishinaabeg and to a few refuges and a few sparse patches of the north woods for the wolves—occurred for both. Like the people, the wolves were brought to near-extinction.

Yet both wolves and Anishinaabeg have returned to the northland. Today, nineteen Anishinaabeg reservations span the north country, from Michigan into Montana. This same territory is today the home of the largest wolf population in the lower forty-eight states. Where there are 60,000 Anishinaabeg, there are 5,000 wolves—both relatives, one with two legs and one with four, rebounding after catastrophic losses.

The Predator Returns

The companies forged of empire in the 1850s are also returning home now, having ravaged the world, fortified their empires, and left memorials to the copper that once was, in the form of huge pits. New mines are proposed throughout the Anishinaabe Akiing. Thus far they have been fended off by citizens and tribal opposition, but the region is incredibly challenged, as Ojibwes note in a letter to the United Nations requesting assistance: "Currently, an aggressive mining boom throughout Anishinaabeg territory, of present-day Michigan, Wisconsin, Minnesota, and Ontario, threatens the water quality and ecosystem of almost every sub-watershed of Lake Superior."

Eagle Rock, known as "the Home of the White Wolf," is a sacred site and prehistoric navigation site on the Keewenaw. It is considered sacred to not only the Anishinaabeg, but also the Hochunk and Cheyenne peoples. The tribes living today in this territory, as well as the National Congress of American Indians, have requested that the rock be protected as a site of religious worship.

Underneath the rock, in a world below, is Miskwaabik Aabinoojiins, or the Copper Child. This copper ore body, appearing in GIS imaging as a baby, awaits its scheduled end like a convict on death row: Rio Tinto Zinc, a UK-based mining company, through its subsidiary Kennecott, plans to mine the copper deposit adjacent to the sacred place.

It has been a seven-year battle for the sacred site, marked by arrests and legal actions, and now by a petition to the United Nations for intervention under the Declaration on the Rights of Indigenous Peoples not only to protect their sacred sites, but to be protected from minerals exploitation, which will destroy the aquatic ecosystems of wild rice and a rich land upon which the Anishinaabeg have lived for five millennia.

The Michigan regulatory authorities, which have taken jurisdiction over the area, have ruled against the tribes, the water, and the sacred site, stating essentially that the site could not be sacred or did not have spiritual significance because a place of worship must be a building. On these grounds, the state approved the mining permit.

Proposals in both Wisconsin and Minnesota would eviscerate water quality laws, with severe impacts on the wild rice or manoomin of the north. In turn, the recent delisting of the wolf by the US Fish and Wildlife seems synchronized exactly with the interests of new mining companies in the region.

But it is a time when relationships are changing. It is ironic that the two largest challenges to the wholesale mining of the north may be manoomin, or wild rice, and the ma'iingan. Tribal communities, joined increasingly by northern residents, have opposed the threats to water and wild rice throughout the north country, and regulatory battles are underway in Minnesota. And, while the wolf has been delisted by federal agencies under the Endangered Species Act, tribal communities are opposing the delisting in their territories. This is significant, as the wolf territories coincide with reservations and the areas surrounding tribal reservations still within tribal jurisdiction due to treaties and court decisions.

In this time, tribal governments and intergovernment agencies in the north pledge to retain their relationship and responsibility to the ma'iingan, and our communities remain vigilant in working to protect the sacred beings from the mines of the predator.

Doko'oo'sliid ... the Mountain of Kachinas & Recycled Ski Areas

To the far south, in the realm of the sacred mountains of the Dine or Navajo people, Dine Bii Kaya, the four sacred mountains, are again facing threats. Mt. Taylor is once again proposed for uranium mining, and Doko'oo'sliid, the Sacred Mountain of the West to the Navajo, is being desecrated for the pleasure of skiers.

This volcanic highland area of Arizona began forming over 6 million years ago with the eruption of nearly 600 volcanoes. The most dramatic of those eruptions created a place sacred to thirteen tribes, a cluster of three 12,000-foot mountain peaks known as the Sacred Mountain of the West, one of four cornerstones marking the borders of Dine Bii Kaya, the land of the Dine or Navajo. The Dine know it as a place where the Kachina spirits emerge. In the proud vernacular of American empire, the sacred mountain is called San Francisco Peaks.

The highest point in Arizona, the only arctic-alpine vegetation in the state, which grows here in a fragile two-square-mile zone, and Arizona's best examples of Ice Age glaciation all can be found here. It has been a place for the gathering of sacred herbs and the practice of religious ceremonies since the dawn of time.

In 1984, the United States Congress recognized the fragile ecosystems and cultural significance of the area and designated the Kachina Peaks Wilderness. Yet here, in this unlikely place, in an ostensibly protected Wilderness in the desert, a ski resort has been proposed, with a plan to pipe treated sewage water from Flagstaff to spray artificial snow on the sacred mountain. There is no water source on the mountain other than what falls from the sky.

Despite the known ecosystem, archeological and cultural issues, and determined opposition from Native nations and conservation organizations, the Ninth US Circuit Court of Appeals recently allowed the Arizona Snowbowl Recreation project to proceed with its plan. Flagstaff-treated sewer water will be trucked to Snowbowl until a 14.8-mile pipeline is complete, and then some 180 million gallons a year of treated effluent from the city of Flagstaff will be pumped up the sacred mountain to the ski area for snowmaking. The treated sewage has been proven to contain contaminants such as pharmaceuticals and hormones. Snowbowl hopes to attract ski-starved desert dwellers to its resort with clever marketing, but it remains to be seen how enticing a mouthful of Snowbowl effluent cocktail might be.

The Snowbowl owners have already clear-cut some 74 acres of rare alpine forest for new ski runs. A 10-million-gallon retention pond and another 12 miles of pipeline will be built to distribute reclaimed sewer water along the ski runs, all desecrations in the eyes of the Dine people. In the summer of 2012, protests continued in defense of a sacred place, in a call for access to water for people and the land, and ultimately in a questioning of priorities.

This is the difference between worldviews, one that views a land as a rich ore body, or a playground, and another that views it as a source of great spiritual and cultural wealth.... This is the story of the time in which we find ourselves.

The Auction of the Sacred

As the wind breathes out of Wind Cave, I am reminded of the creation of humans and my own small place in this magnificent world. Wind Cave National Park in the Black Hills is named for the cave itself, called Washun Niya, ("the Breathing Hole of Mother Earth") by the Lakota People. In the Lakota creation story, it is from here that they emerged to this world.

It is a complex cave system. According to scientists, we may only have a sense of five percent of the cave's volume and breadth, and likely even less of its power. Some might call this the "known unknown." Most Indigenous peoples would understand it as the Great Mystery—that which is much larger than our own anthropocentric understanding of the world—reflecting the understanding that, indeed, there is more than one world surrounding people.

So it is that in 2012, a time of change and transformation signaled in an American election year and predicted in the Mayan Calendar, we find the smallness and the greatness of humans in the much larger world around us coming face-to-face in the Black Hills. A most sacred place, Pe'Sla, in the center of the Lakota Universe, came up for sale, and values and worldviews clashed.

Pe'Sla, to the Lakota, is "Center of the Heart of Everything that is ... one of a small number of highly revered and geographically-cosmolog-ically integral places on the entire planet," according to Lakota scholar Chase Iron Eyes. It is "the place where Morning Star, manifested as a meteor, fell to earth to help the Lakota by killing a great bird that had taken the lives of seven women; Morning Star's descent having created the wide open uncharacteristic bald spot inthe middle of the forested Black Hills. (On American maps,this is called Old Baldy.) The Morning Star placed the spirits of those seven women in the sky as the constellation 'Pleiades' or 'The Seven Sisters.'"

On August 25, 2012, the Center of the Heart of Everything was to be placed on the auction block, destined to be diced into a set of 300-acre tracts proposed for ranchettes, with a possible road through the heart of what has been, until now, a relatively un-desecrated sacred site. "We didn't even know it was going to be sold," Debra White Plume from Manderson told me. "We heard nothing about it until we saw the auction announcement."

America is a country where private property is enshrined as a constitutional right, but the rights of nature, of the natural world, or of unborn generations are not. In the time of the crashing of ecosystems and worlds, it may be worth not making a commodity out of all that is revered. A 2005 editorial in the generally very conservative Rapid City Journal points out that protecting Lakota sacred sites is of interest to all. "Non-Indians have little to fear if familiar sites are designated as sacred; visitors are still allowed at Bear Butte, Devil's Tower, and Rainbow Bridge, even though they are being managed as Indian sacred sites. And in fact, expanding non-Indians' knowledge and appreciation of the Indian lore surrounding such sites could lead to greater cultural understanding."

With less than two weeks remaining before Pe'Sla was to be auctioned off, word spread through Lakota communities (three of which, all Lakota reservations, are in the economically poorest counties in the country), through the use of Facebook, the Internet, and the media, from the Huffington Post to the Seattle Times. The story of the Lakota people, their sacred site, and the proposed auction was repeated in whispers, and then in rallies and in outrage. Using the Internet, the communities raised over half a million dollars, which was then matched by tribal money originating with the Rosebud Sioux Tribe, and other donations.

The auction was cancelled, and the Lakota people have begun to nego-
tiate for the purchase of their sacred site.

It is incredibly ironic, however, in many ways, particularly considering that the Paha Sapa, the Black Hills, was never purchased from the
Lakota but illegally taken by the United States with the advent of gold
mining (the Hearst empire). Though over $105 million was allocated for
the Black Hills by Congress to pay Lakota people for the illegal taking,
that money has never been accepted. Hence the irony: the people must
buy back land they have never considered owned by anyone else.

On a Return to Sacred Lifeways

There is always hope, and for those of us who remain involved in
our ceremonies, there is also faith. That faith is reaffirmed when small
miracles of spirit occur, and the world changes.

On the banks of the McCloud River in Northern California, the
Wintu gather, despite citations and legal opposition by the state of California, to hold their sacred coming-of-age ceremonies for their young
women. This is how life continues.

And, one day, not too far away, those salmon will return home from
Aotearoa. And there will be a celebration of the Nur and the Wintu.

In the northwoods, the Anishinaabeg celebrate one round of opposing
the Beast. In 2012, the huge GTAC mine in the Penokee Mountains
of Wisconsin—the headwaters to the Bad River, the centerpiece of
the Bad River tribal community of Anishinaabeg—was defeated, like
another four before it in Wisconsin. The defeat may be temporary, but
it is breathing room for Mother Earth.

And in 2012, it seems that Pe'Sla will be protected from becoming a
set of luxury ranchettes, and may continue as a place where a people
pray and reaffirm their relationship to Creation.

And then there is the renaming, or the recovery of names. Several
decades ago, Mt. McKinley became Mt. Denali. On the other side of
the world, Australia's Ayers Rock became Uluru, in the name of the
people who live there, not the white man who found it. In 2010, in
Canada, the Haida homeland was formally renamed Haida Gwaii,

eclipsing Queen Charlotte Island, named for a Queen who had likely never seen that land nor understood Haida traditions. And further south, the Salish Sea is emerging in what was Puget Sound, and more reaffirmations of place and history are reframing our understanding of the holy land that is here. These stories join with the stories of a people and their allies who have come to live on this land.

On a larger scale, the New Zealand Courts have recently affirmed the rights of a River to exist, in a court system that emerged from colonial and church authorities. The Whanganui River became a legal entity under the name Te Awa Tupua ("an integrated, living whole") and was given the same status as a person under New Zealand law in 2012.

The industrial predator, however, is unrelenting. Voracious in appetite, greed, and lacking any heart, all that is becomes prey...

If 57 percent of the energy produced in the US is wasted through inefficiencies, one might want to become less wasteful to survive. And if two-thirds of our material-based economy ends up in waste dumps relatively quickly, we may want to cut our consumption. These are economic choices, political choices, and personal choices. And they ultimately have to do with empire, the need for new frontiers, and making peace, omaa akiing, here on this land.

In the din of crashing worlds, it is possible to watch and breathe. In the 2012 deluge of the city of Duluth, rain fell constantly for two days onto the streets of a city with aging infrastructure. The Anishinaabeg remember a great flood from the earliest of memories, after which the world was made anew. The Anishinaabeg watched the flood from our reservations, an island safely away from this deluge and crash.

The tally in economic terms of the 2012 flood is somewhere around $100 million. That figure represents just the beginning of climate-change-related expenses in this year. By March of 2012, there had been over 129,000 recorded weather records on a worldwide scale. World insurance agencies project that we will be spending 20 percent of our GDP on a worldwide scale on climate-change-related disasters.

The polar bear is freed by the Duluth deluge from the zoo, escaping his pen. As the bear headed north from the Duluth Zoo, we Anishinaabeg knew that the time was changing. We watched and we understood that we, as sacred beings in this millennium, have an opportunity to do a righteous and pono thing—to take a good path.

In the time of Thunderbeings and Underwater Serpents, the humans, animals, and plants conversed and carried on lives of mischief, wonder, and mundane tasks. The prophets told of times ahead, explained the deluge of past and predicted the two paths of the future: one scorched and one green, one of which the Anishinaabeg would have to choose.

All of us have the same choice, and somewhere in this time, there is the potential to take a right path.

The Endless Flow of Life

Patrick Levy

It is told that Tupala was a great king who was devoted to his subjects, generous towards the brahmins, gentle with children, respectful of wise men and wisdom, and who followed the rules of good governance.

On one hunting night, leaving his retinue far behind, he ventured far and deep into the forest and lost his way.

At dawn, he arrived in front of a hut where an untouchable was cleaning out the carcass of a bull. As he was surprised to find himself there, the King was about to ask where he was and in which province and hamlet he had arrived, when he caught sight of a dazzlingly beautiful girl. She was simple and smiling, the very embodiment of grace. And of course he fell in love with her.

At the speed of an arrow piercing through space, he forgot about the hunting, his kingdom and government. He was treated with familiarity as if he had been long awaited. He married the girl, and with her came the tannery, the livestock and the forest, the adobe house which had to be patched up after rain, the herd of buffaloes that need taking to the pasture in the morning and bringing back at night, the harvests and monsoon seasons, rough clothes and rope beds. He embraced the worship of the forest Gods and joined with the villagers in prayer. He experienced the peace that follows a hard day's work, and suffered the anxieties of waiting for rain.

His wife gave him a son, then a second one, and then a third. He lived through seasons of happiness and years of misfortune. Sickness took away his eldest son, then his father-in-law, whom he replaced as a tanner. Then came a year of scarcity after a year of drought, and another year there was a great flood, which swept away the cattle. During one monsoon, his beloved wife drowned in the lake. Years had passed, and yet more followed.

One evening, exhausted, he fell asleep in the grasslands and dreamed a strange dream that he was a just and good king, governing his kingdom. One hunting night, he lost his way in the forest, arrived in front of a hut, saw a stunningly beautiful girl, forgot his palace and married her, became a tanner after the death of his father-in-law, lost his eldest son to sickness, then his cattle in a flood, and then his wife by drowning.

One day, his Prime Minister appeared in his courtyard, and threw himself at his feet.

"Majesty, we have been searching for you unceasingly all this time; we have scoured the entire kingdom, from North to South and even the outer provinces to the smallest hamlets; we have covered and searched this vast jungle without rest! Thank God we have finally found you!"

As the king was returning to his capital, escorted by his guards and his Prime Minister, he woke up, astounded to find himself in his palace bed.

It had been a dream.

It had all been nothing but a dream, but this dream had had the taste, colour, texture and charm of reality. During this sleep, the king felt perfectly awake, exactly as he was now.

At this moment who was he? A king in his palace, the tanner in the dream, or the sleeping tanner now dreaming that he is a king? Or perhaps even someone else, sleeping somewhere in a distant universe about which he had forgotten everything, who was dreaming that he was dreaming that he was dreaming. And what of the small house in the forest, and the untouchable, his wonderful wife, the buffalo herd, the rough bed, his sons, the sickness, and the drowning? Were these last years merely a few hours in one night? And is life just a moment of dreaming in eternity? Are we but characters in the dream of a sleeping person? When can one know what is true? When does one wake up? Is truth just a word to be found in the confusion of humdrum existence or is it the continual and indivisible flow of thoughts and dreams?

In the morning, he left his palace in a palanquin carried by four strong brahmins. One of them, uncaring and unconcerned, carried it so roughly, bumping here and stumbling there, that the king could bear no more of it and leapt out to scold him:

"Who are you? And why are you so clumsy?"

"My King, I am tall and fat and rather ugly and I am a brahmin, but tell me, who am I really? And you, who are you? What can you be called? Are you your body? Are you your birth? And why are you a king? Where does this palanquin come from, do you know? Which kind of wood is it made of? Was the tree already a palanquin in the forest? And was the cotton flower already this robe that you are wearing? The air is everywhere, and yet when one blows a little of it in a flute, as it passes through the holes it produces a 'la,' a 'so' or a 're,' and finally a melody. In just the same way there is neither a 'me' nor a 'you,' but only one existence in the endless flow of life."

Having heard this, the king felt the power of truth in his heart beating faster and harder, and was instantaneously freed from birth and the belief in an existence.

The instant of a flash of lightning is all it takes to awaken to truth. Then, all we have to do is go there, where there is neither identity nor the possibility of losing it, neither existing nor the memory of existence, neither birth nor the fatality of death, as if one is endlessly awakening from a dream, and incessantly asking oneself: where am I?

A GREAT URGENCY

CHIEF ARVOL LOOKING HORSE

My Relatives,

Time has come to speak to the hearts of our Nations and their Leaders. I ask you this from the bottom of my heart, to come together from the Spirit of your Nations in prayer.

We, from the heart of Turtle Island, have a great message for the World; we are guided to speak from all the White Animals showing their sacred color, which have been signs for us to pray for the sacred life of all things. As I am sending this message to you, many Animal Nations are being threatened, those that swim, those that crawl, those that fly, and the plant Nations. Eventually all will be affected by the oil disaster in the Gulf.

The dangers we are faced with at this time are not of spirit. The catastrophe that has happened with the oil spill which looks like the bleeding of Grandmother Earth, is made by human mistakes, mistakes that we cannot afford to continue to make.

I asked, as Spiritual Leaders, that we join together, united in prayer with the whole of our Global Communities. My concern is these serious issues will continue to worsen, as a domino effect that our Ancestors have warned us of in their Prophecies.

I know in my heart there are millions of people that feel our united prayers for the sake of our Grandmother Earth are long overdue. I believe we as Spiritual people must gather ourselves and focus our thoughts and prayers to allow the healing of the many wounds that have been inflicted on the Earth. As we honor the Cycle of Life, let us call for Prayer circles globally to assist in healing Grandmother Earth (our Unc'I Maka).

We ask for prayers that the oil spill, this bleeding, will stop. That the winds stay calm to assist in the work. Pray for the people to be guided in repairing this mistake, and that we may also seek to live in harmony, as we make the choice to change the destructive path we are on.

As we pray, we will fully understand that we are all connected. And that what we create can have lasting effects on all life.

So let us unite spiritually, All Nations, All Faiths, One Prayer. Along with this immediate effort, I also ask to please remember June 21st, World Peace and Prayer Day/Honoring Sacred Sites day. Whether it is a natural site, a temple, a church, a synagogue or just your own sacred space, let us make a prayer for all life, for good decision making by our Nations, for our children's future and well-being, and the generations to come.

Onipikte (that we shall live),

Chief Arvol Looking Horse,
19th generation Keeper of the Sacred White Buffalo Calf Pipe
(Wolakota.org)

On Prophecy and Time – part 6

David Spangler to Pir Zia Inayat-Khan and William Irwin Thompson

Dear Zia and Bill,

I'm sorry not to have responded earlier, particularly to your thoughtful comments, Zia. I've been very busy as well, and in the process have strained or sprained my hands from typing, so that I've had to stay away from the keyboard for a few days—hard to do!—and give my hands a rest. Well, it's been a chance to catch up on my reading, particularly W. Brian Arthur's new book on technology which I'm enjoying very much. It's interesting to me how the principles of combination he's describing fit equally well from my point of view in describing the processes of incarnation. I've often said that some of my inner colleagues approach incarnation as if it were a problem in "energetic engineering," and Arthur's book just reinforces that image.

I've been thinking, Zia, about your comments on the muwakkals or "commission holders." These sound very much like a class of entities I've been whimsically calling "underbuddies," because on a developmental scale they are "under" us or less evolved than human beings, and I think of them as allies or "buddies." You see, this is how profound esoteric jargon develops! I've been aware of them peripherally for years but lately have been giving them a good deal more attention. They seem to act at times much like subtle world "bacteria," in that they "fix" subtle energies into the material world in a way that seems analogous to me to how certain bacteria fix nitrogen and other elements into the soil for plants to use. But they also act in response to our energies and can help carry out intentions, at least up to a point. But they have no moral sense at all—they will respond to and mimic negative energies as much as positive ones, at least up to a point. However, I have found that they respond enthusiastically and well to love, which is not at all surprising.

You said, Zia, that "the awakened heart establishes sacred space by appealing to the beset instincts within the myriad entities that populate its mindscape." This is exactly the experience I have with the under-buddies, and it is part of what I call the creation of "Grail Space," i.e. a space or field of energy around us in the immediate environment that can hold wholeness and sacredness—using the image of the Grail as the sacred cup that can hold the blood or energy of Christ.

I do not think of the underbuddies as elementals, however, or as beings such as the djinn or nature spirits. They have a different "flavor" to them. I actually think of them as fellow incarnate beings, residents of the subtle dimensions of the incarnate world. Perhaps physical microbes are their analog, I don't know. But they definitely seem able to help shape and maintain an energetic—and a sacred—space.

There's more I'd like to say, but I need now to rest my hands again. If I write in small bursts I can manage it without causing too much pain or continuing to strain the muscles in my fingers and palms. So I shall write more later.

Interesting how we began writing about the future and about time but have ended up discussing the ecology of the inner worlds.

Love and Blessings,
David

The next letter in this series begins on page 166.

A Physics of Peace

Victor Mansfield

In Middle Way Buddhism, the realization of emptiness—the complete lack of independent existence in all subjects and objects and their profound interdependence with each other and the world—decreases egotism and increases a genuine concern for all of life. If I truly lack independent existence, if my deepest reality is one of mutual dependence upon other life forms and my environment, how can I be concerned with just me? How can I focus only on the needs of simply one intersection, namely myself, among the innumerable dependent relations that define all people and things? Of course, we have no rational justification for our self-centeredness and self-cherishing. Nevertheless, these firmly ingrained tendencies are painfully difficult to uproot.

The greatest obstacle for appreciating emptiness is our inveterate and unconscious belief in the independent or inherent existence of our own egos. Practicing compassion weakens this false belief that blocks the doorway to the wisdom of emptiness. Thus, if we can truly practice compassion, if we can show a genuine concern for both our fellow humans and the environment, then our understanding of emptiness and the implications of its far-reaching interconnectedness with all of life must grow. In this way, the Middle Way's two pillars have a synergistic relationship and encourage us to be responsible for the welfare of all sentient beings and the environment.

I have always wanted to understand more deeply the connection between compassion and emptiness. I actually wanted to derive compassion from emptiness, to see how it flows logically from the lack of inherent existence, like a result in physics. Perhaps my years of doing theoretical physics predispose me to this approach. Emptiness certainly implies compassion. Nevertheless, it was never satisfying to derive compassion from intellectual analysis alone.

Fortunately, life has shown me a little about approaching compassion through the heart. It has shown me how to take in the pain of other people and thereby make a deep feeling connection to them. When I do so I become more open to them and the reality of their suffering. In this way, instead of approaching compassion through emptiness or nonlocality, I try to open up to the suffering of others and then assimilate my profound interconnections with them. The ultimate goal is to expand this openness so that it includes all suffering beings. Such openness to the suffering of others softens my habitual focus on my ego and its needs. The connection is through the heart not through the head. This leads to feeling a realization of emptiness. I then appreciate how connections to others establish my own identity and how without these relationships there is no me at all. Here is a short personal experience from a couple of years ago to convey what I mean.

The Thief as Guru

I am traveling for several weeks in Europe giving lectures and workshops. Despite the terrific extroversion of such activities, I am enjoying the periods of isolation and introversion that travel provides. I have finished reading the books I brought from home, so in a London airport I purchase Ethics for the New Millennium by the Dalai Lama. Although I have heard all of these ideas before, both through reading and oral instruction, the book's direct, clear, and simple message inspires me. With a minimum of technical language, the Dalai Lama shows how our happiness and genuine ethics follow from our effort to alleviate suffering. The root of all ethical action must be our sincere effort to reduce suffering. These well-known ideas have been electrifying me for the last couple of days.

After about an hour of reading in the Barcelona airport, I stretch my legs with a walk among the fancy shops. I continue to reflect on these ideas as I return to the departure gate. On my way toward the departing line, I sincerely vow to work more intensely on practicing compassion. I tell myself, "I can surely do much better."

Suddenly, out of the corner of my eye, I see a fearsome fist fight about 20 meters from my departure line. A policeman and another man are furiously pummeling each other. The policeman is on the floor and getting the worst of it. I instantly decide that this is harming the other man even more than the policeman so I sprint to the fight. I grab the man by the shoulders and pull hard, but I cannot separate them. In desperation, I come up behind the man, wrap my right arm over his right shoulder, grasp his left arm, and give a mighty heave. As the two men separate, the man pinned against my chest gives a powerful two-legged thrust to the policeman's chest knocking off his badge and throwing him flat on his back. The man and I land in a heap with me on my back and him on top of me.

I hug him tightly to my chest, while we struggle awkwardly to a sitting position. He is breathing like a racehorse. His heart is pounding. I feel his beard stubble against my left jaw. Astonishingly, the policeman jumps up and runs to the far end of the terminal and telephones for help. I am very unhappy being left clutching the fighter, but soon other people come to restrain him. I say to him with surprising tenderness, "Just let it go. It is not worth it." These seem like strangely ineffective words, especially since he is unlikely to understand English. I notice that he is about thirty years old, the same age as my oldest son.

In a few minutes, more police arrive and handcuff the man. I get up from the floor and return to the departure line. My tailbone is sore from landing on it. Somebody hands me the Dalai Lama book that had fallen on the floor early in the struggle. As I walk back to the line I think, "The cop didn't even say 'Gracias.'"

Standing in line, a deep sadness overwhelms me. I have to fight the desire to sob uncontrollably. Embarrassed to cry in the departure line, I ask myself, "What is this powerful sadness?" Somebody ahead of me in the line tells me that the policeman caught the man picking somebody's pocket.

That overwhelming sadness has long mystified me. At first, I thought my sadness was due to the policeman not recognizing or appreciating my effort. "I risked physical harm to minimize the pounding that policeman was taking. I want at least a 'Thank you.'" Even more, it embarrasses me to confess my desire to be lionized as a hero. Realizing that my motivation was not entirely pure grieves me, especially when in the book that was just inspiring me the Dalai Lama's writes, "When we give with the underlying motive of inflating the image others have of us—to gain renown and have them think of us as virtuous or holy— we defile the act. In that case, what we are practicing is not generosity but self-aggrandizement." [*Tenzin Gyatso, Ancient Wisdom, Modern World: Ethics for the New Millennium (London, England: Little, Brown and Company (Abacus), 2001) p. 118*]

My motivation was not entirely pure, but there surely is more to it. When I clutched that man in my arms, besides feeling his heart beating wildly, his gasping breath, and even the scratch of his whiskers, I also felt his suffering. A genuine tenderness welled up in me towards him. More than physical intimacy, I directly contacted the broken life that led to the event, a brokenness that was likely to continue well after the prison term that was sure to follow. It is one thing to reflect quietly on suffering while reading a book and another to feel it squirming against your body. I did not have to think about nonlocality in quantum mechanics to make a connection with this man. I only had to be open to his suffering. The Dalai Lama writes,

> *When we enhance our sensitivity toward others' suffering through deliberately opening ourselves up to it, it is believed that we can gradually extend our compassion to the point where the individual feels so moved by even the subtlest suffering of others that they come*

to have an overwhelming sense of responsibility toward those others.
This causes the one who is compassionate to dedicate themselves
entirely to helping others overcome both their suffering and the
causes of their suffering. In Tibetan, this ultimate level of attain-
ment is called nying je chenmo, literally "great compassion." [ibid]

I certainly have not attained anything like the advanced level of nying
je chenmo, but I have seen how opening, even unwittingly, toward the
suffering of others makes me appreciate the profound interconnectedness we all share. Such appreciation through the heart complements
the intellectual apprehension of quantum nonlocality and emptiness.
That man, accused of being a pickpocket, could have been my son. As
much as Einstein and Bohr educated my intellectual understanding, he
educated my heart.

SUFI-YOGI DIALOGUE

DENA MERRIAM

From January 27th to 31st, 2010, Hindu and Muslim religious leaders from India, Pakistan and Afghanistan met to explore forming a spiritual alliance to ease tensions, counter extremism, and set a new tone for the region. Gathering thirty-five leaders from various traditions, the Sufi-Yogi Dialogue took place in a place famous for spiritual seers and sages, Rishikesh, on the banks of the sacred Ganges River in India. Organized by the Global Peace Initiative of Women, the Dialogue was facilitated by Dena Merriam, GPIW Founder and Convener, along with Swamini Pramananda, and hosted jointly with Swami Veda Bharati of the Swami Rama Sadhaka Grama.

During the course of the four days, leaders from the Sufi and Yogic traditions spoke in great depth about the common ground between them, and they expressed great interest in learning more about each other's practices and forming a new partnership for peace. The gathering was not a typical interfaith meeting as the leaders came together not only to talk about mutual tolerance and understanding, but to explore a much deeper engagement as well—to re-discover and strengthen their ancient shared spiritual roots as a means to meet the contemporary challenges of the region and begin to resolve present-day conflicts between the two great cultures of Hinduism and Islam.

The Sufis and Yogis in particular were chosen for this groundbreaking dialogue because they represent the mystical core of the

Islamic and Hindu traditions. As such, they are especially suited to distilling the essence of unity, the direct experience of the Divine, at the heart of both religions—and perhaps ultimately of all religious experience. Tapping into this inner source of unity, common to all spiritual paths at their innermost level, has the potential to guide us to outer unity in our crisis-torn world. Experiencing our true identity with the Divine can then serve as a fulcrum for global healing and harmony.

The Hindu leaders represented Yogic, Vedantic and Kashmiri Shaivite traditions from different parts of India, while the Sufi leaders represented orders in Pakistan and Afghanistan, as well as Kashmir in India. Through the course of the Dialogue, a meeting of hearts as well as minds occurred. In addition to exchanging views, the delegates sat together in meditation, silence and prayer, chanted slokas from the Vedas and recited from the Koran, sang Hindu bhajans and attended a stirring Sufi concert, sat in communion in a holy cave on the Ganges, and emerged with a much deeper sense of unity.

The gathering began with general discussions, formal at first, about the tenets of the two traditions, quoting from the respective scriptures, comparing and contrasting theological points. It was increasingly recognized that beneath the surface differences of language and symbolic expression the Sufi and Yogic traditions showed a great commonality in values, perspectives, and even many forms of practice. The shared historical roots of the two traditions were repeatedly alluded to, along with the fact that they have co-existed for centuries, especially in the Kashmiri region, not only in harmony but in active, fertile dialogic exchange.

Many common points between the Sufi and Yogic traditions were identified. On the spiritual level, both include a focus on interiority, direct mystical experience of communion with the Divine, identification with the Higher Self rather than the ego, and purification practices such as mantra, chanting, silence, fasting and prayer. Both traditions share a rich heritage of aesthetic expression of inner spiritual experience through art, music and poetry. On the social level, both traditions share an emphasis on the values of love, mercy, peace and the honoring of the Divine in all beings—even, and most especially, in the stranger.

As the dialogue deepened in the days that followed, barriers melted away and the growing sense of kinship within the group became palpable. There was a marked shift from theoretical discussions to opening of the heart and a greater trust both in one another and the movement of Divine purpose guiding us. We experienced at a level deeper than words that the outer forms of expression pointed to a shared essence, a spiritual unity at the heart of all existence, cutting across all cultural and ideological boundaries.

In this way, both the unifying essence and its diverse forms were honoured. Bringing together Vedantic, Kashmiri Shaivite and Sufi perspectives clarified that while form, or the manifest world, may be said to be illusion in certain Hindu traditions, it is meant in the sense that the world is not as we perceive it, consisting of solid, separate objects. Rather, it is energy, flowing from a single source of pure consciousness, into many forms.

This Source, whether we call it Allah, Brahman, God or the Divine Mother, is to be realized, honoured and served in all its forms. Here the interconnection between spiritual unity and social transformation came to the fore, the much-needed alliance between spiritual practice and action in the world. It was clearly affirmed that, especially in these critical times, contemplation needs to be accompanied by action. Action, as one delegate said, is a way of expressing Divinity; it is included in the prime definition of Being, and cannot be denied at any stage. The dialogue started to centre around the need for practical steps to bring the power of the collective spiritual wisdom we were gathering from our traditions into effective action for peace and planetary healing so crucial at this time.

This remained a central theme for the rest of the Dialogue, as ideas were generated and exchanged for further networking and collective action in the region. There was an eagerness to disseminate and start to put into practical action the powerful sense of spiritual unity tapped in the gathering. Plans were set in motion to support each other in local and regional initiatives to resolve conflict and restore peace, through education, media, and a continued deepening of interspiritual dialogue, unifying the energies not only of the different spiritual traditions but also the power of spirituality itself with initiatives for social transformation.

A turning point in the dialogue took place with the visit to Swami Veda Bharati's ashram on Friday afternoon. The elegant circular arrangement of the seats, suggestive of our equality in the Divine, in the midst of the large meditation hall resonant with the vibration of many years of collective meditation, set a tone of sacredness, receptivity and inspiration. Swami Veda's heartfelt welcome, his deep understanding, love and affinity for the Sufi tradition, and the life-long desire he spoke of for spiritual unity among the traditions, was profoundly moving for all present. The Sufi delegates, and particularly Said Ahmad Shah, an Afghan Sheikh, melted to Swami Veda, and the two immediately fell into each other's arms, with a deep sense of reunion and a vow to stay connected in the future.

The discussion that followed on the role of Shakti, the Divine Feminine, in spiritual unity and global transformation, was also profoundly insightful and stirring. It was recognized that the Divine Feminine has both an evolutionary and an eternal aspect, both critically needed at this time to bring the mystical core of unity at the heart of the traditions into the healing of the collective consciousness and the planet.

In her interconnective, evolutionary and transformative capacity, the energy of the Divine Feminine can begin to heal the split between spirit and matter, the transcendent and the immanent—between the Divine and all its forms—which has been the root of so much divisiveness on our planet. Turning the evolutionary spiral, she unifies the polarities of spirit and matter through her energy, and through the same energy has the potential to reconcile warring factions, healing the rifts between cultures, nations and religions, between man and woman, and between humanity and nature.

The Divine Feminine is the mediator between all forms, the peacemaker, that which melts all barriers, revealing the essential unity of all existence. In her eternal aspect, as all-embracing Consciousness, She is the space out of which all is born, in which all lives and to which all returns, waiting for us, with open arms, to remember that we were never separate. Women have a large role to play in bringing in this consciousness, along with men who recognize its critical importance and welcome the feminine values of reconciliation and unity into the higher structures of spirituality and society.

This feminine energy was clearly present throughout the conference, weaving a seamless unity. The mystical paths in particular, such as Sufism and Yoga, form a natural alliance with the feminine, since both are about the melting of boundaries, a direct union between the immanent and the Divine. This natural affinity is particularly fertile at this time, when the healing of divisions is so deeply called for.

The awakening of this energy of unity was beautifully exemplified on the group's last morning together, at the Vashishta Cave. The cave, on the shore of the Ganges, where the great sage Vashishta meditated for many years, is sacred to the Hindus. The Sufi leaders entered to the sound of Hindu priests outside chanting the Ramayana. Once inside, the Sufi leaders were awestruck by the cave's powerful energy, and one felt an electric current suddenly surge up his spine. (In Hinduism, this energy of awakening is said to be the Goddess Kundalini.) The Sufis then fell spontaneously into a Zikr, chanting and swaying in their style of prayer, blending with the rhythms of the Ramayana outside. It was a moment of great exhilaration as the two groups wove together in a chorus of communion with the Divine, symbolizing the joining of the two streams in the deeper experience of Oneness that underlies all forms of religious expression, indeed of all creation.

Another theme that recurred through the dialogue was the possibility of working for outer transformation through the collective energy fields in which we are all connected. It is said that when people of deep spiritual devotion join together in prayer or directed intention, powerful vibrations are generated which can flow into manifestation, via the subtle energy fields through which spirit and matter, inner and outer, are interconnected, and influence events on the outer plane. In addition to taking practical outer action for transformation, many delegates expressed the desire to continue to work together on the inner planes, even at a distance, through such group prayer and intention, directing peace and healing to specific areas of conflict in the world, regionally and globally.

In sum, from the start of the gathering, there was a growing realization of our collective spiritual power. When any two groups are aligned in harmony with the One Divine will, whatever their external forms, they can, at a deeper level, act as one, and co-create with the One in its processes of manifestation. In this way, two groups can work in concert, not only with no dispute over their differing forms, but in the sacred recognition that both are emanations of the same Divine One. And because this connection flows both ways—from the Divine One to its forms, and back from its forms to the Divine—the more deeply aligned we are in this Oneness, the more powerfully we can bring its harmony into expression in our world.

In this way the diverse forms become increasingly transparent to their underlying Oneness, in dynamic, responsive, transformative inter-communication with their own Source. The One is the eternal, the forms the evolving aspect, of the Divine, working in dynamic communion to manifest their unity throughout the myriad levels of creation.

At the end of the meeting, the delegates expressed a longing for a deepening and on-going exchange, acknowledging the thread of unity, historical and spiritual, connecting all in the region. There was consensus that a common culture ran through the region joining India, Pakistan and Afghanistan and the participants committed to reviving their shared traditional roots and moving forward with a deeper understanding of the spiritual unity so necessary for resolving regional conflicts. Those present were strongly moved by their experience together and the new sense of kinship that had developed.

A follow-up to the Sufi-Yogi Dialogue is already being planned for April in Pakistan, and possibly in Afghanistan later this year. In addition, specific initiatives are being set in motion for different areas in the region. Inspired by the visit to Swami Veda's ashram, one of the Pakistani leaders, Sufi Rehman Muiyahadeen and a small group, are planning to set up a Sufi practice center in Lahore. In Kashmir, a

Hindu-Muslim youth summit isbeing organized for later this spring by Ms. Ashima Kaul, a Kashmiri Pandit, Dr. Aslam Sahib, a Sufi, and Swamini Pramananda of the Hindu Vedantic tradition.

As our time together drew to a close, few wanted to leave the warm friendships, the momentum of inspiration and spiritual bonds that had been formed. But all agreed that this was just the beginning, with much work to be done together in the future. This first Sufi-Yogi Dialogue is a prologue for what is to come, breaking ground, sowing seeds, and establishing a network of relationships throughout the region through which the spirit of unity tapped here can continue to deepen and grow.

A New Story for Children

Jennifer Morgan

Never forget that you are part of me. You are part of my wild and dazzling dream. Remember, too, that I am inside you.

Every cell in your body is packed with hydrogen made when I was born.

Your bones are hardened with calcium made by stars.

Your backbone was fashioned by fish.

The deepest part of your brain was built by reptiles.

The love you feel for another deepened inside the very first mammals.

Your awe-filled wonder began on starry nights around campfires, long, long ago.

My story lives inside of you and the story continues with you. Every day, you add more to the story. You are me being you, and through you I see myself...a huge restless Universe who loves to morph.

Our adventure has only just begun. There's so much still to come.

Follow your dreams, my dear Earthlings. They are my dreams too.

Love,

Your Universe

– From Book 3, Mammals Who Morph, by Jennifer Morgan

Thomas Berry, in his landmark essay "The New Story: Comments on the Origin, Identification and Transmission of Values" (Teilhard Studies no. 1, 1978), was among the first to express what many already knew but didn't dare say—that the Western creation story no longer serves as a reliable rudder. Based on information people had thousands of years ago, it's no longer adequate for today and a new story based on up-to-date information and knowledge inside a larger context, according to Berry, hasn't yet come into a form that's compelling enough to guide people as to how to live.

Almost thirty years have passed since Berry made this observation, and many are now asking how are we to create new creation stories. What should we teach our children? How can we build upon the wisdom of our elders and incorporate current scientific knowledge into a new cultural rudder? With globalization affecting every aspect of our lives, a metacreation story that retains the wisdom of traditional creation stories while including all cultures is needed. Amazingly, just as the need for a metacreation story is growing more urgent, science is providing just such a story, one that explains the beginning of the universe, including the emergence of life in all its magnificent forms! Science, however, cannot be the sole basis for a creation story because it isn't—nor, I feel, should it be—concerned with the wisdom expressed in traditional creation stories. To what extent, then, can science help produce new creation stories? Can science-based stories serve the same function as traditional creation stories? The answer is, "Yes."

Every culture across the globe has its own traditional creation story. In that these stories increased social cohesion and gave individuals a sense of identity and purpose, they probably also increased peoples' chances of survival—since group identity was particularly important when people competed with other groups for resources. Additionally, these stories most likely inspired people, gave them a deep sense of excitement about life and comforted them during hard times.

If we shift our focus away from particular beliefs in these stories and look instead at the believers, we will see that, across the world, creation stories have elicited some or all of the following responses in children:

1. A sense of belonging to something greater than themselves
2. A feeling that they are not alone
3. Feelings of awe, reverence, and love
4. Connection to a deep mystery that underlies existence
5. A feeling of profound gratitude for existence
6. A sense of identity & purpose, that everyone matters/is important
7. Peace and comfort
8. Zest for life

Creation stories also have provided the following:
1. A context for integrating information
2. The basis for an educational system that includes the transmission of values to children
3. Social cohesion within groups
4. Sanctity of suffering and encouragement of endurance
5. Answers to questions about where things come from

Traditional creation stories provide/have provided the above-named experiences because they inspire. They are deeply moving. Science also can be inspiring, particularly when enfolded in a story that includes the mythic dimensions of traditional stories. But it has been my experience that making science part of a mythic story that evokes the responses listed above makes many adults uncomfortable, if not downright hostile. Some scientists may feel that a "science plus" story compromises science. Some religious authorities may feel that their territory as tellers of the creation story is being usurped. Yet, both scientists and nonscientists are venturing into these uncharted waters, telling science-based stories that do evoke at least some of the responses traditional stories do. Many of today's scientific breakthroughs confirm the wisdom of traditional creation stories, and the evidence these technological advances provide can serve as the basis for an educational system that, among with other things, will transmit our spiritual values to our children. A few of these breakthroughs are listed below along with the subjective responses, or spiritual experiences, they can evoke.

Scientific Evidence #1: The entire Universe is a single entity—
provides a context for integrating information/knowledge.
Spiritual Experience: A sense of belonging.

A science-based story shows that everything is part of a single entity, the universe. Everything—all peoples, all life, and all "nonliving" things—have come out of a primordial fireball. Nothing is separate from the universe. Moreover, it is not possible to fling one's self out of the universe because there is no "outside." There's only an inside... and everything is inside the universe. This scientifically established fact, which is at the heart of many religions, is deeply grounding and enables children to awaken to the here and now. Everything within the system affects other things/objects in the system; everything is interrelated.

In the 1940s, Maria Montessori had the prescience to make a universe story the centerpiece of the Montessori Cosmic Education for the elementary level. In the universe story taught, each thing is situated within the larger universe story. The child learns that it came out of and is part of a universe that transformed itself from clouds of hydrogen into, as Brian Swimme has often said, "giraffes, rosebushes, and humans." The universe story awakens the child (and adult) to the reality that it is part of a universe that is a single entity. Everything that has existed and ever will exist is part of the ongoing dance of the universe.

Scientific Evidence #2: The Universe is a creative organizing force.
Spiritual Experiences: Awe, reverence and love.

Science is providing clear evidence that the universe has its own pervasive creative power that is greater than the child, greater than adults, and bigger than Earth. The universe births stars and life. Tiny bacteria replicate their DNA and reproduce themselves. The magnitude of what the universe does can be dumbfounding. Through creation stories the child can learn to love and understand the universe, to see itself as part of a field of creativity and to see the universe as teacher and guide. It can learn to see, as Thomas Berry said, that the universe is the primary scripture.

Scientific Evidence #3: The Universe is changing. Each thing is
the Universe transformed into that thing.

Spiritual Experiences: Gratitude, connection to a deep mystery.
Sanctity of suffering, encouragement of endurance.

A science-based creation story enables a child to understand that everything—including itself—has resulted from a transformational process that many call "the epic of evolution." It realizes its utter dependence on a chain of innovations spanning 13.7 billion years that happened before it was born or even could be born. The child comes to know that its existence is owed to that chain of events, a process that it did not create—the events created the child. Each child is derived from the universe, and the child is the universe being the child.

The child learns that transformation can be cataclysmic, that destruction is part of creation. Human beings may experience these changes as crises, but such crises can result in innovations, thus propelling the story forward. The child learns not to take crises personally, that they are part of the transformation process. The child thus learns to be and remain empowered during personal and global crises. It learns to look for creativity within crises and to align its own energies with the universe's creative forces. In doing so, the child learns how to endure hard times and further develop its cosmic gifts and contributions to the larger community.

Scientific Evidence #4: The Universe is a web of relationships.
Everything derives its identity from the past and from its relation-
ships with other things.

Spiritual Experiences: Understanding, cooperation, social cohesion,
identity, purpose, a sense that all of life matters.

Through a universe story, a child learns that not only is it dependent upon everything that came before it, but also that its existence in the present depends, every day, upon the Sun and Earth, the universe as a whole, and a web of interdependent relationships. For example, plants and animals cannot live without each other: they exchange oxygen and carbon dioxide; plants feed animals, animals pollinate plants. The knowledge that everything in the universe is interdependent promotes cooperation, not only between humans but with nonhumans as well. The child also learns to value diversity because the universe story illustrates that the universe creates diversity and depends on it for survival. When crises, such as the meteor crash that ended the age of dinosaurs, occur, life continues because diversity increases the likelihood that some beings will be able to adapt to the new conditions created by the crises.

The child learns from a science-based creation story that everything has a cosmic gift and a cosmic task. The gift is the special capacity that each part brings to the whole. Plants, for example, have the capacity to release oxygen into the atmosphere, and that capacity is a gift to the larger community of life because other beings need oxygen to live. Plants do not intend to give others oxygen; but by releasing oxygen, they contribute to the complex web of life on Earth. With the knowledge of where it comes from and an understanding that everything has cosmic gifts and tasks, the child begins to develop a sense of its own unique gifts and tasks and learns to find its place within the larger whole. The result is a lasting and fulfilling sense of purpose.

Scientific Evidence #5: The Universe is changing now. Humans, like everything else, are part of an ongoing transformation process.

Spiritual experience: Zest for life.

A science-based creation story teaches the child that the creative process never stops—that stunning innovations are emerging today. The child learns that such transformations are creative, open-ended, and full of surprises. It learns that humans have become a driving force in the evolution of life. The child also learns that it, too, plays a role in a 13.7-billion-year-old process that unfolds each day with every event, large and small. The new creation story teaches the child the principles of evolution and that uncertainty is part of the process: outcomes are not given; choices can be made. This knowledge may engender excitement and motivate the child. Realizing that it participates in the greatest adventure of all, the adventure of the universe, hopefully evokes in the child what Teilhard de Chardin described as "zest for life."

While traditional creation stories helped provide cohesion within specific groups, the new, science-based creation story provides a basis for promoting cooperation between different groups of human beings and with nonhuman life. With such a "new story," an Earth community begins to emerge—precisely at the time when we need it most. Today's issues are planetary, no longer limited to specific regions or specific peoples. The realization that Earth is a community in which all the parts depend for survival on each other is more imperative now than ever before. Since creation stories have always aided humans to survive, a new science-based story can aid the Earth community (as a whole) to survive. Our children, and all adults as well, urgently need to heed this message if we are to handle global issues in a context that emboldens us while giving us the wisdom we need to resolve those issues. Most importantly, the news that they are part of the greatest adventure of all—a vast and incredible universe that constantly loves to transform—ignites deep within children, and all of us, a fire that will show them and us how to live to the fullest.

INITIATORY RITES

CAROLYN NORTH

A kind friend, knowing I was down in the dumps, offered encouragement by sending me a poem by Rumi (Barks version):

> *Don't grieve. Anything you lose comes round*
> *in another form. The child weaned from mother's milk*
> *now drinks wine and honey mixed.*
> *God's joy moves from unmarked box to unmarked box,*
> *from cell to cell. As rainwater, down into flowerbed.*
> *As roses, up from ground.*
> *Now it looks like a plate of rice and fish,*
> *now a cliff covered with vines,*
> *now a horse being saddled.*
> *It hides within these,*
> *till one day it cracks them open.*

I needed to be reminded of that.

It brought back memories of when I was 47 and in Brittany at the oldest so-called "passage grave" in Europe, Kercado, tucked on a wooded hillside above Carnac, that dates back to at least 5000 B.C. I had seen a picture of the dolmen at Kercado in a book, knew I had to go there, but only learned why when I was there.

It cracked me open.

Standing there on that hillside, I knew this could not be a burial site but was probably an ancient place of initiation. The 'feel' was of life, not death. As I come from a culture that does not prepare its young for enlightened adulthood with initiation rituals, I wondered if perhaps I'd been called to Brittany to do my own version. Otherwise how explain the undeniable pull that had brought me across a continent and an ocean to climb this particular hill to this ancient pile of stones?

It was very dark and silent inside the chamber beneath, and the first time I crawled in I was terrified—so scared I crawled back out and got the hell away from there. But I came back the next day and kept coming back, taking it slow, spending hours in the woods each day in preparation for entering the chamber. Alone in the forest I recalled childhood pain and felt old angers surface, yelling out loud or writing furiously in my notebook about the hurts still alive within me. Then I would eat an apple and, taking all the courage I could muster, crawl back into the dark chamber. I would sit in meditation, often singing softly until the massive stones felt like a womb holding me while the fear sat heavy on my heart. I would sing until the fear dissolved into something like peace, or sleep.

It was as if I were dreaming while awake, descending step by step into an internal otherworld where the secrets of life and death and re-birth were gradually being revealed to me.

I began to become aware of things hidden in plain sight, feeling how my beating heart and my breathing lungs formed their own interlinked rhythms. I felt how the metabolic cycles in my body were connected, how they linked with the cycles of trees and plants, wind and rain, night and day, sun and moon and all life in all the worlds seen and unseen. In the deep dark of the chamber where my senses were deprived of light and sound, another more subtle light gradually appeared, revealing a larger world, initiating me into a many-dimensioned, miraculous universe that had always been there, but had been hidden behind the busyness of the material world and thus invisible to my sight.

It had taken an act of deliberate deprivation to see how it worked. I had to get through the chaos of my terror and be willing to face my memories of suffering and sorrow, my longing for love, even the prospect of my own death, before I could see what lay beyond them all.

I have since learned that there are ruins of initiation chambers from ancient civilizations everywhere in the world. Most of them have been called burial sites but they rarely contain human remains. Even the "sarcophagus" in the Great Pyramid at Giza is famously empty.

I wonder a lot about what these ancients knew that we have forgotten—something about a Dark Night of the Soul, a Valley of Death that has to be experienced if we are to grow into enlightened adults who can meet life's challenges with insight and courage.

For me, it seems to require looking straight into the dark belly of the beast where all is effaced except for my own pounding heart and breath. Though I long for someone to guide and watch out for me, I always seem to do it alone, as if through a glass darkly, face to face with myself.

Alone in a wood facing ancient darkness—facing myself and my fears of the world going crazy around me, the hunger, greed, mayhem, depression, war— I pondered, how do we respond to the horrors of our own time so they do not destroy us?

That time in Brittany was neither the first nor the last time fear forced me to wake up to deeper levels of appreciation for my life and the world I live in, where my inner eyes open and I see that everything cycles, is interconnected with everything else and is ultimately part of one glorious, mysterious, splendid Whole. Everything is part of it—all Time and Space, all ignorance and evil, all life and death, all beings in all the realms trying to learn how to love.

It is happening now as wars heat up around the globe, our government goes even crazier, and we face yet another year of drought in California. The dryness makes it harder and harder for my ailing husband Herb to breathe.

For me, by his side, I feel how every day is a day of grace, how grateful I am for every moment I have with him and the world we have shared for all these years. No matter what happens next in Syria and Palestine, to the oceans and the climate, I know it is all the play of light and dark upon a deeper reality that endures despite our human shenanigans.

What I know is that love literally holds the world together and it is ours to take, whatever else is going on.

To not do so is foolish and not nearly as interesting as looking through the glass darkly and seeing yourself face to face.

ON PROPHECY AND TIME – PART 7

WILLIAM IRWIN THOMPSON TO PIR ZIA INAYAT-KHAN AND DAVID SPANGLER

Yes, David, I agree that a Gaian Humanity is a necessity, and I see this as co-evolving with a new physical biosphere—even earthquakes and volcanic eruptions can be expressive of that.

In this, however, I think, I am more catastrophic than you are (or were?) and see this as similar to the anaerobic/cyanobacteria oxygen shift that Jim Lovelock talked about in his first book on Gaia. But, of course, that shift was not overnight, so these transitions that occur in a

thousand years a frame become rendered by the human imagination into events at 24 frames a second. But these imaginative renderings, of course, are simply movies and metaphors, and not historical events.

I think our lack of a symbiotic consciousness—working in concert with other "Worlds Interpenetrating and Apart"—has caused this current crisis of the climate and biosphere, with its increasing extinctions. Extinction is, of course, part of evolution, so I part company here with our other Lindisfarne Fellow David Abram, who sees the current increase of extinctions as a human mortal sin. I feel he is romanticizing evolution. It is the biosphere that evolves, and not simply species.

I do get the feeling that the Elementals are seeking a dieback in our human numbers because of our thoughtless destructiveness. I remember hearing years ago that native American shamans and kahunas more in tune with the spirit of nature would be willing to invoke natural catastrophes as a form of cultural revenge for Western Civilization's desecration of nature. You can also see this archetype of revenge in the Edgar Cayce prophecies—as I discussed them forty years ago in *At the Edge of History*—that they are the White Protestant and rural biblical vision of the destruction of the cities and the most technologically advanced parts of the planet. The meek shall inherit the Earth, and Kentucky and Idaho will look upon Los Angeles and New York as "cities of the plain."

But I think these apocalyptic visions are not so much prophecies as they are what in quantum physics would be called visions of "quantum potential states." Since our consciousness is also an interactive part of the system, our thought-forms can influence outcomes and become self-fulfilling prophecies.

I see this process in a movie image. Imagine that the artist, cult guru, or self-promoting prophet is Leonardo DiCaprio on the prow of the Titanic, leaning forward with arm extended exclaiming: "I am the King of the World!"

What you would see ahead in the future, however, would not be waves rising on a level sea, but an adaptive landscape of whirlpools as "basins of attraction" with all their different "event horizons" bumping up against one another. In a civilization, the captain of the ship and the time-intoxicated prophet are not the same person, so the prophet like Edgar Cayce cannot steer the ship of our civilization toward one basin of attraction over another. In his state of visionary excitement, the prophet can make predictions and give dates to iron out a complex system into a linear temporal one. So Edgar Cayce predicted that Atlantis would rise in 1968, that New York would be destroyed by earth-quakes in the nineteen-nineties, and that the Eastern seaboard would be inundated around 2000. This kind of error is a "category-mistake" and is endemic to fundamentalisms of any kind—Christian, Islamic, or Marxist. I remember a Jehovah Witness at the windswept corner of Bloor and Avenue Road in Toronto passing out The Watchtower magazine with its cover proclaiming the end of the world for 1984. Recently another Jehovah Witness knocked on my door to warn me that the end of the world was coming in 2012 and that they were going to hold a rally for it here in Portland this year and would I like to come.

Fundamentalism is a disease of consciousness, like aphasia, in which metaphoric language is taken literally. Aphasic people are often inca-pable of abstract and generalized thinking and can only describe things specifically and literally. The fundamentalist condition is like someone so literal-minded that he tries to bottle the blue of the sky. But every time he corks his bottle and looks at it, he sees his bottle is clear. In despair or anger, he buys a blue bottle and tries to convince others in his state of cognitive dissonance that he has now captured the blue of the sky in his bottle.

A myth like the Apocalypse is a horizon and not a location, so if you run toward it, it moves away. In the same way, the blue of the sky is not a thing, but a relationship between two energy streams, solar and earthly atmospheric.

So all these basins of attraction in front of us, when, in the terms of the title of your new book, we "face the future" as Leonardo DiCaprio does on the prow of the Titanic, are quantum potential states. [David Spangler's new book at the time was *Facing the Future*, Lorian Press, 2010 – ed.] How we interact with God, angels, jinn, and elemental natural forces will determine which quantum potential state is activated. So even God, in his gift of free will and freedom to us, does not know how it will turn out. But as we approach one basin of attraction over another, when we encounter the event horizon, then the quantum potential state collapses into a classical system of physical causality. At this point we get the linear events of human time. The cultural transformations of macro-time become infolded into discrete fractal events. The tsunami or earthquake strikes, and we sense that an age has come to an end and something new has just begun. On the positive side of things—to be less catastrophic—it is like falling in love with someone at first sight: an entire future romance and life takes on the configuration of a single face.

Although I recognized my future wife Beatrice at first sight at the magical "power point" of Cluny Hill in Findhorn some thirty-four years ago, even at a distance of one hundred yards or more, I have to admit that "the Magic of Findhorn" has not been enough and that Findhorn animism has not served to right the cultural imbalance generated by industrial pollution. So I feel that a more catastrophic transition seems more likely now, a bumpier ride than might have been the case had we transformed ourselves decades ago. Perhaps all old men think this way and it is our way of saying, "I warned you!" or "We did it better in my day!"

To look on the positive side of catastrophes, sometimes great archangels gather souls into a subtle body when there is a great collective death and create a new world/womb in bardo for their relearning and rebirth. I have explored these visions more in my poetry than my prose, as I did in *Hyperborean Passages*.

Bill

The next letter in this series begins on page 206.

Journaling the Journey

Essays on the Seven Pillars

Deepa Gulrukh Patel

*This chapter originally appeared on **sevenpillarshouse.org** as a series of blog entries posted between December 2014 and February 2016. The author explores the connections between her personal life experience and the process known as The Seven Pillars, a set of universal mileposts in our human journey to a life of meaning. The title and description of each "pillar" (stage) is presented in italics at the start of each section below.*

*The Seven Pillars are fully explored on **www.sevenpillars.org** and in* The Seven Pillars Journey Toward Wisdom, *a multi-media e-book available on Apple and Kindle.*

– ed.

Crossroads

The Journey of Life: Reflecting upon the shared contours of the human experience.

I'm once again at that place in the journey of life where I think I need to make a choice about which direction to take. My mind is buzzing with the usual questions: What if I follow my heart? Will I earn money if do that? Why is this so hard? Can someone help me please? My shoulders slump and my head turns to the ground.

The film in my mind seems to be showing that classic blockbuster of all the times I have been here before, the good times and the bad, where sometimes it was me that made the choice and others where it was made for me. As my eyes look at the ground beneath my feet, I can feel the pressure of getting it right. Luckily a question comes to my rescue: What does it mean to get it right? A chink of light opens through the greyness, but's its not what I imagine. I find myself becoming aware of the sadness that is present in the moment, and just before I slip into the inevitable downward spiral of regret, I catch a fresh whiff of the sadness. It has a dignity to it that I have never allowed myself to experience. It feels as though the sadness is standing up for all those choices that were not taken—the "what might have beens"—because they had fought hard for a place at the crossroads even if they weren't chosen.

A sense of respect starts to emerge for all the steps and mis-steps I have taken or not taken so far, and slowly I raise my head.

Out of the corner of my eye I catch sight of a leaf glistening in the morning frost. I slowly move my head and take in the beauty around me.

I become aware of the taste of honey on my toast, the touch of a hand. I might still be at the crossroads but now there is an engagement with sensing all that appears in this place. A walk with a friend is no longer just another chance to go over the options but a reminder of the companionship that makes it possible to stand here.

As the presence of life soaks into my body, I find myself relaxing; there is no hurry. The anxiety to get it right is replaced by an awakening to the joy of possibility, which in turn allows me to relax more.

After days of searching, an insight appears: maybe it doesn't matter what road I choose, but how I am going to walk.

And then another: maybe all the roads lead to the same place. With that comes a new question: Do I know where it is I am heading for?

The crossroads it seems has turned into an oasis. It is an opportunity to reflect on what has been and what will be, to see how rich and extraordinary this moment is. I am no longer mechanically seeking to get to the right answer, but I have arrived at the very essence of what I am looking for—an authentic and fulfilling life.

Que Suis-Je?

> *The Living Universe: Exploring the nature of the universe and the Earth, and our vital relation to them.*

What am I?

As a young child growing up in Kenya, I was magnetically drawn to the rich, red soil. My love for its sandy softness was a bane to my mother who constantly had to stop me from putting it in my mouth.

Returning to the country I was born in after 20 years, I am struck once again by the beauty of the soil, so different from the stony, dark clunks of mud that I find in my garden in England.

This time round, I am taken with all that grows in this richness, how the leaves here shine with aliveness.

Under the shade of an Acacia tree by Lake Navisha, I find myself gazing at the elegant way in which the giraffe finds its way around the thorns of the Acacia to bite into those shiny leaves. It stops eating as it senses my presence and stares me in the eye. I feel seen, and see, and am left wondering what is it that we have both seen?

On the rest of my walk I come across zebras, monkeys, gazelles, impalas and marabou storks. To walk amongst wild animals is a reminder of my place in the ecosystem. I am no longer the dominant presence, but a member of all the living creatures that share this planet. Here anything can happen, for I am in the hands of nature.

Something in me relaxes, I feel at home. As a Kenyan-born Indian who now refers to herself as a British Asian, this relaxation is felt at a visceral level. I do not belong to a country, but to this land.

Later on, outside my bedroom window I watch baboons start a vicious fight over territory. While we might have taken over their forest, this is still their home. I am reminded of what it means to share this land, and of the battles that are being fought around the world in the name of belonging and identity.

For the last few months the girls who were kidnapped in Nigeria (it's approaching a year since they went missing) and the debates that have raged around the Charlie Hebdo incident in France have been at the center of my attention. And never far from that is the fact that much of Africa is now turning into a dust bowl, which is going to have a devastating impact on all that live here, and beyond. (See: www.common-dreams.org)

So as I watch the baboons fight, I can't help thinking that I have not felt able to put a noun at the end of the two words "Je suis …" I am.

For while the debates and conversations in the fight for justice and understanding have been a big part of my life, and all are critical right now, I cannot find a way to engage with them. I have been desperate to, as Proust says, "see the same landscape with new eyes" that will help me find a course of action.

The feeling of belonging to the land brings a sense of opening to something more than my personhood. The Serbian proverb—"Be humble, for you are made of earth. Be noble for you are made of stars."—accompanies me to my next outing into the wild.

Under the vast night sky, in front of a roaring fire, from the corner of my eye I see the stripes of a zebra walking towards me. Who created this beauty? I am filled with wonderment and a desire to understand how this creature came to be. In a flash, I think of the CERN hadron collider, and I am thankful to the scientists who will help us understand this question of beauty at one level; but I would not be without the artists who allow me to experience this question totally differently, the mystic who chooses to disappear into the question and become it, or the activist who will give her life to save it.

Breathing in the warm night air I feel the infinite power of this creative … hmm, I search for a word ... force? God? intelligence? Maybe the name does not matter so much as the feeling of majestic sacredness, for in this feeling I can sense how our understanding, actions and our enchantment go hand in hand and provide the possibility for a yet to be had conversation.

Here, I am humbled by the intricate simplicity of our living Universe, which is ever unfolding, limitless, contains everything and yet seems to come out of the purity of silence.

Here, I am the living Universe.

From this place I can choose to pursue that sacred mystery that exists in all our current crises and take a stand to behold the opposites while clearly knowing what I am. For in the soil of the unknown we have an opportunity to blossom as never before.

My Sacred Garden

Our Sacred Heritage: Contemplating the rich record of the human encounter with the divine.

To feel the intimacy of brothers is a marvelous thing in life. To feel the love of people whom we love is a fire that feeds our life. But to feel the affection that comes from those whom we do not know, from those unknown to us, who are watching over our sleep and solitude, over our dangers and our weaknesses—that is something still greater and more beautiful because it widens out the boundaries of our being, and unites all living things.

– Pablo Neruda

I am sitting here waiting for the words for this blog to appear. Neruda's quote is the first sign of what is to come as it brings to my awareness the ones who watch over me.

No longer are they unknown to me, for I have been learning how to allow them to guide me on this journey through life. These knowers of Truth—the prophets, prophetesses, saints, and mystics of all traditions, whose words appear in the scriptures and texts that make up our sacred heritage—have become the gardeners of my soul.

As I stare at the blank page, the gardeners start appearing; for a moment I am caught between whether to tell you about the feminine lineage that nurtures me or the masculine one. As I ponder, I think of my friend Theodore Zeldin (www.oxfordmuse.com) who says that the greatest adventure of the 21st century is the conversation between men and women, as it is the first time in human history that men and women are experiencing some kind of equality.

My eyes come to rest on the beautiful painting of Radha and Krishna that hangs on the wall in front of me. As I look at it now, I know it holds a key to unlocking the words that wait in me, for in the story of how this painting came to me is the power of what happens when my friendship with these gardeners comes alive.

My journey toward these friendships began as a child, when I accompanied my grandmother to the ashram of Sri Aurobindo and The Mother at Pondicherry. Once I got bored with playing outside, I would wiggle my way into her lap, pretending to meditate like her. I didn't know then what I was doing, but I loved the feeling of serenity that enveloped the room we were sitting in. I also didn't know then that Krishna was the gardener of Sri Aurobindo's soul. For me he was the butter-stealing God who made me smile, and as for Radha, I had no sense of her.

Through my twenties I tried many paths to serenity, and yet a love for freedom kept me from committing to any particular one. Until on a beautiful summer's day on a mountaintop in the Alps, I found myself once more meditating in the presence of that serenity. This time I realised that if I wanted to truly be free, it was time to stop and stay, which is when Radha and Krishna turned up again.

A few weeks later, in my grandmother's kitchen in India, I found myself asking her the meaning of the word Radha. This question came from nowhere, but as soon as she said it meant soul, I was gripped. Who was Radha?

I started to search through the scriptures for her story, and while reading I experienced all kinds of emotions: indignation at Krishna, sadness at what I perceived to be her search for her place amongst the other cowgirls who Krishna loved, and finally, bafflement—what kind of love was this? With Radha I discovered what it means to be devoted and to surrender to the moment. On days when I don't know if I can trust life, when the ground beneath my feet is not so solid, I call on her to sit beside me so I can breathe in the strength of her commitment to love, and in doing so, find mine.

As for Krishna, at this stage I had stopped being a fan, the best indication that I needed to turn to his story. In the pages of the Gita, I fell in love again, partly because I read them with the commentary from Gandhi, which allowed me to see first hand how the study of a scripture led one of the other gardeners of my soul to action.

I started to appreciate this flute-playing warrior. He showed me what to fight for and how, he reminded me that being myself was more important than trying to be someone else. In the book, Gandhi writes that his secret weapon in the fight for freedom was what he called mute prayer, the silent recitation of a mantra. I took up the practice of repeating the Sanskrit words Aham Prema, I am Love.

On a cold winter's day, as I absentmindedly did my recitations, Krishna's voice said, do you really want to know the power of love? Yes, I said, now suddenly awake to my practice. An image arose in my mind of a man crawling across a desert floor, dying of thirst. As I said the mantra, it felt as though with each repetition he could keep moving, so now the practice was a matter of life and death. I kept going, still unsure how the mantra could save him. At some point I let go of worrying where the water was going to come from and started to feel love, and as I did so I could see that he too was feeling love, and in that moment the desert rose to show him where the water was.

In the world in which we live, it sometimes feels trite to say love has the answers, but the gardeners of my soul are my best reminder that when I pay more attention to how I am being rather than what I am doing, and allow this to govern my actions, then the power of love can truly provide me with what is needed in the moment.

And the painting: It was given to me by a stranger, a customer in a shop to whom my heart had been closed as I had let appearances deceive me. But as she said, "I am looking for a home for a large painting of Krishna and Radha as I have to move," I could feel Krishna laughing at me as he reminded me once more of the gift of an open heart.

What Happens When You Fall?

The Great Mystery: Awakening to the numinous nature of reality.

To live in the Great Mystery is for me the greatest adventure of my life. When we were developing The Seven Pillars e-book, we came up with a series of questions as an entryway into each pillar, and the one for this pillar that was burnt on my heart and mind is: "If the greatest mystery is love, how can I experience all its expressions as love?"

Not long after, I fell into the River Dart while on a moonlit canoe trip. It was a humiliating and cold adventure that plunged me into memories of all the previous experiences that had caused similar discomfort. At times like this one can wallow in the memories or let the Great Mystery come to our rescue and reveal its secret, its love, for there is a saving grace that is ever present in the Mystery.

However to feel its presence it seems one might have to surrender the desire for this grace, and yet when it comes everything is worthwhile, especially the pain and the heartbreak. Then one is able to rest in peace and to dance, as T.S. Eliot says, "at the still point."

Emerging from the River Dart
Burning with the desire for the Real
she threw caution to the wind
and once more set foot on the path of love

Buoyed by the heady pleasure
that comes with certainty
she whispered
I can do this
I can do this

But the Real demands loyalty
to the questions
and answered,
What happens when you fall?

Tumbling into the murky water
she lost her grip on the long held mask
behind which hides all that is unloved and unlovable

Dripping with the tears of exile
separated from those who can
her longing now fully exposed to the moon

in desperation for safety she ran
she ran into the kindness of a stranger
willing to hold her in the grip of loneliness

He walked her into
the silence of sleep

On waking
she found
she had been cleansed
by the forgiveness that resides
in the darkness of night

and by the revelation of the beauty that hides in
the unknown and the unknowable
which is present in each step and mis-step

Now she was ready to set foot
on the pathless path of love
as though for the first time

Wisdom's Cry

The Cry: Opening to the suffering of the world in all its forms.

High in the Swiss Alps, I have felt protected from the constant stream of information about the state of the world by the beauty of the alpine meadows. The grandeur and stillness of the mountains have allowed me to feel cradled by the immense power of nature, and yet the day has arrived when I know that my sense of connection with my fellow human beings and the planet means that I can no longer turn my back on hearing how the world is faring.

As I open the BBC homepage, I am aware that I am holding my breath, as though bracing myself for the worst—images of typhoons, fires, attempted attacks on trains, migrant children caught in the middle of political and economic storms assail my eyes. The timeless purity of my surroundings vanishes in a split second and my shoulders slump as I plunge into a sense of despair and disappointment.

How can we, who have so much potential and possibility, cause such harm to each other and the planet?

I close my eyes, hoping that in the dark silence I will find an answer, but instead I find myself reliving the first moment that I experienced injustice based on something that I have no control over, the color of my skin.

At first I fight with this image, for the pain of others is far greater than this memory. But my surrender to Wisdom as the provider of answers demands that I pay attention to what arises in my inner world.

As I hear the racist taunts of the white boy, I feel the same sense of despair and rage that I feel when I see the image of the child migrants. To this image is added the smiling face of Trayvon Martin, and soon my inner landscape is full of the people who have dealt with and are dealing with oppression.

Now I am aware of how each moment of injustice that I have witnessed and my sense of impotence about what to do have created shells that have hardened my heart. I who have fought hard for a fairer, more just world cannot see a way out of the darkness. I am back in the same sense of isolation that I felt when I heard the taunts as a ten-year-old child.

But this time as I experience the same feelings, I realize that in my desperation to help others not feel the same as I felt, I have often suppressed my tears. I didn't and still don't want the white boy to see my tears. I will not let those that oppress see the hurt they cause.

And yet as a tear hits my chest, I know that a hard heart cannot be the answer. As the trickle turns to stream, I can feel how each tear is not just bearing witness to pain but a reminder that we are not alone.

Here a new hope arises as my heart gets tenderized by the saltiness of the tears. As Chogyam Trungpa says, "Real fearlessness is the product of tenderness. It comes from letting the world tickle your heart, your raw and beautiful heart."

And so today I will let the tears fall and let the wisdom they carry shine. For this cry, it seems, might just be the cry for freedom from all that enslaves us.

The Courage of Imagination

What May Be: Responding with mind and heart to the call of the future.

As I write this blog, I am on my way to Dachau to be part of an honoring ceremony for Noor-un-Nisa Inayat Khan. Noor was a Special Operations agent during the Second World War and became the first female radio operator sent from Britain into occupied France to aid the French Resistance. After four months of exemplary work in extreme danger, she was captured. She was ultimately taken to Dachau, and was executed there on September 13, 1944.

Noor is one of my heroines. I have been studying her life both as an inspiration and an example of what I do with mine. Lately the idea of visiting the place where her life was taken has become like a beacon as I immerse myself in this sixth pillar called What May Be. This is where we turn to the process of re-imagining ourselves, our lives, and our world in response to The Cry, and Noor is a paragon of how to do that.

At the same time, I have a sense of trepidation about going to such a place, particularly at a time when I feel totally bewildered when it comes to the environmental crisis.

I am going with a burning desire to hear the song of "the impeded stream," as Wendell Berry says, for it feels like I have lost my way. I am praying that Berry's words will guide me to a new place.

It may be that when we no longer know what to do
we have come to our real work,
and when we no longer know which way to go
we have begun our real journey.
The mind that is not baffled is not employed
The impeded stream is the one that sings.

In preparation for the trip I am rereading Noor-un-Nisa's stories, for in them I find myself in the realm of imagination and courage. As I randomly open her book titled King Akbar's Daughter, a smile appears on my face.

"'Piwi … piwi' said the two little robins in the forest one day." The thought of her writing this story about Father Christmas and the Two Robins is a reminder. In the current world where it is so easy to see only crisis upon crisis, I rediscover the importance and joy of innocence and play. These qualities seem to awaken the faculty of imagination.

I watch the rain dancing down from the sky. The leaves it seems are shaking with laughter at whatever the wind has said, and the sodden earth squeals with the delight of a child as it starts to turn into a muddy puddle.

As I enter the make-believe world of my imagination, I feel something loosening inside, now I see Noor's smile; with her gentleness and grace she is teasing me out of my dark hole.

How did she bear the torture that was inflicted on her? How does anyone bear that torture? As I ask the question, her smile grows bigger, as if to say, come, I will show you.

Wrapped in her light I feel the grace of the One for whom nothing is impossible, the One who she follows. I am in the land of the heart. Now the question isn't what action can I take, but how do I serve this beauty? In the land of the heart desire lives side by side with surrender, and urgency is able to hold the hand of timelessness. This is fertile ground for imagination to seed action.

And as the question vibrates in this land, not only do I know I would do anything to serve, but I can feel beauty beckoning me with her illusive ways to stand still and listen to the song. Here the next step will come naturally and it matters not whether I make mistakes, for beauty is forgiving. All that matters is that I have the courage to serve with all my heart, and trust the mystery. The mystery where even the last word—which is Noor's case was "Liberté"—can live forever. It carries on, inspiring in me the faith that justice and action are treasures that can be found in every moment. For as Noor said:

> *In my mystery*
> *Deep in my divine Abode*
> *Treasures are bestowed ....*

In Search of a Pledge

The Pledge: Resolving to take meaningful action on behalf of all.

It is hard for me to believe that my first blog post about The Seven Pillars appeared in December 2014. Now, just over a year later, here I am at the last pillar, The Pledge. The crossroads at which I started are replaced by the clarity of knowing where I want to go, and the final act in this journey is to make a pledge. I want a pledge that will act as a torch in the dark times, allow me to celebrate the good, and remind me where I am headed when I feel lost.

I have made many pledges in my time, some that are still alive in me, some that I could not keep, and others that were only meant for a certain period . . . and yet I have a sense of not knowing how to make a pledge. So I decided to read over my six blog posts to mine the map of my journey so they could lead me to the treasure that is my pledge.

At the start I was a woman at the crossroads of life with many questions. By staying there I learned that I needed to give up the mechanics of finding answers for the art of being present in the moment. I learned that by doing this, answers could reveal themselves to me.

> *My pledge needs to have that quality of presence to the here and now.*

In journeying back to the land where I was born, I discovered by connecting to the land and the stars, and wandering beside the living beings who make up the ecosystem, that I belonged to no nation, but instead I am the Universe.

> *My pledge needs to have that sense of wholeness and ever-evolving expansiveness.*

The living Universe opened me to the gardeners of my soul: the prophets, prophetesses, saints and masters (especially Krishna and Radha). I opened to the vast playing field of my inner life. I was no longer alone, accompanied by the illuminated ones of many traditions and none, whose presence acts as a torch on my life's path.

> *My pledge needs to be a companion of light.*

And then I found my resting place by falling into a river! This humiliating experience from which I could not hide led me into the arms of silence. Here I was cleansed and purified by the Great Mystery from which all arises. In this place of surrender, I found the strength to start out once more in search of Love.

> *My pledge needs to reside in the comfort of silence.*

This Love is what enabled me to hear the silent cry of my heart as well as all the cries in the world. As the tears fell, my heart softened until its rawness and vulnerability melted away the fear of the other and gave me the space to taste the freedom that we all long for.

* My pledge needs to be tender and vulnerable so I can fly.

By staying close to those who have fought for freedom, I embraced the courage of our imagination to show us all that is possible when we let ourselves be guided by beauty. Here I rediscovered that innocence and play are essential in the fight against injustice, for they allow us to bear the pain while at the same time we need a steely determination to help us stay the course.

* My pledge needs to ensure that I have no wiggle room, no way to give up.

With each sentence I have written I have felt myself come closer to why and how I want to live my life now. My heart is beating faster as I hear the faint echo of words that will not just be my friends, but will keep me awake and true.

I am not sure if I have found my pledge or my pledge has found me. The most surprising thing is that the intimacy that I feel with these pledging words means that they will remain a whisper in my heart, and will only be revealed through my actions.

Pilgrimage to the House of Wisdom

Janet Piedilato

The idea of a pilgrimage immediately conjures up visions: a long awaited one-time visit, a special crossing taken to a holy site, a journey to Lourdes, to the Kaaba, to the Wailing Wall, or to Chalice Well. Each visit could, to a great extent, be described within the boundaries of a specific history, philosophy or religious tradition. The devotees would likely be following a road well defined and well traveled. For them the goal could represent attaining proximity to the Divine in a space set aside as special, the sum of sacred geometry, the summation of years of dedication to a specific holy role. Each could be clothed in the garments of historical myth and legend. A visitation to such a site could represent for the pilgrim a life's dream. For some it might even be symbolic of their devotion, a badge of their faith more powerful and meaningful than the medallion they wear above their heart. It might grant them special blessings, according to their particular religious tradition, certain benefits as a reward for their efforts as pilgrims of the faith.

I am well familiar with this form of pilgrimage for it was the mystery and magic of my childhood. While others went on vacation, my family went on pilgrimage: St. Anne de Beaux Pre, St. Anthony's Shrine, Holy Cross Monastery, and the like. My tiny knees felt the bite of each of the hundred steps upon which I prayed my way up to the grand cathedral of St Joseph's Oratory. I remember the intensity of my prayers on Holy Thursday during the pilgrimage to the three churches. I journeyed to the garden with Jesus on Good Friday, my lips sealed with inner prayer as my hands kept active in ritual preparations. My parents had a deep abiding faith around which our entire lives revolved. From my mother's continual novenas to my father's daily presence at the Holy Eucharist, as well as morning prayers upon awakening, grace at meals, and evening prayers before we retired, our lives were filled with the presence of the Divine. While we did not have funds to take us to the grand cathedrals of Europe, we visited every church and chapel reached by our humble car.

Back then, among my favorite readings were the many stories of the great pilgrimage sites, the great saints, the great sanctified places, the different localities and diverse traditions where humanity was visited by remarkable unexplainable visitations. Thus I was a seasoned pilgrim of the mind long before my vista expanded and these trips manifested in reality. I simply knew that I could visit each place I read about—in my mind, with my spirit—and so many a summer day found me wandering the great halls of medieval chapels or ancient temples. All this was merely the normal passage of time for the small child I was. Little did I know that it was far from ordinary, far from a common pastime.

As the years passed I was blessed with manifesting in the flesh visitations I frequently had made in spirit. Thus I became a pilgrim in fact, following the well-worn stones laid down by the many that have gone before me. Yet these pilgrimages to sacred spaces all over the world are only little resting places dotting my ongoing pilgrimage of life. For in the end I am still a pilgrim of the heart, still a well-seasoned journeyer of the imaginal, of the inner space that is without boundaries. For me, life is the spiritual pilgrimage and the goal is the House of Wisdom, the ultimate temenos. This life pilgrimage is often not on well-defined roads. I am often alone, often challenged, often lost. And yet I continue, following the tiny glimmer of light that leads me on, ever seeing the ultimate, seeking the House of Wisdom.

The House of Wisdom, just what is it? We all know what a house is, a place which provides shelter, which envelopes us in warmth, a safe haven, a welcoming place to rest, to refresh, a place where we might even interact with others, friends and family, new acquaintances. What then is a House of Wisdom? What is wisdom? What is a wise person? Wisdom, to me, is knowledge of our ignorance, our unknowing! Wisdom is possessing humility enough to see that we do not know everything and especially know little of that which is most important: the very nature of our being, the reason for our presence in this place called Earth in a certain time and locality, in the company of certain people and particular circumstances.

I believe Socrates had it correct. There is a story about how the high priestess at Delphi proclaimed Socrates the most wise of all men. He was baffled by her comment for he knew that he surely was not the wisest. Yet he honored the Oracle and thus set out to investigate her comment by visiting all those he thought to be the wisest. In the end he saw through each candidate's inflation, for each arrogantly believed he was the wisest! Socrates concluded that the Oracle was indeed correct in pointing to him; for although he possessed knowledge, he was humble in accepting his limitations.

Wisdom is not to be confused with knowledge. For that which is welcomed as knowledge today, the sum of many facts gained by much study and reasoning, may tomorrow quickly be overturned by new insights and advanced thinking. Too often today's knowledge becomes yesterday's discarded folly. Unlike such knowledge, true Wisdom lies beyond the boundaries of time, space and human understanding.

Wisdom is perhaps best explained by turning to the ancient idea of Sophia, the Holy Wisdom of God. In early Christian mystical theology Wisdom, Sophia, is embodied as part of the Holy Trinity, infusing the masculine trinity with a feminine aspect. As a biologist, I have always seen Sophia as the essence of all, the Creatrix, the Ultimate Matrix upon which all takes origin. She is the Hidden One, the math behind the art and music of the cosmos. She is the physics of all movement. Sophia, Divine Wisdom, breathed all into cosmic existence and continues to orchestrate the movement of the spheres. Sophia is the Divine Architect who unfolds daily in every event, immanent and transcendent. And thus the Divine House possessing the essence of Wisdom is none other than the House of Sophia.

The House of Sophia is a sanctuary that holds the Ultimate Truth of being. It embodies all answers. It is thus the Ultimate Holy of Holies. It transcends all time and place, for its very existence is at the heart of being, unseen and stable, unlike the shifting panorama of our earthly knowledge.

The House of Wisdom is thus the goal of the wise one, the one who humbly accepts unknowing in the presence of Divine Wisdom.

Lourdes, France

As a devoted pilgrim of the inner path, I find the House of Wisdom within, in the Unconscious, in the inner landscape of the imaginal. A lifetime of prayer and meditative practice makes it accessible. This sacred space of Sophia, this House of Wisdom, is not to be approached without guidance for it is too easy to get lost, deceived, or misled. The founding fathers and mothers, priests and priestesses of sacred traditions, were well aware of the dangers of the interior route and so set out to provide guidance. Today this guidance is found within the mystical traditions of various modern religions as they continue to provide direction for the pilgrim of the inner landscape: Sufism in Islam, Kabala on Judaism, Gnosticism in Christianity, and so on. Like spokes of the Great Wheel, these and other mystical traditions provide paths to the center, to the very same goal of accessing the House of Wisdom, coming into the presence of Sophia.

Such a path was found in the teachings of the ancient Egyptian tradition as well. The priests of the ancient Egypt religion designed their temple complexes not only as spectacular sites for public ritual but also as templates for their private initiatory practices. They believed that Egypt was a model on Earth of that which lay beyond in the unseen dwelling of the Hidden One, creator of all being. While one set of priests were dedicated to producing the great public celebrations, the less public priesthood of the House of Life was dedicated to a more mystical path, a union with the Hidden godhead. While the temple complex was for the former a stage of great productions, for the later is was a pattern of an inner journey. Many ancient Egyptian temple complexes remain standing today, reminders of the ancient ceremonies and beliefs as well as serving as lovely templates for our own reflections upon an inner pilgrimage to Divine Wisdom.

Just as I take pilgrims on physical journeys to the ancient temples of Egypt, I invite you, the reader, to come with me in spirit, to take up the role of an initiate of the House of Life, one devoted to the inner path, seeking the Hidden One Beyond All Names, seeking Sophia, the House of Wisdom, following the path of the ancient temple complex.

Journey with me as we travel to the House of Many Rooms, to our sacred inner space, our Egyptian House of Wisdom, our temple in the sands of the mind. Close the lights upon your earthly environment and for a moment come within. See the path stretching before you. Feel the years melt away. Come with me as we follow the inner road outside of time and space.

Our journey begins with our arrival on the Avenue of Sphinxes. We stand for a moment and peer down the seemingly unending row of towering mythical beings that line both sides of our path. These Sphinxes, with heads of humans and bodies of lions, represent powerful beings, knowledgeable protectors that may offer or withhold their assistance to us. Like the loving yet powerful Ganesh statues that adorn Indian temples, these sphinxes protect the temple complex as well as the pilgrim. For only those of pure heart are allowed to begin this journey.

Our guardians are the angelic beings, the power animals, the deities, the saints in the varied forms that in actuality transcend form, who serve so that we might learn. And so it is that we recognize our teachers, guides and companion spirits, there for us, guiding us on our destiny, our path of recognizing our pilgrimage. For the pilgrimage to the temple complex, the physical House of Wisdom, is but a template of that which is already beyond time and space in the deepest part of our psyche. And so we connect with it in an attempt to understand the meaning of our being, to honor and appreciate all, both the joys and sacrifices of life, to come into the presence of Divine Sophia.

We pause before the Avenue of Sphinxes before we, pure of heart, are allowed to pass.

We come to towering obelisks. These polished granite needles seem to pierce the very sky, reaching right into the heavens with their radiance. The sun reflects off them and we are immediately impressed by their grandeur, connecting the earthly ground and the realms above. The obelisks focus our eyes towards the Unseen, toward the Essence of our being, towards Sophia, Wisdom.

Beyond the obelisks is the enclosure wall of the temple complex. To the right and left of the opening in the wall, there sit two gigantic statues of the reigning pharaoh, He who is the incarnation of Divinity upon the Earth. Each pharaoh was the living Horus, the divine child blessed to rule. We are reminded of the image of Sophia as Divine feminine, as Creatrix, for this same Horus receives power through Her. Like the Christ child seated upon the knee of the Virgin, Horus sits upon the knee of the Divine feminine, of Isis. Our thoughts thus return to Sophia, Wisdom, as we are reminded that all power comes from divinity and is merely a reflection of such; that true teachers are conduits for the message, helping us to cross from the courtyard of yearning through the doorway into the enclosure of understanding. We need to recognize our teachers, being ever aware that the true teacher is often hidden and that the honored celebrity is often a decoy, an imposter leading to a dead end. Thus we pray for the ability to discern the difference between the two. Our eyes move towards the enclosure as we contemplate the teachers who have been manifest in our lives.

We pause for a moment, and as initiates of the House of Life, those truly devoted to truth, to weathering the storms that the earthly powers thrust upon us, we are rewarded, and allowed to enter the enclosure.

Once inside the sacred enclosure we see the temple doorway and the Great Hypostyle Hall. We observe the soaring columns, and their designs from nature, the earliest vegetative forms, for the Hypostyle Hall is constructed to bring to mind the act of creation. In the beginning there was the Hidden One who breathed upon the great Nun, the eternal waters from which all rose and manifested. We thus pause as though on the edge of being, seeing this, the beginning of the manifest, the beginning of all journeys. It is our origin and our destination. Upon this pilgrimage road we return to the great beginning, to the abode of the Hidden One, to Sophia, the Ultimate Matrix. And so this is a journey of the heart and spirit, of the entire being we call the Self. This pilgrimage called life, does not manifest in a day, a week, or a year, for it takes a lifetime of devotion to make all the steps, to suffer the setbacks, to face the challenges, to find our way here, to the very portal of the inner space. We thus rest in awe in the Hypostyle Hall, remembering our origin and our end.

We pause at the threshold of the enormity of our manifestation, recognizing that with our rational senses we can never empirically know the how, why, where we came from. We in humility recognize, as did Socrates, that there shall always be much we do not understand. We can intuitively sense that which is beyond articulation, that which cannot be diminished by the boundaries of language.

And so it is with humbleness that we enter the temple, the holy place in the Unconscious, the dwelling place of Sophia, Wisdom. In awe we enter, remembering that many came before us, and that many shall follow. We are merely part of the flow, the current of the Cosmos, and so we reverently say a brief prayer for all who across time and space join us in this pilgrimage. We then raise our heads and move on.

Slowly we cross the threshold, our heart leading the way, and enter the House of Many Rooms. We take detours, praying our way round the many images that fill the space; the forms that greet us, that arise from beyond the boundaries of defined language; images of deities, of symbols, of sacred events, each directing us inward, connecting us to the Unseen. We feel blessed with these gifts, for each outpouring radiates from Sophia, each but a tiny display of Wisdom's boundless magnificence. To us, limited as we, each sign, each image, is like the birth of a new star in the dark heavens.

Once we have gained access here we may visit easily again as often as we desire. And so the years may stretch until finally, when we least expect it, we come upon the innermost room, the darkest, the most hidden space. We have found the Holy of Holies, the heart of the temple, the soul of the House of Wisdom. We pause at the portal of this dark place, then slowly we enter, feeling our way, for our eyes cannot lead us. We move in the dark cautiously, for the space darkens as we go deeper within it. It is only when we are completely engulfed in blackness that we see it—the Light of the Golden One, Sophia. It is the Light beyond all light, showing us that indeed light most reflects Divine nature. For that light, which defies the rules of time, space and matter, transcending both, best points the way...

In this innermost, darkest and most elevated space of the temple complex, light emanates from a single golden icon, the image of the Deity wherein, symbolically, the ancient priests sought to recreate the dawn of being. In the beginning there was darkness; and the Hidden One breathes light into the darkness, the word was whispered, and all manifest came to be. And so in the darkest hour of unknowing, at a time when all seems lost and most sorrowful, one finds the Hidden Light of Sophia, Divine Wisdom, Ultimate Matrix, source and strength of our being.

As initiates, our pilgrimage is a daily devotion, an ongoing journey weaving through the days of our lives. There are many paths within and many mystical traditions and teachers to gently show us the way. Yet it must be our decision and our feet that make the trip. As initiates we take this responsibility.

The light fills us as we return. Daylight welcomes us as we once again turn to the needs in the waking world, to our earthly obligations. Yet the temple remains within, Sophia, Wisdom, always there for us, waiting for our return, guiding and informing us, infusing us with all we need to continue on, fulfilling the reason for which we were incarnated.

This pilgrimage to the ancient Egyptian temple is merely one path leading to an inner journey to the House of Wisdom, one spoke of the wheel of mystical pathways with different landscapes, different symbols, different names, deities and sacred prayers that in the end all lead to the center, to attaining the presence of Sophia.

No physical location claims sole ownership of this Holy of Holies, although many sanctified places retain recognized and hallowed presences as honored vessels of the sacred. One cannot put boundaries on Sophia! She is both immanent and transcendent to all. She is the Ultimate Matrix. Her House of Wisdom is found everywhere, accessed within the essence of our being, a constant welcome space for our weary spirits, a sanctuary without boundaries.

Our humble quest in search of Wisdom joins us as one—one consciousness, one manifest, one brother, sister, friend and enemy, all part of the Divine plan, the Divine unfolding, all beginning and ending within the safety and welcoming embrace of Sophia, our common birthplace and home, the holy House of Wisdom.

SACRED ECSTASY

An excerpt from "Divine Attunement: Music as a Path to Wisdom"

YUVAL RON

I could hear the seagulls' calls and smell the salty air of the Sea of Marmara from the small café by the grand Blue Mosque of Istanbul. An old man pushed a cart loaded with freshly baked round bread covered with sesame seeds. I felt at home. It was a beautiful warm day in early June 2011, and I was getting ready to start a Peace Mission tour of Turkey. It was a time when I would read one Rumi poem a day and seek wisdom from the great Sufi mystic's timeless teachings. [Jalaluddin Muhammad Rumi (1207–1273) was a 13th Century poet and teacher of the Sufi path, a mystical branch of Islam. His poems have been translated into nearly every language, and many later artists have been divinely inspired by his work. The general themes of Rumi's poetry include the concepts of Oneness and Unity with the Divine, which the seeker has lost and longs to restore.]

I opened my book to a random page and received a gift. I was about to spend two weeks with the Sufis and Roma gypsies of Turkey, and Jalaluddin Rumi's poetry provided me with a much-needed perspective. Eight hundred years ago, he observed that artists—unlike seekers who enter the fire of ecstasy—merely flirt with the Divine, flirt with the Creator, the Source of life.

I often have felt transitory connections to a mysterious energy, during graceful and blessed moments that highlight my concerts and workshops. We, the artists, touch this great mystery momentarily ... and then it is lost. The bliss is there one moment and gone the next. Here it is, and there it disappears. Are we flirting with Source, or is it teasing us?

Whenever we support dervishes with devotional music, as when we participate in the hidden rituals of our Turkish Sufi friends, we provide a runway for which they may fly higher and reach an ecstatic state, the true fire. The sacred ecstasy they experience is above and beyond the mere "flirtation of artists."

This quest for ecstasy has fascinated the Sufis of Islam, the mystics of Judaism (Kabbalistic and Hassidic), as well as the ancient Greeks. Often, ecstasy is connected to music and dance ... the kind that has been practiced for centuries in tribal societies. It is also an important part of Sufism, Hassidic Judaism and the mystical practices of East Asian religions. The terminology may vary, but the essence is the same: It is an attempt to transcend individual perception, the sense of separation between us and our fellow humans and between us and the Creator, and the illusion that the physical world around us is all that exists. [This illusion (or the veil) of the physical world has been called Maya in the ancient Hindu religion. There are numerous references to it in various other mystical traditions, such as Kabbalah, Sufism, and Gnostic Christianity.]

Sacred ecstasy takes us beyond this limited view of life. But the journey toward ecstasy is difficult because of the way we are wired. The nature of our mind, our consciousness and possibly even our physicality belie our connection to the All. [See the research and theories of neuroscientist Vilayanur Ramachandran, Ph.D. regarding phantom limb sensations and the brain. Some of Dr. Ramachandran's studies suggest that physical body parts seem to block brain identification with other human beings outside of us.] Is it possible to go beyond ordinary perception?

From ancient time onward, the motivation for attempting this seemingly impossible quest was always connected to the human desire to utilize and to benefit from a superior creative force. For example, a connection to the Divine was deemed necessary for success in shamanic medicine, music, dance, and other spiritual rituals. If a person could connect with or channel super beings or spirits, he or she could become a powerful healer, magician, dancer, musician, or tribal leader. Thus, the mystics of all traditions have advised that if we go beyond the mere physical, we may unite with the metaphysical, intangible, spiritual aspect of life.

From the Greek, ecstasy means "to be outside of oneself." In other words, ecstasy permits us to transcend individualistic perception, to sense beyond the regular senses which normally lead us to believe that we do not exist beyond our own flesh and mind. When we truly reach an ecstatic state, we are able to feel that we actually exist beyond ourselves. That we are everything!

In a sacred, ecstatic state of mind, we feel connected to all living things. We feel that we are within all of creation, and that all of creation is within us. Some might cry out at such moments, "God is in me!" as some Sufi saints have expressed. But the words are not important; we may call Source anything we like. A deep sense of the unity of all things is what we are seeking—not an intellectual understanding of the idea of unity. It is a gut feeling, a sensation, a perception. Yet, is this a true perception or just another illusion?

The mystics of old have been saying for centuries and in various terms that the unity of all things is the true reality. They have insisted that we do exist beyond our bodies. Isn't it fascinating that recent research is now confirming that our brain neurons actually reach beyond our bodies, connect with, convey information to, and affect living things outside of our bodies! [See various neuro-scientific studies of "mirror neurons"—brain cells that interact outside of our bodies and connect us to others beyond our skin. See also an article at www.Edge.org entitled "Mirror Neurons and Imitation Learning as the Driving Force Behind 'The Great Leap Forward' in Human Evolution" by Dr. Ramachandran (2000).]

Even though the concept that "you are everything" is extremely diffi-cult for many of us to truly internalize, there are numerous ways to experience it. Within ancient shamanic wisdom, it is told that music and ecstatic movement can move us outside of ourselves so that we may reach an altered state of mind—a state of sacred ecstasy—the same goal of ecstatic rituals and celebrations conducted by Hassidic Jews, Sufi Muslims, and Pentecostal Christians.

Therefore, the question arises: Which music and what kind of movement should be used for such an ecstatic journey? It is interesting that both Sufis and Hassidic Jews use circling movements to commence the journey toward sacred ecstasy. The Sufi whirling dervishes take the path of turning around the heart, a practice credited to Rumi, the 13th Century Sufi master. This practice, however, is more ancient than Rumi, as it has been a native practice of the people of Central Asia and the Middle East. [For example, the Tatar people in Central Asia and the ancient Hebrews and Arabs in the Middle East.]

Circling is mentioned in the Hebrew Bible as a form of worship and ritual practiced at the first Jerusalem Temple built by King Solomon. Indeed, the Hebrew word for "holiday"—chag—means, literally, to "turn in a circle." Sacred circling also is a movement used in ecstatic dances at Hassidic wedding parties and by brides during Jewish Kabalistic wedding ceremonies. Similarly, in the Islamic tradition, circling is part of the pilgrimage to the holy city of Mecca—a tradition that dates back to the 7th Century, six hundred years before Rumi. Circling the Kaaba, which contains the holy "Black Stone" of Mecca, likely has its roots in pre-Islamic pagan Arabia. This tradition is one of the most ecstatic and hypnotizing rituals in human history. [This is seen, for example, in the movie Samsara by Ron Fricke and Mark Magidson, *www. barakasamsara.com/samsara*. The soundtrack for the film also includes one of Yuval Ron's tracks from the CD Oud Prayers on the Road to St. Jacque. The track is titled "La Illah aillah la/Nigun le Mashiakh" and can be heard at: *www.cdbaby.com/cd/yuval8*.]

The Sufis, as with all mystics, prefer the deep poetic meaning over the literal one. And so they ask: Why go to Mecca, as the real Kaaba is in you? It is in your heart. Circle your heart. That is the sacred stone on which you should focus your attention. That is where you may find the Beloved (the Creator). They therefore turn and circle around the inner beauty, the inner "honey," around the divine spark of Light (Kabbalistic terminology) [See the DVD *Seeker of Truth* with Dervish Aziz and the Yuval Ron Ensemble at the World Festival of Sacred Music in Los Angeles, CA (2008). On YouTube: *www.youtube.com/watch?v=yJBqAZYIfek*; and on Vimeo: *www.vimeo.com/16682894*], or the Atman (in Hinduism). They circle around their own hearts on the way to sacred ecstasy ... just as atoms circle within all particles of nature, as the Earth spins on its own axis while at the same time circling the Sun, all of which are twirling in our galaxy in an ever-expanding Universe. [At the equator, the Earth is spinning at over 1,000 mph. The Earth circles the Sun at more than 67,000 mph. And the Milky Way Galaxy is turning at approximately 537,000 mph.]

The secret of the circle is its expression of hypnotic repetition. And repetition is crucial for the initial stages of the ecstatic mind-altering process, as we will soon see in the case of ecstatic music. How does it work? First, the lack of new stimuli calms the mind, which then ceases analyzing the sound, movement, or image stimuli. In other words, looping the stimulus tricks the mind into a state of rest. At this point the "guard" is taking a break and the mind is primed to advance toward an altered state, ready to receive a new perception of reality.

Music and audio stimulation provide another great method for relaxing, hypnotizing, and altering moods and mental perceptions. That is why the devotional music of the Sufi and Hassidic traditions includes constant repetition of the same melody. What changes is the rate of the musical pulse or beat. People, especially kids, get excited when music and dance are slowly accelerated. The intensifying rhythms help us forget about our inhibitions and promote release of the intellect.

The lyrics of the Sufi devotional songs, the Illahis, often use poetry from the "School of Love," the work of such masters as Rumi, Yunus and Hafiz, who favor the imagery of lovers—an intimate relationship between the seeker and the Divine. In these poems and songs, the seeker is the lover and the Beloved is the awesome life force behind the reality we see with our eyes. Just as with the Sufis, Hassidic lyrics often express the longing to unite with the Creator. One such song repeats the mantra Tzama lecha Nafshi, which means in Hebrew, "My soul is thirsty for you." In the biblical "Song of Songs" (traditionally credited to King Solomon) and in some mystical Kabbalistic poetry, we find the same metaphor of lovers that Sufi poets often used to describe the ecstatic path to Unity. [See Yehuda Halevi's poem *Yonat Rekhokim*.]

The embrace of lovers that the Sufis seek is called Dvekut by the mystic Kabbalists. This is a difficult word to translate into English. It comes from the root of the Hebrew word devek, which means "glue." In our context, it means "to bond," which suggests strong connections like friendship, marriage, and ultimately Union—all of which are a part of love. This incredibly emotional process of bonding with the Divine— reaching out and attaching one's soul to the Source of life, getting glued to it, and potentially achieving Union—is perfectly encompassed in the loaded Hebrew word Dvekut.

Whether it is an embrace of lovers or a fiery bonding of the soul, the Sufi and Hassidic paths to Union are paved with soulful music, circular movements, and gradual acceleration of the musical pace and the pulse of the human heart. The fire ... the blade ... the drum ... the soulful cry of the reed flute or the singer—all tell the intellect to take a break so that the mind may stop analyzing and allow the soul to fly as high as a dove and to circle, whirl, and entwine itself about the Beloved.

Becoming What You Gaze Upon

Naomi Rose

I cling to Thee with a child's faith, bearing Thy most lovely image in my heart.

I sought refuge in Thy bosom, Beloved, and I am safe, feeling Thine arms around me.

– Hazrat Inayat Khan

I have heard the phrase said in spiritual circles, "God is not our parents." This I have understood as meaning that the full, nothing-with-held devotion and trust we give to our parents when we are born not only gives to them the power of God (when in reality they are "only human"), but also sees in them the God they cannot at that time see, or remember, in themselves. And also that God is much, much more than this.

For years I have been fascinated by the possibility that this might be true, and sought to find out how it could become real for me. I felt that I had lived through "Paradise Lost" both personally and archetypically. For as a young child, I had loved my mother with a complete and utter adoration; an unquestioning, enveloping love that permitted no doubts:

*When I was very young, I loved my mother happily and completely.
I loved her like God must love the morning in spring, when the
mist rises golden on the meadows, when the sun moves a gold hand
through the forest. I loved her like God must love the ocean, its
vastness and depths, its dancing light and gravitational pull, every
wave, every bit of foam, every little treasure it tumbles toward the
shore. Drinking at her breast, searching her dark-brown eyes with
my blue ones, burrowing into the fragrance of her hair, my adoration for her fed my spirit as much as milk fed my growing body.
And in that state, all was good, all was well, all was beautiful.
It was scarcely a breath of difference from her arms to the lake
where she taught me to swim, holding me stiffly from underneath,
and letting me kick and flail and splash. "I'll fall!" I cried; but
her hands stayed with me until my body believed that this invisible,
wet water would actually hold me up. There was a lurch in my
torso when the warmth of her hands went away. But even with my
flailing, the water held me.*

*I swam in the green lake, surrounded by greener trees, watching
the reflected world appear and disappear with a single stroke of
my small, swimming hand. At such times I belonged to everything,
and bliss was too ornate a word for the deep happiness I knew,
just being there, looking, swimming, breathing. There was nowhere
to go, nothing to do. No mountains, no conquering. Why should I
want to conquer what held me up and made me buoyant? Should I
slice the water with a sword? Should I challenge the trees to bend
to my will? No, my beautiful young mother sat on the bank, talking
to a friend and smiling at me. I had been made to lie down in green
pastures; I had been led to the still waters. I swam inside my own,
patient joy.*

[Excerpted from my book MotherWealth: The Feminine
Path to Money*]*

But this paradise was turned upside down by difficult familial life events that followed, and for decades I conflated the loss of that primal bond and support with the loss of all-embracing Love for me. So the original loss was made even more profound and all-encompassing by my extrapolating it out to touch everything, condemning me to inhabit a world in which "God" was not only hidden but essentially untrustworthy. And the even more profound loss was of my own devotional nature; for in losing my adoration for my mother, I lost connection with my original loving, belonging self as well.

There is a wonderful book, Physicians of the Heart, that speaks of the profound wounding that takes place in a child when s/he can't heal the pain of the family s/he is born into, and the sense of deficiency that arises out of that. Authors Wali Ali Meyer, Bilal Hyde, Faisal Maqaddam, and Shabda Khan call this the "secondary narcissistic wound":

> We feel somehow we have failed to fulfill what our family or society has required of us. What makes it narcissistic is our self-identi-fication with the deficiency of this wounded condition. The result of this identification is that we feel deficient in our sense of self, in the sense of our very soul.... As a child ... we felt like a failure because we were not able to heal mother or to heal father.

[Love's Mysteries, pp. 95–96]

This wound, the authors claim, is inherent in the human psyche. So it was not just a personal failure! I took great comfort in this. But there was still the healing of this deep-seated conviction of inherent deficiency to be addressed.

For me, a primary remedy was coming into contact with the spiritual viewpoint that anything you wish you had for yourself and envy (or push away) in others is actually a mirror of what is latent and not yet manifest in you. That once you become conscious of it and start cultivating it, you can become that which you gaze upon. After all, this was the way you developed your conditioned sense of identity in the first place, including the identities you weren't so happy about. But now, by opening to a desired quality or condition that you see in someone else, you give it room—in its infinite potential—to grow and flower from within.

And so I began to gaze upon bringing forth a loving Mother inside me.

Previously, when I would come upon a loving mother and her child—say, at the bank or the supermarket—I would think to myself, "I wish I'd had a mother like that." But now I made the effort to focus instead on how beautiful the child was in her trust of maternal love; how beautiful the mother was in her free and loving giving. This shift from keeping myself familiarly outside the experience to one of appreciating it eventually led me to being able to identify with the experience: to feel at one with the child whose mother was bending down to look into her eyes; to feel at one with the mother whose centering in love naturally opened her arms to embrace the child. And the next development was the capacity to be at one with the Love itself, as it expressed through both mother and child.

Cultivating an appreciation of the Loving Mother and the Deeply Loved Child over time gave me access to both my original innocence and devotion, and the mothering capacities dormant within me. No one was more surprised—or joyful—than I to realize that what I had always longed for actually did exist within me. The mothering I had needed was available from within, from a Beloved who had never left the scene; it was I who had lost heart, left, and needed to return.

To seek to develop the very quality whose absence has marked you and turned you away from the wholeness of Being is to invite the Beloved to blow on the embers of your heart's desire and spark them into life. How extraordinary—and ordinary—to realize, at whatever chronological age, that you are capable of capacities that seemed never to exist before. As I cultivated my connection with the Divine Mother, I recognized that I was in the process of becoming that which I had longed for all along.

Along with the return of the pure, devotional heart that I had experienced naturally but not consciously when young, came the desire to imprint these images in a materialized way. So I began doing drawings of mothers with children—a subject that always had interested me artistically—this time to be actively present with the physical expressions of that maternal-child love. By slowing myself down while drawing as I moved my pen across the paper, I found myself naturally contemplating this sacred relationship more closely. I was especially moved by the postures of love: how the mother inclined her head, held the child in her arms, offered a loving and radiant glance.

Some of the drawings I copied from photos of people I had never met, because something about the mother's postures pleased my heart as well as my eye:

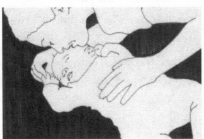

But others I took from photos in my own life; first, of me as a child with my mother:

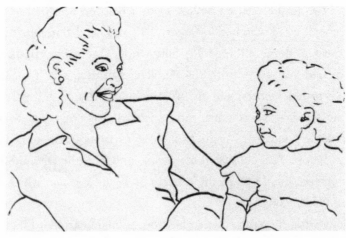

Then, of me as a young mother with my child:

In every case, some "magic" happened as I did the drawing. Sufi teacher Hazrat Inayat Khan has spoken of our conditioning as engraving "grooves" that, like those on a phonograph record, replay the same false self-identities over and over, causing us to forget our true nature. Drawing these images went in the other direction, engraving the lineaments and postures of love into my mind and heart.

Some of us may have been blessed to have been given such a loving and supportive maternal experience that it kept our true nature alive throughout our whole lives. But for those of us who grew up in its absence, it is not too late. Even now, we can invoke and cultivate this sacred foundation, this longed-for birthright. By releasing the self-identification of deficiency and allowing this precious, devoutly wished-for experience to make its way into being, we come to inhabit, embody, and radiate a reality in which this Divine Mother-Love—or whatever the longed-for quality—is alive and well in us, and so also in the world.

On Prophecy and Time – part 8

David Spangler to Pir Zia Inayat-Khan and William Irwin Thompson

Yes, Bill, I think you are more catastrophic than I am, though my sense of the future is that a dieback is coming, but not, I think, in the immediate future, perhaps not even this century (though about that I cannot really say as it's very hard to configure these intuitions into time, as you rightly point out).

I am aware that there are "factions" in the subtle worlds, with some factions promoting the expansion of human population (though not indefinitely) and other factions seeking a dieback (a few even desirous of our extinction as a failed experiment). Those that seek expansion are those who believe that the sheer mass of human consciousness in incarnation will trigger a "revelation" event, a consciousness shift. However, as I understand it, this shift is not a sudden movement into enlightenment on the part of everyone—that is pure fantasy. But it is an energetic phase shift that allows, even requires, a new Gaian human to appear, much like a certain threshold of heat and pressure produces a diamond from carbon—but not all carbon suddenly turns into diamond, yes?

As for apocalyptic prophecies, I feel that if we want to face the future creatively, then, as I say in the new book, the apocalyptic imagination is like giving yourself a lobotomy. This is my main objection to something like the 2012 prophecies, which even the native Mayans don't recognize and even see as one more example of white society appropriating Indian culture. While they make for a fun disaster movie with Woody Harrelson dancing on the lip of an erupting supervolcano that wipes out all of Yellowstone Park, on a larger scale such prophecies and expectations are a distraction from any creative engagement with the challenges that do face us. They diminish us and once again encourage us to give in to waiting for some outside force to save us. It ain't gonna happen, folks. Besides, almost all apocalyptic scenarios, including at times the seemingly benign ones that only predict a "consciousness shift," are a thin covering over a darker and uglier face of hostility, hatred, anger, fear, and revenge. Apocalypse is simply a revenge scenario writ large, the dream of people who feel powerless to stick it to a world that has marginalized them.

My non-physical mentor, John, always said there would be "rolling disasters," each of which would send a shock through the global system but no one of them would push it over the edge. Katrina and New Orleans is a good example of this. He was adamant that there was no great planetary apocalypse descending upon us, and that is still the information that I get in conversations with non-physical colleagues. But a lot of body blows that destabilize the global system and make changes possible, yes, I think we will see that.

The real joker in the deck, though, is human energy and intention. Here there are two major forces at work. There are the large waves set into motion by mass consciousness and habit—which can be very destructive but potentially can be very constructive as well. The problem with these waves of energy is that they possess so much inertia. It's why, as you say, the influence of a Findhorn doesn't have a more dramatic effect (not that it's the only reason, of course). It is frustrating to see on the one hand the increasing documentation and physical evidence of climate change and its dire potentials, and a blind resistance on the part of people, particularly in the United States, to anything that will make them change their world view and lifestyle. But this isn't an American fault; it's a human one at the moment. We get into ruts and we stay in them even when they lead us off cliffs.

The other force is the small ripples set off by individuals which, because of the nonlinear dynamical characteristics of the planetary system, can have profound, emergent, transformative effects that can be unexpected. The individual is not helpless. Under the right circumstances, any of us could be the butterfly whose fluttering wings set hurricanes into motion thousands of miles away.

My perception is that there are a lot of individuals all around the world who have come into incarnation precisely for this moment in history in order to be transformative butterflies to create both stabilization on the one hand and transformation on the other. This is why Pir Zia's work with Seven Pillars is so vital as it holds the promise of stimulating, inspiring and energizing such individuals. However, the very nature of this dynamic is that it cannot be organized into a movement; as soon as that happens, it becomes subject to the larger, mass waves I spoke of and vulnerable to being swamped by older habits. So a different kind of organization is needed, one essentially structured by love and the resonances of the winged heart that can transcend differences and space, and does not need an administrative structure or membership rituals to do its work. It lives in the individual, and it's the flutter of those wings in the unique phase space of that individual that can work the transformative magic.

These two forces are constantly affecting each other as the influence of an individual shifts and shapes a collective wave for a time, but the inertia of the wave can swamp or dampen out the individual effort. Very challenging. It's why none of the inner beings I work with attempt to proclaim prophecies. The overall "ecology of time," about which I write in my new book, is so filled with variables and volatility.

So I see a catastrophic outcome as only one of many possibilities, though perhaps the one with the most energy in its "attractive basin" at the moment. I absolutely agree that not God, and not the World Soul or any of the great planetary or cosmic beings know exactly how things will work out. This is both scary and very wonderful, for it opens up possibilities.

In my own case, I can feel almost every day the resistance of aspects of the world to change, to the invocation of the Gaian Human, and also to what I'm trying to do and bring through in my own work and life, even while I feel support and encouragement as well. I don't say this trying to claim any particular significance to myself or my work; I don't think that way, as you know. I can't claim like the Dalai Lama to be just a simple monk, but I can sure claim with much justification to being just a simple person!

It's just an energetic fact that I live with that in many ways the inertia of the collective waves works against the particular task I've been given and that many of us have been given. This is one reason we need each other for mutual support and encouragement when the going is rough and the wave seems to swamp us.

However, to paraphrase Pir Zia's new concept of Chivalry that is part of the Seven Pillars House of Wisdom, the fact that there's opposition or resistance to what we do, some of it deliberate (and not all coming from the human realm by any means) but most of it reflecting just pure inertia and habit, doesn't mean that I or any of us don't press ahead on doing whatever we can to bring the Gaian Human into being and to develop new patterns of incarnation. Heaven only knows, Bill, you have been courageously (and chivalrously) doing this as long as I've known you. So did Pir Vilayat, and now, so is his son, Pir Zia.

For me, this means that I need to work with an attitude of success, though not with blind optimism or a denial of the dark possibilities that surround us. Along with my inner colleagues, I have no doubt that the Gaian transformation of humanity will occur not just for a few but for the greatest possible number. I could not do my work otherwise, for it is this attitude of success that gives the energy to proceed.

There are, as I said, many factions at work, and most of them in the subtle worlds really do have human and planetary well-being at their heart. Then again, some of them have planetary but not human well-being as a focus; and some aren't working for anyone's well-being, and unfortunately some of the latter have taken root within humanity. I trust that out of this fluidity and current maelstrom of possibilities, we will in partnership with the Great Ones as a kind of collective or planetary equivalent of your Entelechy, sort it out and bring all of planetary life to a good place.

Blessings, my friend,
David

The next letter in this series begins on page 230.

HEAVEN IS NOT A ZIPCODE

OMID SAFI

W hat if we have gotten Heaven all wrong?

Many Christians, Muslims, and some Buddhists imagine a heavenly place as an eternal reward for the faithful. While this place is often described as a garden of serenity and tranquility, we often see many faithful arguing about who can and cannot have access to this place in ways that are in no way serene and tranquil. Not only do we argue about the place, we also argue about who can get in, and who is locked out.

What if we have it all wrong?

Some mystics have actually dared to ponder that. They realize that it is not about heaven as a place, but about a heavenly state of being, a state of the heart.

One of these mystics, a famous 8th-century Iraqi lover of God, Rabia, is remembered as having gone through a city in the middle of the bright day with a lit torch in one hand and a bucket of water in the other. It's a paradoxical image, this woman who combines the opposites of water and fire. The puzzled people of the city asked Rabia what she was doing. Rabia responded that with the lit torch she was going to burn down heaven, and with the bucket of water she was going to quench the fires of hell—so that people would have no reason left to worship a god other than God.

There have always been a few who are in it not for the garden, but for the Gardener; not for heaven, but for the Lord of Heaven.

How do we get back to looking beyond salvation and getting into Heaven, and arguing over who can (and cannot) get into Heaven, and reflect more about being in a heavenly state here and now, already in union with the Divine Beloved?

One mystic who did so was the great, incomparable Rumi. Rumi, the great master of love poetry, was also a deep lover of the Qur'an. In fact, he called his masterpiece (the Masnavi) the "Unveiler of the Qur'an" (kashshaf al-Qur'an), an erotic metaphor that compares the scripture to a beautiful veiled bride. The bride of scripture has to be unveiled (kashf) before a love-union can take place.

In his masterpiece, Rumi offers a brilliant reading of the Qur'an, in which he imagines heaven to be not a "place" that we enter, but nothing short of a state of being taken inside the heart of a fellow human being. He focuses on a beautiful passage of the scripture in which God addresses the tranquil souls of those who are about to enter Paradise:

O soul at peace!
Return to your Lord,
You well-pleased with God,
God is well-pleased with You.
Enter in my servants
And enter My heavenly garden.
(89:27–30)

It's a simple and beautiful passage, often recited in funerals to offer a prayer that the departed will be among those with whom God is pleased, and will enter the heavenly garden (Jannat).

There is the beautiful reciprocity of a human being reaching a state of joy and tranquility with God: we're pleased with God, God is pleased with us. This state is characterized by pleasure.

The magical mystical twist, the "Rumi take," comes in a brilliant mystical reading of the simple Arabic preposition "in" contained in the phrase, "Enter in my servants and enter My heavenly garden." Yes, it really does depend on what the definition of "in" (Arabic, fi) is.

Most people read the verse as "Enter in, my servants." In other words: Come on in, y'all... and enter God's Heavenly garden.

Rumi reads the same verse literally: "Enter in my servants, and enter my Garden." As in "Enter into my servants, and you've entered my Garden." Enter inside my servants, and you're already in Heaven.

In Rumi's poetry, there are dozens of references to "come on in," "come inside," and many of them harken back to this beautiful interpretation.

Heaven is not a place. Heaven is to be found inside the hearts of those who are already at peace with God. When one of these souls loves us and takes us inside their hearts, we are taken into a heavenly state.

Heaven is not a zip code. Heaven is a not a place with walls and pearly gates. No guardians to keep us in, or out. We ourselves are the guardians keeping ourselves out of that heavenly state.

Heaven is about a state of peaceful tranquility. If and when we achieve it, including here and now, we are already in the Garden.

We alone can reach this state, yet we do not reach it alone. It is possible that we cannot reach it alone. We reach it when we take in other human beings into our hearts' inner paradise, and when others take us into their hearts.

There's a beautiful tale of a man who went to see a sage. The sage lived on top of a hard-to-get-to mountain. When the man climbed the mountain, he saw the sage sitting in meditation, in a blissful state of serenity. He approached the sage and asked: "What is hell?"

The sage looked at the man, still huffing and puffing from the climb, and said, "Why would I reveal such secrets to someone as fat, ugly, and immature as you?"

The man turned red in anger, and uttered some nasty words to the sage. The sage took a deep breath and said to the man, "Feel the heat rising from inside you. That heat, that anger, that resentment—that is hell."

The man understood what the sage had done. He sat down next to the sage, and took in a deep breath. He felt the breath enter in his heart center, and come out of the heart center. His complexion changed. His heart's beating slowed down to a tranquil state. The sage put his hand on the man's arm, looked at him with the glance of compassion, and said, "This feeling of tranquility, this calm, this peace, my friend, this is heaven."

What if we can cultivate an awareness of heaven not as a place that we go to somewhere after death, but rather as a state of having a tranquil heart that we can—and must—achieve here and now?

What if what we are meant to do is not to get into heaven but to get heaven into us?

REMEMBERING LYNN MARGULIS

DORION SAGAN

Lynn Margulis, my mother, had a stroke on November 17, 2011 and died five days later in her own bed. The following text is slightly modified from a reading, written for my nieces and nephews, given before scattering her ashes in a private family ceremony at Puffers Pond in Amherst, Massachusetts.

Grandma Lynnie is dead. But what is life? Where do we go when we die?

It's a funny thing: Death is the opposite of life. But so is birth. Your birth continues the life of your parents—here Zach, Jenny, Robin, and Jeremy—just as your parents' lives continued the life of their parents.

What does this mean? It means that life and death are not so simple. Although a body may disappear, its form—with some changes—continues. We are one of the changed forms of our parents.

Your grandmother studied an organism—it may look like a plant, but it's a bryozoan, an animal—named Pectinatella magnifica—in this very pond. It is a funny-looking, puffy creature that looks kind of like a brain on a stick. And she made a discovery: it lives with other organisms, purple bacteria I think, that help it grow. She was still working on this when she died.

When a caterpillar becomes a butterfly it changes, and when a butterfly lays its eggs, it changes again: We say the butterfly dies when the body that lays the eggs dies, but, if you think about it, the cycle goes on. We could say that the caterpillar dies and the butterfly is born.

Focusing on this idea, we could say that her body died, but part of her—you and me—has already been born again: not in a religious sense but as your bodies and minds, which don't know as much as her yet, but do contain some of the same thoughts and feelings.

So we should not be so sad. You are not just a grown up who is twenty or thirty or forty years old, or a kid who is 8 or 9 or 10 or 11 or 12 years old. You are part of a collection of microbes, including symbiotic bacteria that joined forces—fast ones and slow ones, oxygen breathers and those that could live in the mud, green ones and transparent ones—billions of years ago. Life on Earth is 3.8 billion years old and it has not stopped reproducing since it started. You may disappear but you may also become part of a new form—not a ghost, but a grandchild.

She and I wrote about this in What is Life?. We tried to show that life is not just a thing, a body, but a process—and that looking at it this way was not make-believe, but scientific.

"'What is life?' is a linguistic trap. To answer according to the rules of grammar, we must supply a noun, a thing. But life on Earth is more like a verb. It is a material process, surfing over matter like a strange slow wave. It is a controlled artistic chaos, a set of chemical reactions so staggeringly complex that more than 4 billion years ago it began a sojourn that now, in human form, composes love letters and uses silicon computers to calculate the temperature of matter at the birth of the universe."

Your grandmother was so smart, talked so fast, and about so many subjects that hardly anybody—maybe even not she herself—could always understand everything she said.

She said: "Evolution is no linear family tree, but change in the single multidimensional being that has grown to cover the entire surface of Earth. "

She said: "The idea that we are 'stewards of the earth' is another symptom of human arrogance. Imagine yourself with the task of overseeing your body's physical processes. Do you understand the way it works well enough to keep all its systems in operation? Can you make your kidneys function? . . . Are you conscious of the blood flow through your arteries? . . . We are unconscious of most of our body's processes, thank goodness, because we'd screw it up if we weren't. The human body is so complex, with so many parts. . . The idea that we are consciously caretaking such a large and mysterious system is ludicrous."

She said: 'The notion of saving the planet has nothing to do with intellectual honesty or science. The fact is that the planet was here long before us and will be here long after us. The planet is running fine. What people are talking about is saving themselves and saving their middle-class lifestyles and saving their cash flow."

She said: "We are walking communities. . . Of all the organisms on earth, only bacteria are individuals."

By that she meant that we are not who we think, just animals, but also bacteria, and other microbes. These bacteria help us make vitamins, they live in and on our bodies, and, though they sometimes make us sick, they also come together to make new forms of life. The amoebas and Paramecia and Pectinatella that Grandma discovered in this pond, which she swam across every day this summer, are examples of such creatures that bring together bacteria and other kinds of life in their bodies. They are connected. So are you. We are connected not only to the beings inside us, but also to the beings outside us, of which we are a part. So remember this—and when you think of grandma gone and are sad, remember also that her body is going back to the water and the ground, and that her memory is now part of you, and you are part of her, and that in a sense she is not leaving us but coming back to us in another form..

FROM VISION TO ACTION

How We Can Fulfill Our Call to Higher Service

CHRISTINA SOLARIS

> *God: Please Use Me. Let me be an Instrument. Let my Life be for Something. Reveal my purpose to me!*

I was down on my knees, uttering one of the deepest, most treasured prayers of the human soul. And I refused to get up until I had an answer.

You see, I was on a quest:

We are born with a great sense that our lives are for something BIG, something important, something greater than ourselves. Something of significance, a part of some effort or some saving grace that will be a benefit to the whole.

Because if we aren't meant for something big, then what on earth is this whole journey of life for?

The world's scriptures tell us that we are made in the image and likeness of our innermost essence, which is Spirit. We are forged by the Supreme Being at the center of all things. Because we are made in the image and essence of the Ultimate, at the deepest level we share its divine characteristics. We can therefore emanate expanded consciousness, deep unending love, grace, mercy and a profound devotion to all of creation.

When we awaken to the divinity within us, we begin to have visions of what may be possible. We begin to have flashes of a healed Earth and a loving world. We have insights into how we can re-imagine old decaying systems and traditions in new life-giving ways. We begin to see how to become instruments of the highest good of all. We know that the old ways of doing can be remade to convey higher conscious-ness. We have visions of creating a World that Works for Everyone, including the Earth herself! This urge to be part of the great solution is nothing less than our innermost divine essence yearning to express itSelf. It is a fundamental urge of the divine to express its Light, Love and Life outwardly. [We wish to acknowledge the profound work of Howard Wills, who developed a contemporary language of prayer in the continuum of Infinite Light, Love and Life.]

That fateful day, after hours of prayer on my knees, I finally received a vision. It was a clarion call to my highest destiny. I was shown a path that I would not have dared to imagine for myself. A life more wonderful, a vision more vast, a service more meaningful, a relation-ship more fulfilling, than I had ever dreamed of before. Wow!

Even as I proclaimed, "Yes! Yes! Yes!" to the divine in that small meditation room, my mind chimed in with the question: How on earth is this going to be possible!? You see, the vision I received was so far removed from my small-feeling life at the time that I could not wrap my head around how it would become a reality. It was so vast and beautiful, and I had no idea how it would be possible.

So this became my next prayer: Spirit, I say Yes! to this vision, but please show me How!

We may have great visions, but are we truly ready? We may be yearning, but are we fit to fulfill them?

What does it take to go from visualization to actualization?

Is a visionary or enlightened moment enough?

To paraphrase the sage Sri Yukteswar (guru to Paramahamsa Yoga-nanda): A single enlightened soul can effect a greater positive change than a thousand humanitarians. And so, the goal of enlightenment has become the most popular prize on the spiritual path. For the last several thousand years, humanity's spiritual journey has focused on enlightenment, awakening, liberation. The ascetic, monastic, celibate traditions of the East and the esoteric Mystery Schools of the West have called humanity higher out of its material morass. As a result, humanity has begun to lift its head from a dull slumbering existence into its higher potential. We have begun to awaken out of our limited personal identities and are becoming aware that there is a deeper sense of Self.

There is a soul within us which bears profound talents, expertise and new horizons, and it is just waiting to participate fully in our lives. We realize that our divine nature has been waiting for us to come along, honor, participate and claim it. Once we have tasted this nectar of divine meaning, we seek out the teachers, disciplines, and modes of propulsion towards the Supreme Source. We seek to merge with our innermost essence—that from which we have never been separate—Source, Spirit, Omnipresence.

For so long, this remembrance of Divine Union has been the ultimate prize—the reason we have incarnated, the pearl beyond price, the capping reward, God's golden ticket out of what has been called samsara and back to the God realms, back Home. As a result, transcendence, the upward outward expansive movement into the Ultimate, has been the most desired journey.

But this is only half the story.

Anyone who thinks it is the end ...

Is about to have yet another awakening:

Enlightenment is just the beginning.

Those who have had glimmers of unity consciousness, who have cultivated it, and are establishing themselves in the Supreme, have an inkling that this is just the beginning of a deeper mastery where we not only merge with the infinite but begin to fully function from it. Where we integrate the expanded self into our daily activities. From samadhi in action we are able to serve and make an even greater contribution, because it is now coming from expanded consciousness. As the saying goes: chop wood, carry water.

In truth we have not just incarnated to awaken to our true nature. When we awaken we assimilate more of the qualities of the Divine. Among the qualities of the divine are that it answers prayer without ceasing, dispenses mercy without end, and is continuously working to uplift and evolve itself through creation. When we remember our divine nature, we re-energize these qualities. We begin to act as the divine would act: self-effulgent and overflowing with life force and blessings.

This is the deeper reason why we have incarnated. Not just to awaken, but to become a living, breathing Answer to Prayer. To become a physical manifestation of divine mercy in action answering the Cry of our Souls and the Cry of the World.

And so begins the second phase of this giant journey: Embodiment. In the quest for enlightenment, many of the world's religious and spiritual traditions left the body and all materiality behind for thousands of years. The body was relegated to worlds of shame, separation, illusion and samsara.

Indeed, the body and all things associated with it (women, wildness, earthiness, darkness) were not just "conveniently left behind." The Body was repudiated and denigrated (that word is deliberately used here to convey the fullness of its prejudicial intent). It was persecuted. It was guillotined, burned at stake, hung from scaffolds. It was bought and sold as chattel, its natural carnal functions were rendered abominable. Entire empires were raised and toppled on the following of repressive codes of bodily conduct that made all things carnal and fleshly the depth of sin. Finally, it was commodified in the name of profit and exploited as a hollow sketch upon which hauntingly soulless material fantasies could be projected.

This separation between source and the body is a false separation whose purpose has run its course. The pendulum had swung so far towards transcendence, that it has now become it's return journey towards embodiment.

When we dare to follow this natural renaissance and reclaim our embodiment, we begin to experience the power of the divine light when it is actualized. We move along a spectrum from Light to Love, and into Life itself, as a force and intelligence which moves every particle on earth in its own mysterious and majestic dance. Shakti. Shekinah. She.

But the reclamation of the body and our embodiment is not a mental exercise. "Visualizing," "meditating on," or "praying for" embodiment (which are some of the preferred, known and comfortable methods of transcendental evolution) are akin to a car spinning its wheels while being suspended on a lift at the mechanic. There is no traction with the earth, and it won't go anywhere.

Embodiment must be invited physically through healing action. We can reclaim the body through dance, movement, drumming, sensuality, bodywork, womb healing, cellular cleansing and detoxification, spinal alignment, fascia release, and so many other ways. This depth of self-healing and self-care is a massive departure of the indoctrinated exploitation of the flesh in the name of progress and profit.

It is for this reason that deep self-care is still a radical and subversive act, and why we must reclaim it regardless of whether others think it is necessary, appropriate, or worth it.

As we do so, we make space for the light, love and life of source within our very own bodies and limbs. We begin to root to the source rising up from the ground of Being that holds us, and we begin to see its blessings made manifest. Our health, security and prosperity improve. And as all of this occurs, we strengthen, renourish, grow, and begin to come into overflow.

Humanity is now in the age of collective awakening and embodiment. It is time to reclaim the Source within, and then to actualize it by grounding to it in our physical beings. Earth. Embodiment. The Final Frontier.

Why is this important? For eons humanity has often chosen service through martyrdom. We have made a difference, yes, but through suffering, self-denial, depletion and self-harm. These are the hallmarks of an era founded upon the transcendental journey of enlightenment, which generated sacred service and fulfillment based on the denial of the body.

This is no longer tenable. We are coming full circle, and as we step into divine embodiment we realize: That in order to fulfill our callings, we must truly be living examples of divinity made manifest, of radiant health, wellness, blessing, and peace. We are called to become examples of what divinity could look like actualized in form. When we cultivate this overflowing embodiment, we grow into a state of being and having "more than enough," so that we can begin to be a blessing to others too.

This is where our ultimate fulfillment is born: When we have more than enough, we can become a sustainable blessing to others. We graduate from enlightenment to embodied fulfillment. Our souls begin to truly be of great benefit. We can begin to nurture our dreams, visions, and sacred call.

That day on the meditation cushion, a miraculous process began to unfold. When I asked Spirit to show me how these visions could become possible, I was given a series of answers. Over the course of the next weeks, months, and yes, even years, I was given a progressive revelation of the steps towards divine fulfillment. A sort of spiritual "connect the dots" prayer system that links the life we have now, with the life our spirit would choose for us.

A process by which we can Awaken. And then Embody. A full-circle cycle of evolution that guides us through each phase in a way that is utterly unique to our own individuated soul.

It took eight years to internally receive this series of 24 principles or prayers, who bring us full circle to our divine fulfillment. Each and every one of these prayers was so powerful that it took months to integrate. And as I integrated each new prayer, my life utterly transformed.

Within 18 months, my life not only fulfilled the vision I had received on the meditation cushion, but it had surpassed it. And in time my service grew to reach souls on six continents, and I began to share these powerful prayers.

The beauty of this process is that it can be used in virtually any faith context. Whether you invoke the prayers for yourself, or they are adapted for congregations, these powerful principles translate across interfaith lines allowing their blessings to be received in the unique language of our own hearts and souls.

I finally asked Spirit if this series of prayers and principles had a name. The Omega Codex has since been shared with conscious leaders, visionaries and change makers around the world. It has helped countless people move from their vision to its fulfillment. The prayers and principles have allowed so many to clear out old obstacles, transform difficulty, and emerge triumphant in their life's purpose.

The most important thing I have learned from these 24 prayers is this: When we pair transcendence with embodiment, we have the fullness of divine human flourishing. The prayers are structured with nine upward prayers and nine downward prayers. When we master them, we can inhabit our bodies as source ensouled. We are able to make the greatest possible difference by bringing the full power, blessings and grace of the divine source all the way through into the physical!

And everything thrives because of it.

THE CHIVALROUS PATH

DAVID SPANGLER

What is the chivalrous path? If I seek to embody chivalry in my life, particularly as a spiritual practice, what might that look like?

My first steps in taking a chivalrous path is to re-imagine chivalry, freeing it from a glossy glamour of gallantry, heraldry and privilege by drawing on the virtues central to traditional knighthood and finding their personal and universal applications. In this sense, chivalry is not a code to which to aspire but a description of our innate capacities, an expression of qualities intrinsic to being human. If I understand this, then acting chivalrously means paying attention to and expressing those qualities and virtues, all of which I can find within myself already if I choose to look.

How might I do this? We may find some clues by going back to the very roots of this idea, back to the origins of chivalry itself. A chivalry was essentially a cavalry, men on horses. This is a partnership. The life of the knight or mounted trooper depended on the well-being of his horse and his skill in blending with his animal partner. Lack of care for his horse or lack of ability to ride it could leave him dismounted and vulnerable. At the heart of chivalry, then, is an image of partnership between two very different beings, two different types of sentiency, who depend on each other for their well-being. It is a symbiosis based on respect.

In our day, skills of creating symbiosis and mutual well-being between humanity and nature are becoming increasingly vital. We may call these ecological skills but they are at heart "chivalrous" as we seek to find a new partnership between human beings and the planet we ride, the nature we inhabit. This is not a glamorous chivalry of knightly virtues but the same practical, down-to-earth, daily necessity that every mounted troop had to deal with: the need to take care of and respect the other lives with which I am in partnership.

For a cavalry force, care for their horses was paramount, for the life and ability to function of the group depended on it. I don't have horses to care for, but I am in partnership with this world and all other lives upon it. We all are. If we damage or destroy the ecology that carries us upon this world, our own well-being will soon follow it into disaster. But at heart, it's not an issue of not doing damage as much as one of caring and partnering. No member of a chivalry or cavalry would deliberately damage his mount, but he had to learn how to care for it and how to be a good partner. He had to learn to ride. We have to learn to be good riders of our world, as well.

The "knightly virtues" also emerged out of the life of the cavalry as a military unit designed to wage war and win combats. Certain attitudes and skill sets were needed to be a success at this. One needed courage so as not to flee when the enemy appeared. One needed martial skills to triumph over a foe. One needed loyalty in order to build a cohesive fighting unit. And one needed a willingness to sacrifice oneself for one's comrades-in-arms so that warriors knew they could depend on one another in the heat of battle.

These are combat skills, and sometimes in thinking of how chivalry can be applied to the spiritual path, we may be tempted to think in terms of "spiritual combat" or "defeating" unwanted and negative tendencies within us. But more to the point, one could say that successful chivalry entailed developing the skills appropriate to one's task, drawing upon innate human capacities and virtues. For a military unit, such skills, capacities and virtues are those needed to succeed at combat. But the "chivalrous path" could look very different for a different set of tasks. For the spiritual path, for instance, we may need skills like respectfulness, compassion, attunement, forgiveness, and the ability to create wholeness.

To walk the chivalrous path, then, I want to consider what virtues and skills I need for the tasks that I must meet. They might be "heroic" or "knightly" virtues; they might not. But whatever they are, they are essentially human virtues innate in me. They may benefit from training and disciplined development, but I possess them not because I am a knight or a scientist, a gentleman or a priest, or anything else, but because I am a person.

This also is a kind of partnership: a partnership between me and my tasks. For example, I am a teacher and writer. The skills that make up my "chivalry" are those that enhance my ability to communicate. There is nothing particularly heroic about them.

But there's also more to it than just matching skills to tasks. Chivalry implies a third kind of partnership, the partnership between oneself and a larger whole—or a larger wholeness. A chivalry wasn't simply a band of mounted warriors riding here and there, fighting as the whim took them. As cavalry, they served the larger whole of the kingdom or, as in the quests of Arthur's knights for the Holy Grail, they served a larger vision. They did not ride, in other words, for their own benefit alone but in dedication, loyalty and service to something greater than themselves.

It is this connection and partnership with something larger that gives chivalry its power as a noble ideal and as a spiritual force. Even while respecting who we are in our uniqueness and sovereignty, it also calls us to look and to act beyond ourselves. Thus, in the chivalry of my teaching, I seek to serve those who are my students and the larger vision of what we are all capable of.

I now have three signposts for walking a chivalrous path. First, I am in partnership with the world around me. How can I care for my world? Second, I want to identify the tasks I need to do on a daily basis. What are the skills and virtues that enable me to do them well, honoring both myself and my tasks? Third, I am in partnership with a larger wholeness in the world and its emerging potentials. How can I serve that larger whole and that emergence in the context of my daily life?

Considering these questions, two things immediately come to mind. The first is that none of these questions ask how heroic I am. It may well be that to do any of these three things I will have to act with courage and in heroic ways; I may well have to rise to meet challenges within myself or within my world. But I can be chivalrous without needing to be heroic. Heroism is one of the skills and virtues that chivalry may call forth because my specific task in the moment requires it. But this is not necessarily so. A different skill or virtue may be needed.

The second point follows on from this. What is at the heart of all these questions concerning chivalry is love. Indeed, love may be seen as the heart of chivalry itself. To act chivalrously is to act with love. We can see this in the evolution of chivalry from military unit to code of conduct. The mounted trooper had to love his horse, at least sufficiently to respect it, care for its well-being, and find that mutuality of partnership that good riding embodies. The knight had to love his companions to be loyal and faithful to them and to be willing to sacrifice himself for their well-being. And he had to respect his foe, a form of loving, in order to meet him in honorable battle according to the rules of knightly and chivalrous combat. And to the extent that knightly virtues also express an attitude of service to a larger whole or a greater cause—that, too, is a form of love that takes one beyond oneself.

Love can certainly be heroic. We meet many unlovable situations and people in our lives; engaging with them with grace, compassion, caring, and respectfulness for all involved can call upon us to reach deep and reach high to find the inner spaciousness and openheartedness to do so. But not all love requires feats of inner heroism, even when meeting the challenges of the world. Opening my heart to the waitress who serves me and honoring her as a fellow human being doesn't require heroic efforts on my part, but it does require me to be aware and attentive to what is going on around me. I can be chivalrous without being heroic. No glamour or drama is required. But in the moment a partnership of mutual blessing between the waitress and myself—a link along which a spirit of wholeness may flow—is created.

The chivalrous path is, for me, one of loving partnership in action. It can still resonate with the gallantry and pageantry of the many stories of heroes and heroines, of quests and adventures, and the meeting and overcoming of great odds that have come down to us through history and fiction. That part is fun and inspiring. I will always enjoy tales of chivalry, whether of Arthur's knights, or George Lucas's Jedi, or the real-life heroism of people like Gandhi and Martin Luther King. But the greatest tale is the one each of us tells as we shape our lives each day in partnership and love with the world around us. It is this natural chivalry of our personhood that holds the power to bless and heal our world. Expressing it, we discover that the chivalrous path is not simply something we walk, but what we are in the loving fullness of our being.

On Prophecy and Time – part 9

William Irwin Thompson to Pir Zia Inayat-Khan and David Spangler

Dear David,

Well, I can see that we are not really that far apart, for I certainly agree with John's description of "rolling catastrophes" as the operative model. Extinction is a thought-form in the ether, as are others, but they are all multiple basins of attraction in the adaptive landscape. Since our consciousness of the system is now part of the system and affects it, everything is unpredictable by its very nature as a complex dynamical system.

The Dreamtime is an "Everpresent Origin." Cultural transformations are rendered by the human imagination into events, but they are rarely that. Remember how George Trevelyan and Peter Caddy at Findhorn were constantly saying that the flying saucers were going to land on Pine Ridge very soon—"Surely, I come quickly," as St. John said of the Second Coming. Neither Edgar Cayce, nor George, nor Peter ever lived to see the events they kept predicting. So Findhorn started out as a flying saucer contactee cult and evolved into something else—thanks to you! And even I played my small part by introducing the ideas of "the planetary village" and ecology to Findhorn and by bringing many of the Lindisfarne Fellows there.

You were brought up on religious traditions of manifestation and positive thinking with Myrtle and others. I was brought up on literary modes of exegesis with their tragic narratives of rise and fall. So, yes, I am a little "darker" than you are; you are vanilla and I am chocolate! And so we can ask Pir Zia to be the strawberry of the pink Sufi heart and have the last word.

Bill

The next letter in this series begins on page 249.

THE END OF THE AGE OF RELIGION AND THE BIRTH OF SYMBIOTIC CONSCIOUSNESS

WILLIAM IRWIN THOMPSON

Through my collaboration with the chaos mathematician Ralph Abraham in designing an evolution of consciousness curriculum for the Ross School in East Hampton, New York, I began to understand that the shift from the linear causation of Galilean dynamics in the early modern era to the complex dynamical systems of our era also expressed a shift from linear modernist ideologies and religions to planetary ecologies of consciousness in which diversity was affirmed. In the evolution of the catastrophe theory of the 1960s—with their images of saddles and butterfly folds—to the images of fractals and Lorenz attractors in the chaos dynamics of the 1980s, our cultural Imaginary was given a gift of a new alphabet of symbols. Dynamical systems were given geometrical portraits of their behavior [Ralph Abraham and Christopher D. Shaw, *Dynamics, the Geometry of Behavior*, Reading, MA: Addison Wesley, 1992], and these were therefore called phase portraits. The linearity of left-brain thinking was now to be balanced with a right-brain activation. This emergence of a new visual mathematics expressed, in effect, a return on a higher turn of the spiral to hieroglyphic thinking.

It all started with Poincaré in Paris in 1889 when he showed that the clean and consistent system of Kepler in which the planets rotated around the sun in neat ellipses was not correct, that the solar system was actually a chaotic system. You can date the birth of complex dynamical systems with Poincaré and say that the new era begins with his mathematical revisioning of the geometry of behavior of the solar system. At about this time the premodernist esoteric cosmologies began to experience what Marshall McLuhan called "cultural retrieval," and thinkers like Rudolf Steiner, Hazrat Inayat Khan and William Butler Yeats began their visionary careers. The linear reductionism of modernism was going to be challenged by a cultural retrieval of animism on one side and higher mathematics on the other. The composer Satie was a Rosicrucian, and the painters Kandinsky and Mondrian were Theosophists. Clearly, complex dynamical systems began to impact on the cultural evolution of human spirituality.

What could this new planetary culture possibly look like? First, egocentric monumentality and the extensive clutter of industrial civilization could be eliminated. We could shift from industrial object to ecological process—as foreshadowed in the "Living Machines" of John Todd [Nancy Jack Todd and John Todd, *From Eco-Cities to Living Machines: Principles of Ecological Design*, Berkeley, CA: North Atlantic Books, 1994]. Some buildings through the effectiveness of nanotechnologies could become ephemeral and evanescent; enduring structures could be more ecologically embedded in their setting—like the Shire of the Hobbits in the writings of Tolkien. We could become electronic nomads who pitch their tent, and then pack up and move on. Buildings could become appliances that we turn on with a switch, and then turn off to make them disappear in the forest or meadow, and this would enable the human and animal domains to coexist more peaceably. Think of this as an electronic version of the Arthurian Lady of the Lake who used enchantment to keep her settlement hidden to mortals so that it appeared to the local inhabitants only as a lake.

Our machines could become intimate and ensouled by the elemental beings whose presence we might rediscover in the coming period of intense volcanic and tectonic activity. We will all have a chance to become animists again—like the present population of Iceland or the kahunas of Polynesia—those people who have been living with volcanoes for some time. The kind of being that once was envisioned as ensouling a sacred mountain could now be seen to ensoul the noetic lattice of crystals in electronic and quantum computers in a new cultural Imaginary. As these computers are worn on and in our bodies and our body-politic, our sense of "in here" and "out there" would be transformed as a cube became a tesseract or a sphere became a spiraling hypertorus in which the inside and outside surface are continuous through the spiraling axis.

Our consciousness could become symbiotic, as elementals become to us what mitochondria are to nucleated cells. But this symbiotic consciousness need not simply be restricted to human and elemental or animal realms, it could also be extended to involve the celestial intelligences. To imagine these "software" beings that are made out of music and mathematics, we need once again to go back to the end of the film 2001: A Space Odyssey (which I discussed with Arthur C. Clarke over breakfast in New York long ago in 1971). When the astronaut approaches the monolith in orbit over Jupiter, he sees coming toward him rotating crystals of light and complex pulsing topologies. These are Stanley Kubrick's technological envisioning of what esoteric initiates would recognize to be the Neoplatonic "celestial intelligences"—the Jinn of the Moon and the Angels and Archangels of the planets and stars. For Kubrick's and Clarke's vision, however, it is these high tech cosmic beings who serve as midwives to the astronaut's rebirth as he moves out of history into myth.

To draw a circle one moves from the point to the line; to draw a sphere, one pulls the circle up into the third dimension; to create a hypersphere, one rotates the sphere into the fourth dimension. Our physical body, or what the yogis call our food sheath, has three dimensions, but our other bodies or sheaths have more dimensions, and it is in the facets of the topology of these dimensions that the celestial intelligences can interface with us and participate in the field of our consciousness. The brain may be a three-dimensional volume, but neurons in separate parts of the brain can fire together in the neuronal synchrony of the range of 40 Hertz. The geometry of the synchronies engage as facets of the higher-dimensional geometries of the subtle bodies—where both the Dalai Lama and Rudolf Steiner say memory is stored—so the play of consciousness should not simply be reduced to a section of the brain [*Sleeping, Dreaming, and Dying: A Conversation with the Dalai Lama*, ed. Francisco Varela, Boston: Wisdom Publications, 1997, p. 174]. Cultures have in the past called this process of consciousness, imagination or intuition, but whatever one calls it, it is basic to the creative process in art, science and spiritual contemplative practice.

Mediating between the elemental and human on one polarity and the celestial intelligences on the other is the realm of the soul, which for men is often figured as a feminine being—a Tara or Beatrice. (Jung maintained that for women this contrasexual "animus" was male— the Christ of Saint Teresa of Avila or the Krishna of Mirabai.) This being appears regularly in the intermediate life of our dreams—and here one needs to understand that dreams, as Sri Aurobindo pointed out for his generation, are very muddled memories of higher spiritual experiences blended with the proprioperceptions of the physical body and the brain's return to waking consciousness. As the spirit returns to the confinements of incarnation, it can start to dream it is in a confer- ence, or a crowded airport, and as it becomes aware of the body's full bladder, it will begin to dream that it is looking for the restroom in the airport. To interpret these dreams with Freudian or Jungian symbolic systems is, at this level, a category mistake. The imagery is taken from personal memory and is being used as metaphors for the reactivation of specific brain modules that are operative in the cognitive functions of the waking mind.

Shamanism was the form of spirituality that evolved in the oral culture of preliterate societies. Religion was the form of spirituality that emerged with literate societies and their new temple-based read- ings of the stars and sacred texts. Though traditionalists may wish time to stop, it does go on, and now in our global electronic society, a new transreligious form of spirituality is emerging, one that will not replace religions, anymore than the nucleus of the cell replaced the mitochondria, but will envelop them in a much vaster form of consciousness. In this futuristic ontology, we are already beginning to glimpse an evolutionary Entelechy—a symbiotic consciousness of human, elemental, psychic and celestial intelligences. In the smuggled esoterism of children's literature, comic books and science fiction, an archetypal group of four becoming one is being foreshadowed. For example, we see this grouping expressed in Fantastic Four and The Wizard of Oz.

In preindustrial animist cultures, the human would establish a place for the elementals to cohabit or participate in its human life through the intermediary use of a magical object—a magical ring or stone, an Aladdin's lamp or an ensouled sword such as Roland's Durendal or Charlemagne's Montjoie. Like the needles used in acupuncture, this numinous object can interact with its possessor at the subtle-physical or etheric level—the level of qi or prana. In shamanistic cultures, the individual would project out of his or her body and travel in a spiritual or astral world. If one is able through meditation to remain watchfully awake in the state of deep dreamless sleep, then one experiences a vast magenta sea of cognitive bliss in which one hears the music of every-thing—every existent being in the universe sounding its presence. This is the world of the Holy Spirit that is "above" or "below"—remember these terms express a merely Euclidean geometry—the psychic realm of dreams or astral out-of-the-body travel. In the astral, one travels, but in the realm of celestial music, the center is everywhere and the circum-ference nowhere, so there is no need to move. One simply joins in this Hallelujah Chorus to the nth power by listening and sounding one's ontic note. In this sense, music is not a representational art of mimesis, but an ontological performance.

The human is the ordinary ego in time, but in the completion of our emergent evolutionary spiritual process the ego becomes trans-human, "anointed" or Christic. For esoteric Christians, the prophet Jesus became the Christ at the time of the baptism by John, and this narrative of the Son of Man describes the process of enlightened indi-viduation. For Buddhists, this process is seen more like a wave than a particle, one in which egohood is transformed in dependent co-origina-tion (pratityasamutpadha) of enlightened Buddha Mind.

Now you may have noticed that one thing that results from this ontology of symbiotic consciousness is a non-locality in which "out there" is "in here" so that it is no longer necessary to put three-dimensional bodies in expensive tin cans and space suits and try to propel them to the stars. We may be able to go to the Moon, and my Lindisfarne colleague James Lovelock's proposed atmospheric and bacterial "greening of Mars" would certainly be a worthy project for sublimating the nations' defense industries into a transnational technological project with Europe, Russia, Japan and China, but I think it is highly unlikely humans could travel in physical bodies to the stars. Indeed, that is precisely what the astronaut of 2001 discovers in his transformation from technological man to star child. So the Christian fundamentalist notion that we can trash the Earth and move on, and that whatever mess we make here is permitted because Jesus will play the role of a suburban mom coming in at the end of the day to clean up our room for us and then take us away in a vacation rapture to some theme park heaven is an expression of folk superstition and the limited three-dimensional thinking of religion.

Jean Gebser taught us that when a new evolutionary form becomes efficient, the old becomes deficient [Jean Gebser, *The Ever-Present Origin*, Athens, OH: Ohio University Press, 1984, pp.93ff]. When religion emerged, shamanism decayed into sorcery and black magic. Now that a new planetary spirituality is emerging, religion has become a toxic dump, as witnessed in the recent [2008] terrorist attacks in Mumbai.

But the religionists are right in one way; it is the end of their world, but that also means the end of the age of religion and the beginning of a unique/universal self-similar architecture of consciousness that is based upon individual experience and not upon priestcraft, rigid dogma and collective forceful indoctrination. If we can avoid the dark age of religion that now stares us in the face, we may discover a more surprising and delightful politics of Being behind the mask.

THOUGHTS ON MYSTICISM AND THE VOICE

BISAN TORON

I often wonder at the range of emotion engendered by our relationship with our voice, from giddy delight to deep shame. Or interestingly, there might be a neutral attitude toward one's voice, or even a total removal from knowing it at all, so that one never takes the time to consciously feel its nuances, leaving that to the experts and approaching it only as a means to an end: communication, usually of a verbal kind. Perhaps something in us understands the power of our voice to bear witness, to answer the call, and perhaps most shattering of all, to call forth.

To sing "on the breath" means that voice and breath ride as one movement; the voice becomes an amplification of breath, no longer withheld from it (or from one's truth). The process of "voicing" has the potential for bridging the chasm between our inner movements and what actually comes out of the mouth as expression. The mystical dimension of sound does not lie in the finished bridge, but in the ongoing bridging—the active intent of revealing ourselves in each changing moment: an active, ongoing 'yes.' Where voice and mysticism meet is in the churning toward transparency. And toward is enough. Toward is what we are.

Providing there is the will and the listening required to do so, everyone can experience their voice as a portal into the eternal: the bare moment lived through the transparent voice. The question becomes, 'is the sound as free as it can be?' 'Whatever the tone characteristic, is it present to its fullest capacity?' 'How do I need to be to fully support physically and imaginatively this moment in sound?' One's entire presence is placed at the service of the freedom of this one tone.

And herein lies the possibility of spinning mystery around like a bath of vibration in the mouth and body. Mysticism of sound is play. Perhaps it's the sort of play that requires years of practice, but mostly it only needs a willingness to open into the quotidian moment and to allow it to live through one's voice. One tends to the bubble of this moment through the sound gestures that pierce it.

Technique is for the support and "holding" of that moment: freeing tensions that create closure, knowing and feeling the form of a vowel before singing it (another miracle: can it be that the sound impulse begins within?) and quitting it at the height of its openness, where it can continue to thrive and dissolve into the air. It's a type of poetic dignity, this art of opening to receive an inhalation, spinning the vibration in your body, and releasing it, with a giving intention. And then there's the potential of losing track of giver and receiver.

I love the thought that "mysticism" of sound (or of anything) is not a polished concept that is outside the realm of myself, with all my wounds and incompleteness. Perhaps the mystical dimension of sound arises in the authentic utterance of a moment that thrives on the understanding of things as unfinished: the shape of the sound morphing as each becoming moment.

What I find astoundingly beautiful is that the potential miracle of sound springs from the decision to abundantly feel in oneself an impulse and the desire to make oneself known. This is what makes a sound resonate in undeniable clarity: one sees the sound. And then the sound somehow sees itself.

WHEN THE WHOLE WORLD IS FOR SALE

The Maker of Things is The Revolutionary of the Age

WENDY JEHANARA TREMAYNE

In 2006 I quit my career job, left my home in New York City, and headed to rural New Mexico to discover a life less reliant on money. I wanted to become a maker of things instead of a buyer of things. I didn't know exactly what I was getting myself into, but I knew that nothing in the future would be the same.

I gripped an important imaginary object, an ideal that I'd been holding up against the world for as long as I can remember. Old and well worn, I considered the ideal a barometer of sorts. It helped me to track when the world was falling short of my hopes for it. I had never seen this ideal materialized, and though an imaginary thing, I valued it. By having the courage to start an adventure I learned that the ideal I carried was key to learning what I have to offer to the world—my own call to action.

After leaving New York, I advanced into an unknown future step-by-step, curiously lifting veil after veil. The journey's demands shape shifted me, and before long the disappointment I'd felt about the world turned malleable. A wonder world of my own creative visioning replaced it.

What lay ahead was a world of grandiose possibility.

I fulfilled the wish that I left New York with. I became the maker of things I imagined I could be. I learned to do things like weld, wildcraft, forage, make biodiesel fuel, hack electronics, build structures out of paper, grow food, make medicine, and many other things that I needed to live. These things taught me about value, value is not a thing. It is responsibility; the life preserved in the process of making anything.

The adventure helped me to materialize my ideal. Today I see my ideal on the inside and on the outside.

All of our stories must be different, but some things about them are the same. Adventures have a rhythm. Often they invite us to a cliff's edge and ask that we take a step without knowing what will come. It is natural to wonder, "will I fall and meet my doom?" Like a bedroom window on a breezy spring night, wisdom needed for success blows into our hearts and settles. We need simply to begin. As with all things worth having, in order to obtain something, something else must be given up. One might give up familiarity and comfort—things that slow down adventures. The only real mistake is to think that the jump is too big to consider.

Here is a snippet from my adventure. When you're done reading it, I hope you will consider the ideal that you have been carrying around. What standard have you held the world to that you wish to see materialized? What step must be taken to start out on an adventure?

Excerpt

A year of building in the desert had made me capable of having sophisticated conversations about building with people like Clyde, and yet the door that divided the cozy life of Eve's Garden from the unforgiving desert was all that prevented me from being as useless as a sapphire cocktail ring. In the desert I felt as though I were on a ship stranded at sea and didn't know how to swim. I had learned about building shelter, but I still didn't know how to survive in the world outside of it.

Cooking and sleeping outdoors, knowing how to find drinkable water, and reading upcoming weather conditions by looking at the sky were not skills I had yet. More than 30 years of acculturated knowledge made me perfectly able to operate a bidet, avoid paying retail, and get a free parking spot almost anywhere in New York City. But I could not understand that a 50-degree change in temperature was possible in the same day, nor was I prepared for it when it happened.

I remembered the stories told days before by the sturdy desert dwellers who sat around the fire. There was one about living in the back of a pickup truck with a dog for 10 years, working a stint counting trees while residing in a tent deep in a forest for several months, and serving as a firewatcher in an 8-foot by 8-foot cabin miles from the nearest road. My contribution to the conversation sounded something like, "Put me in any New York City neighborhood any time of night and I am not scared." I had no idea that city folks are notorious for saying these kinds of things (lest their value go unrecognized by those who wield a different variety of knowledge). Desert dwellers knew such things as this: after becoming dehydrated out in the desert, the first sip of water should be used to wash the toxins out of your mouth and spit on the ground. Or what to do if a forest fire broke out and there was no time to run from it. You could jump into a water tank. If the fire passed quickly and you got out before the water boiled, you might survive. I was not a New Mexican yet. I did not have a dog of the heeler variety or a nonworking toilet serving as art in my yard, although both were soon to come.

With my ego stuffed deep in my pocket, below the pack of hand-wipes that it had become my habit to carry in case I was offered another hole in the ground to poop in, I thought about the image I had crafted of myself as the outdoorsy type and reviewed where this impression came from. In day camp, my group twice won the best campsite award because of a fence, a fire pit, and a swing that I designed. As a little girl, I had imagined tending a garden and filling an odd lot of dusty bottles with exotic plant remedies. I built sturdy forts in the woods behind my house. At Burning Man, I made an impressive outdoor shower that everyone wanted to use. Many people who knew me thought I was really tough. But I'd been hanging out in French restaurants too long.

I definitely couldn't light a fire without a match. The only plant I had ever grown was fruitless and died on my fire escape back in Brooklyn.

This is what I came for, I thought to myself. To find the edge, the point at which my knowledge ends. I was exactly where I wanted to be: uncomfortable. What I was itching for was something new. It was common sense. I didn't mind feeling ill at ease as long I was getting nearer to it. I considered the ways to acquire common sense: by living close to nature, by playing, by making mistakes, by taking time for contemplation, by trial and error, by listening, by building, by problem-solving, by maintaining relationships, by hiking, by growing plants, by cooking. Really, I didn't know. But I suspected that it would come from experience and not just from reading books or hearing of it being told.

SPIRITUAL PRINCIPLES IN ACTION

A Story for a Younger Generation

LLEWELLYN VAUGHAN-LEE

In answer to a question from a 31-year-old person, "What advice do you have for people my age in dealing with a world that tells us we are nothing but material mechanisms, and has almost no concept of the soul?"

Chapter One

I grew up in an England still dreary in the post-war years. It was a grey world aspiring to middle-class materialism—a TV, a washing machine, even a car! Then in the mid to late sixties, another color entered the spectrum of consciousness. The Beatles went to India to meditate with the Maharishi, and orange-robed Hare Krishna devotees could be seen dancing and chanting on Oxford Street in London. Spirituality in all of its flavors and colors began to arrive in the West.

This awakening spirituality was part of my adolescence. When I was sixteen I began to practice Zen meditation, and experienced an inner dimension of emptiness completely different from the world of my schoolboy classrooms. When I was eighteen I practiced hatha yoga (until I damaged my knee from sitting too long in the lotus position) and became macrobiotic, learning to bake my own unleavened bread.

I studied sacred geometry and built geodesic domes. I attended one of the first Glastonbury Festivals, where the pyramid stage was supposed to transmit spiritual vibrations. Then, when I was nineteen, I met my spiritual teacher, a white-haired Russian lady who had just come back from India where she had been trained by a Sufi master. My heart became awakened to a love I never knew existed. Many friends at the time followed similar paths—exploring Buddhist meditation in the monasteries of South East Asia, reading Tibetan texts, chanting Hindu mantras, or whirling with Sufi dervishes. We felt that we were part of a spiritual movement that was going to change the world. Something was alive in a new way, a new spark of consciousness was present.

Looking back over almost half a century, I can see how our journey, the story of my generation, was to help bring these practices and teachings to the West, to help something come alive in our materialistic Western consciousness. Meditation groups formed, ashrams were built, and many of us practiced ways to access different states of consciousness. We were naïve and optimistic, expecting this infusion of spiritual consciousness to change the world. Sadly, or more realistically, while it changed our world, the world around us only became more enamored of materialism, technology, and the "toys of triviality." And, as the seventies moved into the eighties and then the nineties, many of the gurus became corrupted, mainly by sex or money, and many sincere seekers disillusioned. The innocence of those early years faded into the harsher light of daily life.

But something remained. There was a shift in consciousness—this new color in the spectrum remained—along with the various spiritual practices and texts that had come from the East. Those of us who remained true to our practice, who lived our meditation and spiritual values, held this shift in consciousness, and integrated it into our daily life. We listened to our dreams and our hearts, we opened to inner experiences beyond the physical. We lived the story of our soul.

Then, at the beginning of the twenty-first century, something within me shifted, and I was shown how spiritual values belong not just to the inner journey of the individual, but have a vital part to play in the outer world. Traditionally the seeker turns away from the outer towards the inner, seeking the truth that, for example, in Sufism can only be found within the heart. Through meditation and prayer, going deep within, we find something beyond the illusions of the outer world— we dip into love's infinite ocean. We experience the reality of the Self and the oneness that belongs to all that exists—what the Sufis call "unity of being," and for the Buddhist is experienced as Buddha nature with its awareness of the interdependence of existence ("dependent co-arising"). But I began to realize that this "consciousness of oneness" was needed in our outer world, that our world was suffering from a misguided consciousness of separation, which is the consciousness of the rational self and ego: we are separate from the Earth and separate from each other.

This focus on awakening to oneness gradually evolved into my Spiritual Ecology work of recent years, giving a spiritual perspective to our present ecological crisis. When I began this work over a decade ago, "oneness" was still a fringe "spiritual" idea. Spirituality and ecology were rarely associated. Environmentalists thought spiritual practitioners were "new age" and not activist enough, while apart from a few "engaged Buddhists" and others, spiritual practices and teachings were focused on self-development and the individual inner journey. But I am very happy that in the last few years, oneness, interconnectivity, or what the Buddhist monk Thich Nhat Hanh calls "interbeing," have become much more part of the mainstream, and central to understanding the ecological crisis—that we need to respond from an awareness of the Earth as a living organic whole.

As Pope Francis expressed so beautifully in his encyclical, *On Care for our Common Home*, we need to listen to "the cry of the earth and the cry of the poor." We can no longer afford to live in a way of exploitation and division. We need to take full responsibility for our world and work together to return to a balanced and sustainable way of life for humanity and all of creation—to care for both the soil and the soul.

Chapter Two

As I have mentioned, condensed into these paragraphs is almost half a century's journey of living, and also holding, a quality of consciousness radically different to that of the environment I was born into. In its broadest terms this consciousness is *the awareness of a spiritual reality whose values are very different to the ego-driven material focus of our present civilization.*

Sadly the materialistic values of the fifties have now morphed into a global monster, exploiting and ravaging the Earth in a way that can only result in mutual self-destruction. Still, while there are those continuing this nightmare of "business as usual"—the global corporations and politicians who pursue only economic growth or greed—there are others who have real "care for our common home," who hear the cry of the Earth and the pressing need to live from a place of unity. Maybe we have already passed the "tipping point" of unforeseen ecological consequences: temperatures rising, rivers and oceans polluted, and air made toxic. But spiritual consciousness still has a vital role to play as our world spins out of balance.

Yet I believe it is no longer enough just to hold this awareness—*we have to bring it into action.* Many people who read my book *Spiritual Ecology: The Cry of The Earth* responded, "What should I do?" The next chapter in this story of spirituality must be to bring these values, this quality of consciousness, into action to help heal and restore our dying world. I firmly believe that this is the calling for the next generation, for those who have the energy and passion to act from a place of service and love for the Earth—and, especially important, from a place of unity. [Spiritual Ecology: The Cry of the Earth is a collection of essays by spiritual teachers, scientists and others, that proposes the need for a spiritual response to our present environmental crisis.]

This is the challenge facing those of the millennial generation who sense that life is something more than the accumulation of "stuff," who have heard the cry of the Earth, which is also the cry of their own soul. How can we help the world in this time of transition? How can we participate creatively in our lives and communities? There is much work to be done, a work founded upon the principles of oneness and unity, a work that recognizes that all of life is sacred and whole. Life is calling to us and it desperately needs our attention; around us are what Thich Nhat Hanh calls "bells of mindfulness," which we need to hear and then respond to—hear with our hearts and respond with our hands.

There are many ways to participate, to work towards ecological wholeness, from forming a community of urban gardeners, to developing new economic models based upon generosity and sharing rather than acquisition, such as "pay it forward." It is for each person to find the community and initiative that speaks most to their nature, their unique offering. And central to this work is that we are here to help each other and to help. And I firmly believe that—while some global initiatives are vital, like reducing carbon emissions—most initiatives should be small groups of people coming together in different ways. Governments and politicians are too bound to the idea of continued "economic growth" to commit to real change. Instead the world needs to be regenerated in an organic, cellular way, the way life recreates itself.

I also believe that it is important for anyone committing to this work to develop their own spiritual practice—especially helpful is a meditation practice that is done every day. It can be a mindfulness meditation, watching the breath, the Christian practice of centering prayer, or a Sufi heart meditation. It could also be walking in a sacred manner, being aware of our connection to the sacred Earth with every step we take. What matters is that our practice connects us to what is most deep and enduring within us, a Source beyond the illusions of the ego and the many distractions of the outer world. This practice can support and protect us, and inwardly guide us in our work.

And if I have learned anything from my journey, I've learned what matters most is love. Love is the most powerful force in creation, and it is our love for the Earth that will heal what we have desecrated, that will guide us through this wasteland and help us to bring light back into our darkening world. As in the words of the poet Wendell Berry, "The world ... can be redeemed only by love." Love links us all together in the most mysterious ways, and love can guide our hearts and hands. And the central note of love is oneness. Love speaks the language of oneness, of unity rather than separation.

ON PROPHECY AND TIME – PART 10

PIR ZIA INAYAT-KHAN TO DAVID SPANGLER AND WILLIAM IRWIN THOMPSON

Dear William and David,

At the start of his Stoic handbook, Epictetus makes a distinction between the things that are in our power and the things that are not. I find this discrimination useful when it comes to pondering apocalyptic themes. Some apocalyptic scenarios are utterly beyond our control, like asteroid impacts, solar storms or volcanic eruptions. There is no point losing sleep over such things since there is nothing we can do about them.

But then there are the scenarios in which we are implicated, like climate change and the specter of nuclear Armageddon. Epictetus wrote, "Jupiter has not made you dispenser of the winds," and that was true at the time. But today our consciousness, mediated by technology, melts glaciers and sends hurricanes hurtling across the Gulf of Mexico.

The Mayan calendar has been generating a lot of buzz lately. What deserves more attention, I think, is the emerging picture of the collapse of the Mayan civilization. According to Jared Diamond, that collapse was the result of overpopulation, deforestation, drought, war, and political inertia. In other words, Mayan history mirrors our contemporary reality with eerie precision. Of course the stakes are incomparably higher today since the whole human species (seven billion people) is on the line. And not only humans: E.O. Wilson estimates that if current trends continue, half of Earth's animal and plant species will be rendered extinct by the end of this century.

I recognize that the line between what is in our power and what is not can be a blurry one. As you know, over the last several years James Lovelock has become increasingly pessimistic about the chances of averting calamity. His latest book—bearing the ominous subtitle, "A Final Warning"—makes the case that, whatever we may do, a catastrophic climatic jump is now inevitable.

I always come back to the hadith of the Prophet Muhammad (peace be upon him): "Even if you know the world will end tomorrow, plant a tree." Whatever may happen around us, the choice to live in symbiosis with the visible and invisible beings that compose Earth's living systems is an act of love and a state of grace. If we become Gaian Humans in our bodies, hearts and souls, whether we flourish or perish we will have been true to our promise.

Thank you, dear and respected colleagues, for sharing your deep insights with me and with the Seven Pillars community. I look forward to further chapters in this conversation.

With every best wish,
Zia

BIOGRAPHIES
ABOUT THE CONTRIBUTORS

Christopher Bamford

Christopher Bamford is Editor-in-Chief for SteinerBooks and its imprints. A Fellow of the Lindisfarne Association, he has lectured, taught, and written widely on Western spiritual and esoteric traditions. He is the author of *The Voice of the Eagle: The Heart of Celtic Christianity* and *An Endless Trace: The Passionate Pursuit of Wisdom in the West*. He has also translated and edited numerous books, including *Celtic Christianity*, *Homage to Pythagoras*, and *The Noble Traveller*. An essay by Mr. Bamford is included in the HarperSanFrancisco anthology Best Spiritual Writing 2000 by Philip Zaleski.

www.steinerbooks.org

Felix Idris Baritsch

Felix studied cello in Paris, international law in Geneva, natural medicine in Germany, and recently acquired an M.A. in comparative philosophy. He founded the Intercultural Association for Holistic Medicine in France and Germany, and teaches natural and holistic medicine all over Europe and America. He has run a permaculture farm and medical practice in Hamburg since 1992. He guides retreats, pilgrimages, Universal Worships, and inter-religious dialogs. He helped found the Peace University in Brasilia, the first Buddhist center in Sao Paolo, the Buddhist Religious Community of Hambur, the Music for Peace Association in Freiburg, and various cultural associations in Germany. He has been a board member of the Seven Pillars House of Wisdom, a council member of the Tibetan Center Hamburg and the German Buddhist Union, and a delegate of the European Buddhist Union and the

Council of Europe. He regularly translates the works of His Holiness the Dalai Lama, Pir Zia Inayat-Khan, and many other holy masters into German, French, Spanish and Portuguese.

www.baritsch.de

Hathaway Barry

Hathaway Barry has worked with kids and served as a mediator—and she has done a lot of listening. Inspired by her personal experience and the turmoil of the planetary situation, years ago she began a whole new inquiry. The result is *BOY: A Woman Listening to Men and Boys*.

Robin Becker

Robin Becker, MA, RSME, is an internationally recognized teacher, dancer, choreographer, and founder of Robin Becker Dance. She became an authorized teacher of Continuum, an innovative process of movement education, in 2001. Her teaching weaves together her lifelong experience in dance, 35 years of experience as a student of the Inayati Order, 26-year study of Continuum with Emilie Conrad and Susan Harper, and 14 years of study with Gary David in Epistemics and Affect Script Theory. She has served as both a Guiding Voice and member of the Wisdom Council for Seven Pillars House of Wisdom.

www.robinbeckerdance.org

Devon Shahana Beckett

Devon Shahana Beckett has worked in local and state governments, corporate communications and marketing, museums, service learning and environmental conservation. She is an ordained UCM minister, a Suluk graduate and a gardener. She participated with her parents in the inaugural weekend and has served as a Trustee for Seven Pillars House of Wisdom for many years.

Diana Beresford-Kroeger

Diana Beresford-Kroeger is a world recognized author, medical biochemist and botanist. She has a unique combination of western scientific knowledge and the traditional concepts of the ancient world. Orphaned in Ireland in her youth, Beresford-Kroeger was educated by elders who instructed her in the Brehon knowledge of plants and nature. Told she was the last child of ancient Ireland and to one day bring this knowledge to a troubled future, Beresford-Kroeger has done exactly that.

Her Bioplan encourages ordinary people to develop a new relationship with nature, to join together to replant the global forest. Her books include "The Sweetness of a Simple Life", "The Global Forest", "Arboretum Borealis", "Arboretum America", and "A Garden for Life". Diana Beresford-Kroeger was inducted as a WINGS WorldQuest fellow in 2010, she was elected as a fellow of the Royal Geographical Society in 2011. More recently, in 2016, the Society named her one of 25 women explorers of Canada. In addition, in 2011 she was named one of Utne Reader's World Visionaries.

Denise Boston

Denise Boston, Ph.D., RDT, is Dean of Diversity and Inclusion, Professor and adjunct faculty in the School of Professional Psychology and Health, with concentrations in Expressive Arts Therapy and Community Mental Health. Over the past 25 years she has devoted her teaching and research to the increased understanding of urban trauma and expressive arts therapeutic approaches to address mental health care disparities of people of African descent. With a culturally relevant approach toward mental health and wellness, she is known for her dynamic, interactive presentations. Denise earned a B.F.A in Drama from the University of the North Carolina School of the Arts, an M.A. in Psychology and Counseling from Goddard College, and a Ph.D. in Counseling Psychology from Walden University.

dboston@ciis.edu

Adam Bucko

Adam Bucko is an activist and spiritual director to New York City's homeless youth. He grew up in Poland during the totalitarian regime, where he explored the anarchist youth movement as a force for social and political change. Adam emigrated to the US at 17, but his desire to lead a meaningful life sent him to monasteries in the US and India. His life-defining experience took place in India, where a brief encounter with a homeless child led him to the "Ashram of the Poor" where he began his work with homeless youth. Upon returning to the US, Adam worked with homeless youth in cities around the country. He co-founded The Reciprocity Foundation, an award winning nonprofit dedicated to transforming the lives of New York City's homeless youth. Additionally, Adam established HAB, an ecumenical and inter-spiritual contemplative fellowship for young people which offers formation in radical spirituality and sacred activism. Adam is a recipient of several awards and his work has been featured by ABC News, CBS, NBC, New York Daily News, National Catholic Reporter, Ode Magazine, Yoga International Magazine and Sojourner Magazine.

www.reciprocityfoundation.org
www.adambucko.com

William C. Chittick, Ph.D.

William C. Chittick, Ph.D. is distinguished professor of Religious Studies in the Department of Asian and Asian American Studies at the State University of New York, Stony Brook. He has lectured around the world and published 30 books and numerous articles on Islamic intellectual history, concentrating on the interface between Sufism and philosophy. His books include *The Sufi Path of Love*, *The Sufi Path of Knowledge*, *The Heart of Islamic Philosophy*, *Divine Love*, *The Unveiling of the Mysteries*, and, with Sachiko Murata, *The Vision of Islam*.

Robert Peretz Corman

Robert Peretz Corman is a member of the Seven Pillars House of Wisdom Board of Advisors. As president of Applied Concepts, he provides executive coaching and whole systems thinking leadership to senior nonprofit leaders. Previously, Robert led the National Partnership for Social Enterprise, which focused on market-driven approaches to social issues and the Gallup International Institute, where he helped launch the Health of the Planet Survey. Beginning as a criminal and environmental lawyer, he became president of The Fund for New Jersey, starting various organizations, including a community foundation with assets now over $500 million. A practitioner of Nondual Kabbalistic Healing and student of shamanic traditions, Robert currently chairs A Growing Culture, an NGO that is building an online agroecology knowledge commons for global farmers.

Charles Eisenstein

In 2013, journalist and author Rory Spowers described Eisenstein as a "refreshing new voice", saying that he's young, fresh, well-informed, humble but articulate, with a very spiritual perspective. He added that Eisenstein is too intelligent to be confrontational but that, through his works, especially *The*

Ascent of Humanity and *Sacred Economics*, "he's really moved the whole thing along in a number of ways."

Eisenstein's most recent book is *The More Beautiful World our Hearts Know is Possible*, and he hosts a podcast called "*A New and Ancient Story*". In advance of appearing on Oprah's Super Soul Sunday on July 16, 2017, Eisenstein published an essay titled "The Age of We Need Each Other."

charleseisenstein.net

Nambaryn Enkhbayar

Nambaryn Enkhbayar has been the Prime Minister of Mongolia since June 2005; he served as speaker of the Parliament 2004–5 and as prime minister 2000–2004. A graduate of the Moscow Institute of Literature, he has also studied at Leeds University in England. Enkhbayar worked for the Mongolian Writers Union as an editor-translator, and was their secretary general and vice president. He has translated Mongolian epics as well as a number of works of European literature, Dickens among them. Enkhbayar has also translated Buddhist teachings into Mongolian.

Darakshan Farber

Darakshan Farber is a member of the Board of Advisors of the Seven Pillars House of Wisdom. He serves as a connecter immersed in regenerative community, new culture, and emerging spirituality. He was a software architect for thirty years, co-founding Sandpiper Networks, which developed Internet technologies that were an early part of what is now called "the cloud." He is a graduate of Suluk Academy and the Nine Gates Mystery School, created the Seven Pillars Journey of Wisdom, an immersive transformance experience based on the Seven Pillars, and recently launched a website for language play. He lives a technomadic life engaged in a world walkabout.

www.floetry.s

Jennifer Ferraro

Jennifer Ferraro, MFA, is a poet, teacher, artist, and writer/translator of *Quarreling with God: Mystic Rebel Poems of the Dervishes of Turkey* and a collection of her own illustrated poems, *Divine Nostalgia*. She has led workshops and has presented poetry performances combining poetry, dance and music in innovative ways. For four years she toured with a Turkish music ensemble performing percussion, dance and sacred poetry all over the world. Her work is particularly concerned with presenting poetry as a sacred art and in illuminating Beauty and the wisdom of the sacred feminine. Jennifer lives in Santa Fe, New Mexico. Her newest work, *Sophia's Book of Wisdom: 25 Illuminations of the Soul* is forthcoming in 2018 on Kindle.

www.jenniferferraro.com

Angela Fischer

Angela Fischer, of German heritage, has led spiritual seminars and medi- tation retreats since 1982 and is the author of several books on feminine spir- ituality, the oneness of life and the healing of the feminine and the earth. She has followed the Sufi path for thirty years and dedicated her life and work to taking care of a meditation center, speaking, writing and finding ways of living a mystical life in the present time of transition and global crisis, with an emphasis on living the sacred in daily life. Central to her work is reclaiming a genuine feminine spirituality which leads to living women's spiritual respon- sibility for the well-being of the world and future, as well as recovering the feminine principle in both women and men, in service to life.

www.oneness-of-life.org

W.H.S. Gebel

William Hassan Suhrawardi Gebel received a Ph.D. in astrophysics from the University of Wisconsin and was a member of the faculty at State Univer- sity of New York at Stony Brook. He received his training in the Sufi path from Pir Vilayat Inayat Khan and Pir Zia Inayat-Khan, served as Secretary General of the Sufi Order International (now The Inayati Order) for 8 years, and is currently a senior teacher and retreat guide. He is the author of *Root Speaks to Bud: Fulfilling the Purpose of Life*.

Jane Goodall

Dr. Jane Goodall is a renowned primatologist best known for her 45 years of studying and living among the chimpanzees in Tanzania. She's an ethnologist, a conservationist, and a United Nations Messenger of Peace. She spends about 300 days a year on the road speaking with students and children and government officials about animal conservation issues and the threats to the chimpanzees of Gombe National Park, which is one of their last remaining refuges on the planet.

She is the founder of the Jane Goodall Institute, and its Roots and Shoots program to motivate young people to learn the important challenges that face their communities and to implement projects to solve them. She was named the Dame Commander of the Order of the British Empire, and awarded the Prestigious Kyoto Prize in Japan, and the Gandhi King Award for nonviolence. And she has written many books about her chimpanzee research, wildlife conservation, mindful eating and postmodern spirituality, including *Hope for Animals and Their World: How Endangered Species Are Being Rescued on the Brink*.

www.janegoodall.org

Lafcadio Hearn

Lafcadio Hearn (June 27, 1850–September 26, 1904), born on the Greek island of Lefkada to a Greek mother and an Irish army surgeon. Until the age of 19, he was raised in Dublin by an aunt after being abandoned by both parents. He was known as Koizumi Yakumo in Japan, for his many books about that country, especially for his collections of Japanese legends and ghost stories, such as *Kwaidan: Stories and Studies of Strange Things*.

The noted playwright and novelist, Roger Pulvers, considered Hearn America's foremost ethnographic documentarian of the 19th century, citing the hundreds of articles he wrote about America's black and Creole subculture during his 18 years as a reporter in Cincinnati and New Orleans. A world traveler, it was a Harper's Magazine assignment that took him to Japan, where he spent the last 14 years of his life writing nearly a book a year about his adopted country.

Pir Zia Inayat-Khan

Pir Zia Inayat-Khan is a scholar and teacher of Sufism in the lineage of his grandfather, Hazrat Inayat Khan. He received his B.A. (Hons) in Persian Literature from the London School of Oriental and African Studies, and his M.A. and Ph.D. in Religion from Duke University. Pir Zia is founder of Seven Pillars House of Wisdom, and also of Sulūk Academy, a school of contemplative study with branches in the U.S. and Europe. His most recent books are *Saracen Chivalry: Counsels on Valor, Generosity and the Mystical Quest* and *Caravan of Souls: An Introduction to the Sufi Path of Hazrat Inayat Khan*, both published by Sulūk Press, an imprint of Omega Publications.

www.pirzia.org

Lee Irwin

Lee Irwin is a Professor in the Religious Studies Department at the College of Charleston where he teaches world religions with an emphasis on Native American traditions, western esotericism, hermeticism, contemporary spirituality, mystical cosmology, and transpersonal religious experience as related to dreams and visions. He is the Vice President of the Association for the Study of Esotericism (ASE) and a board member of the Sophia Institute. He has been a workshop leader and group facilitator for over twenty years, particularly in the areas of visionary cosmology and the development of the sacred human. He is the author of many books and articles, including: *The Dream Seekers, Visionary Worlds; Awakening to Spirit: On Life, Illumination, and Being; The Alchemy of Soul; Coming Down From Above: Prophecy, Resistance, and Renewal in Native American Religions; Meditations on Christ; Reincarnation in America: An Esoteric History.*

Robert Karp

Robert Karp is a writer, thinker and social entrepreneur informed by the insights of the Austrian philosopher and social activist Rudolf Steiner. Robert is the former executive director of Practical Farmers of Iowa, the Biodynamic Association in North America and is the founder of New Spirit Farmland Partnerships, which helps organic and other conservation minded farmers secure long-term access to farmland by facilitating partnerships with social investors. Robert's writings include *A New American Revolution: Associative Economics and the Future of the Food Movement* published by Hawthorne Press in *Free, Equal and Mutual-Rebalancing Society for the Common Good* and *Community and Agriculture: An Iowa Pilgrimage*, published by Free River Press in *Eating in Place: Telling the Story of Local Foods*.

www.robertkarp.net

Satya Inayat Khan

Satya Inayat Khan is a freelance web developer, martial artist, and chivalry practitioner. She resides in the San Francisco Bay Area with her husband and son.

satyakhan.com

Sister Joan Kirby

In 1994, Sister Kirby found her true passion when she became the director of the Temple of Understanding (TOU) in New York, an interfaith organization affiliated with the United Nations. The TOU works to educate adults and young people across cultures and religion to create understanding and peaceful co-existence.

In 2010, the Temple of Understanding presented Sister Kirby with the Interfaith Visionary Lifetime Achievement Award, "for promoting interreligious values at the United Nations, her lifelong commitment to addressing human rights and ecological issues, and her passionate devotion to the development of young leaders."

Satish Kumar

Satish Kumar is a spiritual ecologist, an earth pilgrim, a vegetarian who led a civil disobedience movement in efforts to restore humanity's sense of community. At the age of 9, Satish renounced the world to become a wandering Jain monk, but dissuaded by his inner voice at the age of 18, he left his ascetic life to embrace Gandhi's visions of land reform and global peace. Influenced by the great British philosopher Bertrand Russell, especially his anti-nuclear war philosophy, he undertook an 8,000-mile peace pilgrimage, walking penniless from India to America to deliver packets of peace tea to the heads of government of the four nuclear powers, the Soviet Union, France, UK and the United States. He settled in the United Kingdom in 1973 and is now editor of the prestigious magazine Resurgence, which highlights many of our world's greatest thinkers and visionaries. Influenced by the "Small is Beautiful Movement" of economist E.F. Schumacher, Satish has founded pioneering schools and colleges that introduce ecological sanity and spiritual values into their curricula. He has written six books and received two honorary doctorates from prominent British Universities.

www.resurgence.org
www.schumachercollege.org.uk

Winona LaDuke

Winona LaDuke (Anishinaabe) is an internationally acclaimed author, orator and activist. A graduate of Harvard and Antioch Universities with advanced degrees in rural economic development, LaDuke has devoted her life to protecting the lands and life ways of Native communities. She is the

Founding Director of the White Earth Land Recovery Project and Honor the Earth. The author of six books, including *Recovering the Sacred*, *All Our Relations* and a novel—*Last Standing Woman*, Winona LaDuke is widely recognized for her work on environmental and human rights issues. She is the recipient of numerous awards including the Thomas Merton Award, the Ann Bancroft Award and the prestigious International Slow Food Award for working to protect wild rice and local biodiversity. LaDuke is also a two time vice presidential candidate with Ralph Nader for the Green Party. LaDuke lives with her family on the White Earth Reservation in northern Minnesota.

Thea Halima Levkovitz

Thea Halima Levkovitz is a member of the Board of Advisors of the Seven Pillars House of Wisdom. Her career and passion arise from a deep delight and connection with wilderness. She became an environmental policy analyst and activist after living in the Alaskan bush and witnessing first hand the environmental and human devastation from the Exxon Valdez oil spill. She led outreach in the Pacific Northwest for The Wilderness Society, Washington Association of Churches and convened the Washington state-based Partnership for Religion and the Environment, where she created value-driven campaigns for clean car legislation, Wild Sky Wilderness and climate change policy. Thea has a M.S. in Botany from Humboldt State University, served on the Board of Directors for the National Wildlife Federation and co-led mindfulness retreats for environmental leaders.

Patrick Levy

Patrick Levy is a strange phenomenon in the world of writers on spirituality. He claims to be a zealous atheist but is very interested in religions and spiritualities. "All that belongs to humanity belongs to me," he says to justify his curiosity.

He is the author of *Sadhus: Going Beyond the Dreadlocks*, *110 Tales of Wisdom from All Over the World*, and *Le Kabbaliste*, which was awarded a Special Distinction prize by the panel of judges of "Spirituality Today" in 2002.

site.patricklevy.free.fr

Chief Arvol Looking Horse

Arvol Looking Horse was born on the Cheyenne River Reservation in South Dakota in 1954. Raised by his grandparents, Lucy and Thomas Looking Horse,

Arvol learned the culture and spiritual ways of the Lakota. He speaks both Lakota and English. At 12 he was given the enormous responsibility of becoming the 19th generation Keeper of the Sacred White Buffalo Calf Pipe, the youngest in history. Arvol has felt, on many occasions, overwhelmed by inheriting such a responsibility of the Lakota, Dakota and Nakota Nations at such a young age. He was raised in an era and bore witness to the suppression of his peoples' spiritual practices. He decided to "work for change and let the world know how beautiful our way of life is, so the seventh generation can have a better future."

wolakota.org

Victor Mansfield

Victor Mansfield (1941–2008) was Professor of Physics and Astronomy at Colgate University and a student of Tibetan Buddhism. He published widely in physics, astronomy, and several interdisciplinary fields, studied and practiced with teachers in the USA, Europe, and India, and lectured widely in the USA and Europe. In 2008, Professor Mansfield published *Tibetan Buddhism and Modern Science*, with an introduction by His Holiness the Dali Lama.

Dena Merriam

Dena Merriam is the founder and convener of the Global Peace Initiative of Women (GPIW), as well as Vice Chairman and partner in the public relations firm Ruder Finn, Inc. Her work at GPIW aims to create a global platform for women religious and spiritual leaders, and to engage Hindu and Buddhist leadership more actively on the world stage. Merriam began working in the interfaith movement in the late 1990s, when she served as Vice Chair of the Millennium World Peace Summit of Religious and Spiritual Leaders held at the United Nations in New York. She previously served as executive editor of Sculpture Review. In 2014 she was awarded the Niwano Peace Prize. Merriam holds a M.A. from Columbia University.

www.gpiw.org

Jennifer Morgan

Jennifer Morgan is an author, teacher trainer, and founder of the Deep Time Journey Network. Her Universe Story Trilogy—*Born with a Bang, From Lava to Life,* and *Mammals Who Morph*—for children won the Teacher's Choice Award and was endorsed by Jane Goodall, Neil de Grasse Tyson, and numerous world renowned scientists. The Deep Time Journey Network is a worldwide social partnership for educators, clergy, artists and others that offers professional development for teachers.

www.universestories.com
www.deeptimejourney.org

Carolyn North

Carolyn North loves to write and dance, and uses these forms as a vehicle for her work as a healer. She defines her purpose as an aide in making the transition from a materialistic culture to one that recognizes that we are all connected with each other, with the Earth and with the cosmos.

www.carolynnorthbooks.com
www.healingimprovisations.net

Gary Null

Dr. Gary Null is the host of the nation's longest running public radio program on nutrition and natural health, founder of the Progressive Radio Network, a New York Times best selling author, and a multi-award-winning director of controversial documentaries, including *Gulf War Syndrome: Killing Our Own*, *The Drugging of Our Children*, and *Autism: Made in the USA*.

www.garynull.com

Deepa Gulrukh Patel

Deepa Patel is passionate about music, young people, fighting injustice and poverty and nurturing equality and creativity in our world. These areas have been the focus of her work. Her past roles have included work as a music education producer for the BBC, a campaigner on HIV/AIDS for ActionAid, and as a Managing Director of Creative Partnerships (a national UK Government Initiative on creativity in schools). She currently facilitates programs on the art of collaboration and conversation and is Co-Director of Slow Down London, a campaign on how to appreciate and enjoy life at a different pace. Deepa is a former member of the Seven Pillars Board of Trustees and lives in England.

Janet Piedilato

Janet Piedilato is a transpersonal psychologist, a complementary health care consultant, and an ordained minister. She holds a doctorate in biology from New York University and a doctorate in transpersonal psychology from Saybrook University. She took her herbalist training at David Winston's Center for Herbal Studies. Janet holds the distinction of being the first woman practitioner to present shamanic ritual at the Harvard Divinity School Conference on Reinterpreting Shamanism. She offers workshops and lectures on dreams, ancient mystery tradition, and shamanism at the Journey Within Spiritualist Church in Pompton Plains, New Jersey. She is the author of *Pieda's Tales, Stories Old As Time*, and the founder of Immaginal, a company that grew from her practice of creating scent memory experiences during relaxation therapy protocols. She resides at Temenos, an environmental sanctuary, co-founded with her husband and soul mate, Iggy.

http://www.janetpiedilato.com

Yuval Ron

Yuval Ron is an Oscar-winning composer, Grammy nominee, and peace activist. His multi-faith ensemble performs "Peace Tours" around the world, including the Seeds of Compassion Festival for His Holiness the Dalai Lama. Bonding people of all nationalities and religions, Yuval's career includes work in film, television, radio, dance, theater, and teaching at leading universities. He recently published *Divine Attunement: Music as a Path to Wisdom*.

www.yuvalronmusic.com
www.theoracleinstitute.org/DivineAttunement

Naomi Rose

Naomi Rose is the author of *MotherWealth: The Feminine Path to Money* and *The Portable Blessings Ledger: A Way to Keep Track of Your Finances and Bring Meaning and Heart to Your Dealings with Money* (www.rosepress.com). A writer, book developer, and "creative midwife" based in Oakland, California, she helps people bring forth their heart's expressions in the spirit of "I was a hidden treasure and I longed to be known". Her "Writing from the Deeper Self" approach assumes that deep listening will bring out the best of what is uniquely yet universally true in the writer, and therefore in the reader. This also is the focus of her book, *Starting Your Book: A Guide to Navigating the Blank Page by Attending to What's Inside You*.

www.naomirose.net

Omid Safi

Omid Safi is a leading Muslim public intellectual. He is the Director of the Duke Islamic Studies Center Omid is a professor of Islamic Studies, and specializes in contemporary Islamic thought and Islamic spirituality. He is the recent Chair for the Islamic Mysticism group at the American Academy of Religion, the largest international organization devoted to the academic study of religion. He is the editor of the volume *Progressive Muslims: On Justice, Gender, and Pluralism*. In this ground-breaking volume, he inaugurated a new understanding of Islam which is rooted in social justice, gender equality, and religious/ethnic pluralism. His work *Politics of Knowledge in Premodern Islam*, dealing with medieval Islamic history and politics, was published in 2006. His *Memories of Muhammad* is an award-winning biography of the Prophet Muhammad. His next book is called *Radical Love*, and will be published by Yale University Press.

islamicstudies.duke.edu

Dorion Sagan

Dorion Sagan is a science writer, essayist, and theorist. He is author of numerous articles and books translated into at least eleven languages, including *Death and Sex*, and *Into the Cool*, coauthored with Eric D. Schneider. His writings have appeared in the New York Times, the New York Times Book Review, Wired, and the Skeptical Inquirer. His recent book, *Lynn Margulis: The Life and Legacy of a Scientific Rebel*, is an anthology of essays about the late Lynn Margulis from scientists and philosophers around the world.

David Spangler

David Spangler is an internationally known spiritual teacher and writer, and was instrumental in helping establish the Findhorn Foundation community in northern Scotland in the late 1960's early 1970's. Since then David has traveled widely within the United States and Canada giving classes, workshops and lectures. His themes have included the emergence of a holistic culture, the nature of personal sacredness, and our participation in a co-evolving, co-creative universe. He has also focused on partnering and working with spiritual realms, the spiritual nature and power of our individuality, and our calling to be of service at this crucial time of world history. Many of these themes come together in his primary work, which is the development of a spiritual perspective and practice called Incarnational Spirituality.

www.lorian.org

Christina Solaris

Christina Solaris is a spiritual guide, source conduit, and new paradigm wisdom teacher who has founded multiple methods for accessing and embodying expanded consciousness, including The Omega Codex. In her first career Christina served with the United Nations and other organizations in Sub-Saharan Africa as a human rights advocate. It was in the world's largest refugee camps that she witnessed the incredible overcoming power of the Human Spirit, causing her to turn towards the divine with her whole heart and soul. She serves leaders, luminaries and pioneers on six continents and supports them to fully deliver their gifts. She holds a Master of Divinity degree and Fellowship from Harvard Divinity School and is devoted to blazing the new consciousness needed to create a whole Earth and a more loving world. She currently calls the Yucatan Peninsula and the indigenous lands of the Maya her home.

www.christinasolaris.com

William Irwin Thompson

William Irwin Thompson is a poet and cultural philosopher who has made significant contributions to cultural history, social criticism, the philosophy of science, and the study of myth. Early in his career he left academia to found Lindisfarne, an association of creative individuals in the arts, sciences, and contemplative practices devoted to the study and realization of a new planetary consciousness, or noosphere. Thompson lived in Switzerland for 17 years and describes his most recent work, *Canticum Turicum*, as "a long poem on Western Civilization, that begins with folktales and traces of Charlemagne in Zurich and ends with the completion of Western Civilization as expressed in *Finnegans Wake* and the traces of James Joyce in Zurich." With mathematician Ralph Abraham he has designed a new type of cultural history curriculum based on their theories about the evolution of consciousness. Thompson now lives in Portland, Maine.

www.williamirwinthompson.org

Bisan Toron

Bisan Toron is a vocal artist and voice teacher. Born in Syria and raised in Paris and New York, Bisan studied classical voice performance at NYU, holds a masters in Ethnomusicology from the University of London School of Oriental and African Studies, and studied voice and improvisation with the Roy Hart-based company, Pantheatre, in France. Her music is informed by a multitude of cultures and vocal traditions, which she threads with vocal articulations that arise from the moment. She has released two CDs, *Backstage Reveries* and *Toward the Roar*, and was the featured vocalist or the acclaimed film, *NYsferatu*. She currently performs and teaches independently across the United States and Europe and makes her residence in Richmond, VA.

www.bisantoron.com

Wendy Jehanara Tremayne

Wendy Jehanara Tremayne was creative director in a marketing firm in New York City before moving to Truth or Consequences, New Mexico, where she built a sustainable off-the-grid oasis with her partner, Mikey Sklar. She is the founder of the textile-repurposing event Swap-O-Rama-Rama, which is celebrated in over 100 cities around the world; a conceptual artist; a yogi; a teacher in the Inayati Sufi Order; and a writer. She has written for Craft's webzine and Make magazine and, with Mikey Sklar, kept the blog Holy Scrap. Wendy Jahanara is a graduate of Suluk Academy, and retreat guide. In June 2013 she released her first book, *The Good Life Lab: Radical Experiments in Hands-On Living* (Storey Publishing, 2013).

www.gaiatreehouse.com

Llewellyn Vaughan-Lee

Llewellyn Vaughan-Lee, Ph.D. is a Sufi teacher and author. In recent years the focus of his work has been on Spiritual Responsibility at a time of Global Crisis, and the emerging subject of Spiritual Ecology. His most recent books are *Spiritual Ecology: The Cry of the Earth*, *Spiritual Ecology: 10 Practices to Reawaken the Sacred in Everyday Life*, and *For Love of the Real: A Story of Life's Mystical Secret*.

www.workingwithoneness.org
www.goldensufi.org

A Discussion and Exercise Guide

FOR *Journeys and Awakenings*

As an anthology, *Journeys and Awakenings: Wisdom for Spiritual Travelers* offers an enormous array of opportunities for rich csonversation as well as exercises that deepen your experience. This Reader's Guide offers some suggested questions to stimulate individual and collective thought for individuals, small groups and/or book clubs. Perhaps you will find the Guide helpful in stimulating your own inquiries for discussion or tailor some of your own strategies for shared exercises as you reflect alone or with others on the writings.

One possible place to start is to relax and ponder the following question and suggestion:

1. What feeling first surfaced in you when you saw the title of the book?

2. If it was very rich and textured, consider writing a paragraph (or more) or a short poem that captures what you felt.

3. If you are in a group, share your response to #1 or you writing in #2, or both.

Another place to start or continue your interaction is by asking:

1. What two or three chapters among the ones you have read most touched you personally?

2. Were there themes present in those writings that seemed particularly alive for you in your life, or, perhaps opened you up to new arenas of thought and exploration?

3. Conversations around these questions and variations of them may prove enjoyable.

Alternatively, you may wish to identify a few titles in the book that you have not read and ask:

1. What do you think they may be about?

2. Share your thoughts with others, if you are in a group comparing your varied views.

3. Then read the chapter and deliberate on its meaning, the surprises you found and the alignment between what you (and others) anticipated or the lack thereof.

You may choose to focus on a particular chapter and frame some question or hypothesis for further thought, discussion or as an exercise. For example:

1. If you read *The Mystery of Trees* interview of Diana Beresford-Kroeger (page 31), you may ask "What is your historical relationship with trees?"

2. How might it change, if at all, upon reading about the merging awareness of "infrasound," or how trees produce a phenol to help heal injured trees in their family of trees?

3. Consider going into a forest and sitting quietly and listening deeply in the way suggested. Can you sense the presence of the "infrasound"?

The word "chivalry" appears in no less than three chapters and offers up interesting opportunities:

1. What is your personal concept of "chivalry"?

2. How is your view different from the way it is used in the writing

of Felix Idris Baritsch, *Shooting Arrows Blindfolded* (page 9) and Lee Irwin, *Wisdom and the Way of Awakening* (page 100) and David Spangler, *The Chivalrous Path* (page 225)?

3. A group may want to explore in small breakout subgroups, what is the role of chivalry today, asking anew that now proverbial question, "Is chivalry dead?"

The book has many contributors who directly express opinions based on their journey about what issues need real attention. These offer opportunities to the reader and groups, such as:

1. What are the ecological implications for you of Jane Goodall's comments on poverty and over consumption in *Meetings with Remarkable Minds* (page 83)?

2. Numerous contributors draw the link between science and spirituality. A group may wish to identify the various examples of them and discuss which examples are found most or least compelling. Consider, for example, Jennifer Morgan's *A New Story for Children* (page 155) or W.H.S. Gebel's *Does the Universe Have an Inner Life* (page 73)?

If you enjoyed this book, you might want to read the *Seven Pillars Journey Toward Wisdom*, a multimedia production available as an iBook from Apple and as a Kindle book from Amazon.

You'll find more articles of interest on our website:

www.sevenpillarshouse.org